TOWARDS A CHRISTIAN POETICS

TOWARDS A CHRISTIAN POETICS

Michael Edwards

William B. Eerdmans Publishing Company
Grand Rapids, Michigan

First published 1984 by
THE MACMILLAN PRESS LTD
London and Basingstoke
Companies and representatives
throughout the world

First American edition published 1984
through special arrangement with Macmillan by
WM. B. EERDMANS PUBLISHING CO.,
255 Jefferson S.E.,
Grand Rapids, MI 49503

ISBN 0–8028–3596–1

Printed in Hong Kong

Library of Congress Cataloging in Publication Data
Edwards, Michael, 1938–
    Towards a christian poetics.

    Includes index.
    1. Christianity and literature.   I. Title.
PN49.E32   1983   809'.93382   83–20629
ISBN 0–8028–3596–1

For Rodney Hillman

Contents

Acknowledgements

Earlier versions of many of the chapters, or parts of chapters, in this book appeared originally in the following periodicals, to whom acknowledgement is due: *Adam International Review, Critical Quarterly, PN Review, Prospice, The Times Literary Supplement.*

The author and publishers are grateful to the following for permission to reprint material in this book: Faber & Faber Publishers and Harcourt Brace Jovanovich, Inc. for extracts from *Collected Poems 1909–1962* by T. S. Eliot.

1 Literature, Language, Life

I want to consider literature in a rather steep perspective. This will involve asking a number of questions that have a touch of extravagance about them, questions like 'what is literature?', 'why is there literature?', 'what and why is language?', 'what', even, 'is life?' It would be wiser, no doubt, to refrain from pushing too far. To follow the bearings of literature all the way they lead is to put oneself at risk: one may dissolve the subject, or find oneself mute or with phrases that merely resound. It is also, however, to encounter possibility, in the form of wider understanding, in a variety of fields; and part of my aim is to explore the kind of world in which literature occurs, and in which risk and possibility are met with. If the move is foolish, I can only say that the Fool is a hero in my book.

I believe in any case that to write – or rather, to write while at the same time being conscious of what is entailed in the act of writing – is inevitably to open oneself, via language, to everything essential: to the issues of the self, of the world, of the other, of God. To read, in that knowledge, is to realise that we are unable to grasp literature effectively unless we relate it to the largest matters that bear in on us. We do not understand literature without a theory of language, and we do not understand either without a theory of life.

The 'theory' underlying the study that follows will be Christian. I should like to discover what we can learn about literature and language by viewing them in terms of Christianity – to discover specifically, in the light of biblical teaching, what literature and language mean. The enterprise may well seem bold, or worse; to link writing with theology is certainly somewhat *insolite,* where links with sociology or psychoanalysis, for example, with the politics of Marxism or the ethics of humanism, are more expected and acceptable. I could argue that it would be only natural to examine in this way the literature and the language that have operated within a European and meta-European civilisation historically Christian, in which the Bible itself has figured for centuries as the supreme Book. That is not, however, my concern; I shall be discussing later what I consider the delusions at work in the notion of a 'Christian civilisation'. (I might add that even the idea of the natural is suspect for the Christian, as for the Marxist.) I realise, moreover, that most readers of this book are not going to be Christians, and that for them the concepts of Christianity are a highly unstable basis for a discussion of literature, or of anything else. I must also add that I shall be admitting the Bible on what I understand to be its own terms. This means, to take the opening chapters of Genesis as the most delicate instance, that however 'mythic' the conversation, say, between Eve and the serpent, and whatever the circumstances of its composition and its redaction, I shall assume that its teaching about language is rigorously exact. What I ask is that the reader forego for the time being his demand for hard theory (reflecting perhaps that theories which delve no further than psychology, social practice, language function or literary technique may actually be quite softly and superficially founded), and his conviction that this kind of submission to the Bible is outmoded, to see if the approach, combined with a dogged attention to literary and linguistic matters, doesn't illuminate these nevertheless.

What I shall be offering is the adumbration of a Christian poetics. Surprisingly, given the richness of Christian inquiry in other areas, I am not sure that the basic questions about literature and language have been asked – despite the fact that Christianity foregrounds language by its doctrine of the Word, and literature by the centrality of the Scriptures. Any answers that I suggest will, I appreciate, be severely limited, not to say, for reasons that are theological as well as intellectual and historical, blinkered. In all my assertions, therefore, there should be overheard some such recurrent phrase as 'it may be that . . .', 'it seems to me that . . .'

So as to articulate the sense of things from which I shall be working, I should like to focus not on a biblical writer but on Pascal. In particular, I am concerned with his uncovering, in the *Pensées* and elsewhere, of what he calls the *grandeur* and *misère,* the greatness and wretchedness, of the human condition. He lights on something in a way extremely simple and perfectly evident in Christian theology; yet he draws from it a conceptual device for the most wide-ranging exploration, a precise pattern for understanding the pattern of everything. All that is great about a man derives from his 'first nature',[1] given to him in 'the state of creation'. His wretchedness – blindness, 'concupiscence', mortality – is constituted by his 'second nature', which has resulted from the original sin of Adam. A man is therefore no longer a 'simple subject'; his condition is double, and he will appear plausibly great or wretched according to the perspective in which he is viewed. In Pascal's dual perspective, he is at every moment both himself and the opposite of himself; ravelled in contrarieties, he is 'chaos', 'prodigy' and 'chimera'. The two elements that compose him, moreover, are so involved that to see one truly is also to see the other. Greatness can be deduced from the quality of the wretchedness: 'all those very miseries prove his greatness. They are the miseries ... of a dispossessed king.' Wretchedness can be concluded from the fact that the greatness is merely latent, the 'capacity' for goodness, truth and happiness remaining 'unfilled'. Perception is swung giddily from side to side, and at no point can it find rest.

Because of the contradictions that work him, Pascal names a man by – or more strictly, as – a crucial figure of speech: he is a 'paradox'. Paradox governs the fundamental thinking of the *Pensées,* and it also structures many of the individual fragments. This is most remarkably the case in fragment 130, where Pascal describes, presumably, his intended relation to the reader in the Apologia which he was projecting (and for which the *Pensées* were, of course, the notes). Whether owing to Pascal or to his amanuensis, the fragment looks astonishingly like a piece of free verse:

> S'il se vante, je l'abaisse;
> s'il s'abaisse, je le vante;
> et le contredis toujours,
> jusqu'à ce qu'il comprenne
> qu'il est un monstre incompréhensible.

(If he vaunts himself I abase him/if he abases himself I vaunt him/ and gainsay him always/until he understands/that he is a monster beyond understanding.)

The contradiction in the syntactic patterns – *he ... himself, I ... him* and *vaunts ... abase ... abases ... vaunt,* which is particularly complex and also a chiasmus – culminates in the paradox of *understands ... beyond understanding.* The paradox is further emphasised by the kind of 'rhyme' that clinches it.

One notes the density of the language. And there is more: in the very middle of the piece Pascal identifies his strategy as that of literally gainsaying, or 'saying against', his reader. It is beautifully appropriate that Pascal's logic should issue in that rhetoric, since I shall hope to show later that, in a fallen, contradictory world, all writing, in one way or another, is writing against.

The Fall, of course, is what determines Pascal's reading of the human condition. His dualism implies, not independent and absolute principles of good and evil, but history and change. Contradiction emerges from an event in time that altered humanity, with the result that a man is 'no longer in the state in which God formed him'. Hence his alienation from himself, his first nature having been his 'true nature'. Hence also his alienation from God. The thinking is again paradoxical. The fallen world, and ourselves as part of that world, neither reveal God evidently nor evidently disprove him – they point to him as being not there: 'nature ... everywhere indicates a lost God, both within man and without'. In the sign constituted by the universe, God is present by his absence.

The analysis of 'greatness' and 'wretchedness', however, is only the beginning of Pascal's persuasion. Because his dualism is based on the Fall, and describes a dynamic rather than a static world, it also opens to the future. The thesis of *grandeur* and the antithesis of *misère* are in motion, both logically and historically, and they culminate and are exceeded in Jesus Christ. Jesus is the supreme paradox. In his two natures he unites the greatness of God and the wretchedness of fallen man. He combines human greatness, in his sinlessness, with human wretchedness, in his suffering and mortality. Divine, he undergoes death. Yet in reconciling the contraries he also draws beyond them. By the extreme greatness of his extremely wretched death, he overcomes wretchedness, and initiates a renewed greatness.

Pascal's shaping of experience suggests a ternary process, in which a positive is reversed by a negative, which is then reversed by a new positive far more powerful than the original. The suggestion can be confirmed by a more detailed scanning of the Bible. A ternary process, a strong dialectic, governs each level of biblical revelation, in cosmology, history, anthropology and theology.

The cosmology of Christianity is creation, fall and re-creation.

The threefold pattern involves, moreover, not one point of encounter but two. The first, between creation and fall, occurs when a creation repeatedly pronounced 'good' through the open-ing chapter of Genesis is 'subjected to vanity' and 'corruption', in Paul's phrasing,[2] because of the disobedience of Adam and Eve. The move from creation to fall points to the radical, primal nature of greatness and wretchedness; its happening with such speed (from one chapter to the next in the biblical telling) points to their amazing proximity. The move is also highly significant for litera-ture: it speaks, as it were, volumes, since it engenders the rest of the Bible. The Scriptures, from Genesis to Revelation, are writings occasioned by the collision of opposites.

The second point of encounter, between fall and re-creation, involves the negative becoming absolute so as to be replaced, with the same speed, by the positive transformed. According to an apocalyptic vision of Peter, the mortality of 'the heavens and the earth' will be taken on the day of judgement to the extreme of total destruction. Then, out of that reverse of creation and from the fire which accomplishes it, there will appear an entirely new creation, consisting of 'new heavens and a new earth'.[3]

The transformation is described more closely in a Pauline apocalypse, to which I shall be returning on a number of occa-sions. Referring not to the change in the universe but to the change in Christians, Paul writes that the 'natural body' will be raised at the end as a 'spiritual body'.[4] My contention is that part of the function of language and literature is to strain towards that spiritualising of the body.

It is also significant that Paul presents the change by means of the logical device of analogy. He compares the relation between the natural body which dies and the spiritual body which it becomes with that between grain and the equally prodigious and unforeseeable corn. Either he is merely employing a handy, familiar illustration to make his meaning clearer, or, as I believe, he is implying that the transworldly change to the hardly imagin-able 'body that shall be' is already visible in this world, in the process of vegetable change. In the latter case, he lays the basis for a Christian theory of the sign, which I shall explore.

By naming the transformed world as a 'spiritual body' he is also using a highly significant linguistic device, which goes, in fact, beyond analogy. His tense and surely astonishing oxymoron dispels the reality we know and allows the glimpse of another reality, related to it yet founded on different categories. Among the figures of speech, the oxymoron leads even further than paradox into the complex and knowing eloquence of language.

Biblical history is disposed according to the same ternary pattern. Relative to the place we inhabit, it proceeds from the Garden of Eden, through a fallen earth where the ground is 'cursed' because of Adam's fault,[5] to the higher garden of Paradise. Within Eden grows the tree of life; after the Fall the way to it is barred, to prevent Adam from reaching its fruit;[6] the barrier having at last been removed, its fruit can be eaten,[7] and the tree, according to a rhythm in advance of this world, yields its crop not every year but every month.[8] Relative to God's dwelling, on earth and beyond, the progress is from the temple in Jerusalem, through its destruction, to the Church as the new and spiritual temple. Relative to the people of God, it is from Israel, through Israel's scattering, to the Church as the new Israel.

Biblical anthropology, in the strict sense of 'discourse about man', is similarly triadic, and could again be described in a number of readings. The design would be: unfallen man, sinner, Christian, in terms of a man's state; nature, 'flesh', spirit, in terms of what constitutes him; goodness(?), sin, grace, in terms of the forces at work in him. In terms of the representatives of man, it would be unfallen Adam, fallen Adam, and Christ, who replaces the 'first Adam', or first man, at an infinitely higher level, and so is described as the 'last Adam' and the 'second man'.[9]

It is here that the dialectical nature of the conflict between *grandeur* and *misère* has the most urgent practical consequences. According to this elucidation of him, a man, having fallen from greatness into wretchedness, carries with him memory and vestiges of his former state, and is impelled towards a future state, which Paul explicitly calls that of the 'new man',[10] and which is to begin, moreover, here and now. This differs entirely from a static dualism, in terms for instance of a 'lower' and a 'higher' nature, or of the fixed contrarieties in Pope's only in part Pascalian *Essay on Man*.[11] It differs, most importantly, from the ethic, the reading of the future and the sense of possibility to which such a dualism gives rise.

Finally, the same pattern articulates biblical theology, once more in the strict sense of the term. It is not, of course, God's nature that changes but his relation to us. In Genesis, he 'blesses' the first humans, as he blesses the creatures. After the Fall, although he continues to bless and to promise blessing, he also displays a new face in 'wrath'.[12] In the sending of Jesus, he climaxes the revelation of his 'love'. God too approaches us dialectically, as Creator, Judge and Redeemer.

It is, surely, a vast and exact vision, and one that touches us at all turns of our experience. I presume that it can also appeal, and appear true, to someone who rejects the specifically Christian doctrine that subtends it. The two instants of contradiction – between the greatness and wretchedness of the self and of the world, and between that wretchedness and hints, glimpses, partial enactments of a new splendour – drive deeply and variously enough into our reality to be recognised, whatever the source and the meaning we assign to them. And in each of the subtly related areas, and underneath them all, there is a fundamental process at work that perfectly defines our happiness, our unhappiness and our desire: a process of life, death and resurrection.

Outside of Christian belief, the process is at least true to the need of the human condition, or to its dream. Inside, it achieves a profoundly elegant, and moving, and awesome focus. All the many instances of dialectic have their ground and origin in no less than the experience of God himself, being exemplified and crowned in the life, death and resurrection of Christ.

This reading of the Christian reading – in which you will have realised that, if the term 'dialectic' has been lifted from Hegel, it has also been, not for the first time, adapted – emphasises that wretchedness is a stage: from one perspective it closes off a past, but from another it opens to a future. It signifies destruction, yet at a climactic moment it changes sign, and signifies a possible re-creation. It marks a fall and gives rise to possibility. The future, moreover, is larger than the past. In specifically Christian terms, possibility is not merely recovering what was lost and being reinstated into the condition of Adam. After physical and spiritual death, after exile and judgement, a way is opened towards a relation of sonship to God, towards living 'in Christ' and being lived in by the Holy Spirit, and even, according to a heady expression of Peter, towards 'partaking of the divine nature'.[13] *Misère* is ultimately opportune, as an ancient liturgical cry – *O felix culpa!* – famously and aptly asserts. The cry is steeply dialectical, since it reverses Adam's unhappy guilt into a source of happiness. It is also paradoxical, in its collocation of 'happy' and 'guilt'. If paradox governs the involvement of greatness with wretchedness, so it governs the involvement of wretchedness with possibility.

We are so placed within the process, however, that the fulfilling of possibility, the transcending of an initial greatness, is for the future. We experience, at most, only its beginning. Although the world will be renewed, it continues in the meantime to fall around us. The earth will become paradise, but continues cursed. Besides, the property of a dialectic is that its resolution is incomplete, its third term becoming the thesis of a further triad and the origin of a new conflict. Such is the case here. The Resurrection brings not immediate bliss but another series of contradictions, between the forces of rebirth and the death which still asserts itself – between, in the same individual, the 'new man' and the 'old'. As Pascal saw,[14] the logic and the language remain oppositional, and one has to conceive of the spiritual/carnal, of grace-and-sin, of the Christian sinner.

At this point above all the dialectic reveals itself as more than a pattern. It is no external and alluring aesthetic object to be submissively contemplated rather than lived through. The world is 'in the midst' and we are in the midst, still involved in *misère,* inhabited by desire and confronted with choice. Either we live, as it were, in a perpetual Saturday, between the Friday of death and the Sunday of resurrection; or we live, during the 'last days' between Christ's resurrection and his return, in the witholding of the final transformation. In terms of that other and corresponding ternary process, of past, present and future, ourselves and our history are poised between, implicated in actions and transactions, within a present always dialectically and spiritually fraught.

Language and literature, I believe, advance through that same process, and from it derive their power and urgency. Language allows us to become aware of the process; literature is a privileged means of enacting it, and especially of contesting the Fall and of reaching towards possibility.

As the Bible expounds its dialectic, language accompanies, remarkably, each of the moves. It is present at the outset, in Eden, and even constitutes the only action of Adam there which Genesis narrates. This is specifically, of course, a naming: as God brings them to him, Adam names 'every beast' and 'every fowl of the air', and then names the first woman.[15] That initial, momentous linguistic act, which still continues to excite, we must be ultimately incapable of understanding. One guesses that 'bird' – or whatever

Adam said: but the point is that we can no longer say as he said – rather than being, in Saussurian parlance, arbitrary, a sign problematically linking a signifier to a signified in the mind and being linked itself even more problematically to an object in the sky, met with the flying creature truly. As Milton has it, voicing the interpretation common to his time, Adam 'rightly named' because he 'understood the nature' of the animals.[16] Sharing with them in a single substance – the beasts and birds had been formed out of the same ground as himself, while Eve had been made from his rib –and emerging along with them from the word of God,[17] he could name them in such a way that the creatures, his understanding of them, and the mental and physical properties of his words, would perfectly rhyme.

Perhaps we should add, from insights of our own time, that by naming the animals Adam must also have brought to them something of himself: the quality of his mind, the sounds of his body. In biblical terms, he didn't create a world, since creativity was the prerogative of another, divine language; but his language did have power, through being related to that other language by analogy – by the analogy that permeated him as a man made in God's 'image'. After God's all-powerful divine language had created the world, Adam's powerful human language, by naming it, could mingle with it and modify it.

Adam's would be a really Edenic naming, for us, by being both true to the nature of things and charged with human significance. And one notes that the references to his language in Eden concern, not communication, but a response to reality, as if the fundamental of language is its relation to a world. In Eden the relation was, by implication, 'good': rather than there being an Edenic world plus an Edenic language, words and world would presumably interpenetrate with ease. At the naming, therefore, the world, which was derived from God's language and was God's (spoken) text, now became Adam's text also.

His words, moreover, were not only related truly to their objects: the relations among them also corresponded to the relations of the real. In two instances, Genesis records the actual names that Adam gave – or rather, the writer suggests them by means of Hebrew – and in both cases he is shown deriving the name phonetically from the name for a corresponding person or idea: he called the woman 'Woman' because she was taken out of 'Man', and 'Eve' because she was the mother of all 'living'. (The

King James translators, one sees, took advantage of the fact that the same word-play is available in English, as did Jerome with respect to Latin : in the *Vulgate* he linked 'Virago' with 'de viro' and 'Heva' with 'mater . . . viventium'.) As Adam bound word and object, so, in the Genesis story, he bound word and word.

In turning from the *grandeur* of language to its *misère,* one might expect to encounter Babel – which I shall indeed be considering throughout this study, as the sign and moment of a particular fall of language, into the 'confusion' of multiplicity. Before Babel, however, language is present at the Fall itself, for between the languages of God and of man there intrudes the language of the serpent. God has told Adam that, if he eats of the tree of the know-ledge of good and evil, he will 'surely die'; the serpent tells Eve that they will 'not surely die'. It is another momentous deploying of language, which reverses the greatness of Adam's naming into the wretchedness of contradiction and ambiguity. In contradicting the words of God, the serpent produces a language at odds with the world, opposed, that is, to its Creator and to its fact, since Adam and Eve *will* die, and also at odds with language itself. He opens, in language as in life, a chasm of terrible possibility. His contradiction is plausible, moreover, through being ambiguous. It conceals God's meaning, that the humans will die at once spirit-ually and at length physically, and advances a meaning of its own, that they will not instantly fall dead. The serpent's phrase is the beginning of semantic obscurity, and since it was effective it has left us a world in which meaning is no longer evident, and a language equally uncertain, as we interpret it and as we use it.

An abuse of language, a fallacious gloss, brings about the Fall, and it is a fallen language that the now mortal pair take with them into exile. Fallen, but not merely wretched. The first recorded utterances outside Eden, which occur within a few verses of each other, are in fact sharply antithetical. Naming her son, Eve main-tains a relationship with God, by acknowledging his hand in her child-bearing: 'she . . . said, I have gotten a man from the Lord'. Cain, on the other hand, when God asks him where Abel is whom he has just murdered, notoriously denies a relationship : 'he said, I know not : Am I my brother's keeper?' The contrast of their human *grandeur* and *misère,* which also focuses pointedly on giving birth and killing, is conveyed in their language: Eve's is open, to the highest truth, while Cain's reiterates the language of the serpent, through being a lie.

Such, if the Bible is correct (and my reading of it accurate), is the language that we inherit, and such also, I believe, the language that we encounter in actual experience. We do have a sense of language in an Edenic condition of efficacy and plenitude, at one with the world and with ourselves, fulfilling our desires as speakers and writers, and doing so with ease. We recognise it at times as a quite prodigious power. On the other hand, we also know, perhaps more clearly in our century than ever before, that language has been subjected, like the human and non-human world to which it belongs, to 'vanity' and 'corruption'. The Edenic harmonies being lost, our access to it – as to everything else – is troubled, and our engagement with it a form of our exilic labour. It no longer meets the world inwardly, and in our mouths and under our hands it falls short of evidence and necessity. Languages even die, through disappearing from use, and they half-die by altering, and so alienate us from their, and our own, pasts. Words, in Eliot's paradoxically memorable phrase, 'slip, slide, perish'.

If the world is no longer (as we can imagine it having been) a coherence of expressive signs to be read as Adam read it, so we lack the expressive language by which to perform the reading. And while words and world disjoin, it is equally true that, obscurely, they are mixed one with another. Since they combined, in biblical terms, through Adam's naming, and since they suffered the Fall in common, the world is indeed a single text, but a corrupt one. Having borne the stamp of Adam, it now bears the stamp of fallen Adam, that is, of ourselves. It is only legible in part, and part of what we read in it is our own fallen condition.

We arrive after generations of shady complicity between language and the world, to find ourselves in an inextricable yet incongruous texture of words, self, things. The incongruity of language, however, is precisely our chance. The flaw between word and object, the flaws within words (the apartness of sound and sense, for example), and the complex obscurities of meaning, impel the imagination. Explored, language becomes a domain of suggestions, fragments of a novel reality emerging with fragments of a novel speech. No longer blocking or clouding the issue but pushing restlessly at a multivariety of unexpected doors, contradiction and ambiguity change.

It is this possibility, of re-naming, with which I shall be mostly concerned. I am proposing that language, by hints of its own renewal, adumbrates no less than the renewal of reality, of our-selves, of the disrupted harmonies. As it witnesses to Edenic creation and to the Fall, so it witnesses to re-creation.

Here too the Bible gives the lead, in the narrating of Pentecost. Pentecost is the third term in the biblical dialectic of language, after the greatness of Adam's tongue and the wretchedness of the serpent's tongue, and of Babel. It is a linguistic move that once again accompanies a major existential move. On this occasion, however, language is foregrounded as never before. For if the Spirit comes at Pentecost as a beginning and a pledge of the future transformation of the world, his sign is the miraculous transfor-mation, very pointedly, of the apostles' speech.

This theology of language presents it as dialectically charged, motivated by heaven and by hell and capable of the processes of possibility. The realising of its potential: the renewing of language, and beyond, in acts of renaming, is the work of writers. Literature engages with the dialectic on a number of levels. It may articulate it, or moments along it, by its plot. This is the case, I believe, in what are arguably the two primary 'kinds' within Western literature, that is, tragedy and comedy. Considered not as, say, types of play but as two related clusters of approach to the shaping of experience and the shaping of a literary work, both tragedy and comedy seem thoroughly dialectical, and it is with their study that I shall begin.

Of course, most tragic and comic writers, and indeed most writers, have been indifferent or hostile to Christianity, and far from anxious to proceed according to its tenets. I am not unaware that Sophocles, say, or Molière, or Bashō for that matter, were not functioning as Christians. What I do suggest is that, if the biblical reading of life is in any way true, literature will be drawn strongly towards it. Eden, Fall, Transformation, in whatever guise, will emerge in literature as everywhere else. The dynamics of a literary work will be likely to derive from the Pascalian interplays, of greatness and wretchedness, of wretchedness and renewal, of renewal and persisting wretchedness.

I also suggest that the dialectic informs literature more in-wardly. Literature occurs because we inhabit a fallen world. Explicitly or obscurely, it is part of our dispute with that world, and of our search for its and our own regeneration. It begins in alienation, and stands over against a reality which it perceives as exilic and mortal. Or rather, even when its first impulse is to record, to mimic, to celebrate, it immediately disturbs reality, and draws it into itself. Whatever the strictness or even fidelity of its representation, it delights in a new world produced by its own powers of fiction: of narrating, imaging, combining, changing. It is, inherently, contention and quest, battle and journey, *Iliad* and *Odyssey*. Its fundamental moves can be followed in story, which I shall also be exploring, and which is perhaps its most ubiquitous component.

In its depth, however, which is also its surface, literature is governed by dialectic since the language that it deploys is dialectical. Literature is the working of language; it is the process by which an altered, 'vain' and 'corrupt' speech is revealed and transformed. If literature exists because of our desires for reality and for ourselves, it also exists because of our desires for language, and our impatience to enter its domain : its art, its play, its possible world. This is particularly true of poetry – literature at its most verbal – which attempts more single-mindedly than other forms of writing to convert language from a 'wild wood' to a paradise. And there is one poetry of special significance here: that of T. S. Eliot. Eliot had a highly conscious theory of language, which could be described, I believe, as dialectical; and his practice allows one to follow a writer actually engaging with language in terms of its fallen state and its possibilities of rebirth. I shall therefore concentrate on his poetry at the centre of this book, and make of it a bridge to a systematic study of the abusive and re-creative manoeuvring of language in literature. This will involve considering a number of other varied and fundamental matters, such as rhetoric and translation.

What is true of life, moreover, will be true not only of literature but of all the arts. Each art will derive from what I have called the Christian dialectic, and may be studied in its light. Though neither a musician nor a painter, I hope to be able to illuminate both music and painting in these terms; I shall glance at them briefly, to indicate how I believe a more expert inquiry might proceed.

2   The Dialectic of Tragedy

1

That tragedy deals in 'greatness', of a particular kind, in actions and characters of extraordinary elevation, is of course a commonplace. What concerns us here is the meaning of this greatness and its function in the over-all design.

A place to begin might be the fact that it has a surprising and exact expression in grammar and rhetoric. One notes from play to play that, in Sophocles, Oedipus is 'the best of mortals', 'the greatest man', and Heracles in *The Women of Trachis* 'the best of all'; that in Euripedes Alcestis is 'the best of women under the sun', that Milton's Samson is the 'Strongest of mortal men', and Racine's Mithridate 'le plus grand des humains'. Shakespeare's Julius Caesar, for Brutus 'the foremost man of all this world', is for Antony 'the most noble blood of all this world', 'the noblest man/ That ever lived in the tide of times', while Antony himself, in *Antony and Cleopatra,* can be called 'the best of men' and the 'Noblest of men'; an anonymous Lord says even of Timon that he carries 'The noblest mind . . . That ever govern'd man'; Coriolanus 'is simply the rarest man i'the world'.

The speakers of such encomia are sometimes expressing a personal intention rather than presenting the facts as seen by the play as a whole. The point, however, is that tragedy encourages this manner of singling out its heroes. And when hyperbole is present, that too is to be expected, since, if the status of the hero is superlative, it is also hyperbolic. These are the terms, for instance, in which it seems natural that Racine's Alexander the Great should be addressed:

> Quand l'Océan troublé vous verra sur son onde
> Achever quelque jour la conquête du monde;
> Quand vous verrez les rois tomber à vos genoux,
> Et la terre en tremblant se taire devant vous . . .

(When the troubled Ocean sees you on its main, crowning one day the conquest of the world; when you see the world's kings fall down at your feet, and the earth tremble and fall silent before you . . .)

In his *Andromaque,* one can actually trace in Pyrrhus the process by which a 'hyperbolic' hero is created. Pyrrhus' confidant is made to see him as 'le fils et le rival d'Achille', while Hermione claims that his exploits have 'effaced' those of his father. Pyrrhus is the son of Achilles according to fable; he is the rival and, startlingly, the exceller of Achilles in accordance with the needs of tragic celebration.

Not to labour the point, hyperbole is particularly abundant in Shakespeare, as one might guess. Caesar bestrides the narrow world 'Like a Colossus' and Antony is the 'demi-Atlas of this earth'. Desdemona is a woman so excellent that, in the essential vesture of creation, she 'tires the ingener', while Coriolanus appears to his followers 'like a thing/Made by some other deity than Nature,/That shapes man better'. Her Gentleman even senses in Cordelia 'a daughter/Who redeems Nature from the general curse/Which twain have brought her to'.

The hyperboles natural to lovers also take on a deeper significance here. Antonio's eulogising of the Duchess of Malfi in Webster – 'She throws upon a man so sweet a look,/That it were able to raise one to a galliard/That lay in a dead palsy' – means all that it does because it occurs in tragedy.

We know that, historically, the greatness of the hero has its source in social experience, ritual, religion. While this accounts for his difference and power, it does not account for his utter singularity in terms of the whole human race and the whole earth. Oedipus needs, for the ritual as we understand it, to be the first in the City and of another order from the common Thebans; he does not need to be 'the best of mortals', 'the first of men in the incidents of life and the circumstances created by the gods'. Is there a shadowy presence behind tragic heroes, in the person of 'Adam', the first and greatest man? Adam is certainly their archetype, as Chaucer's Monk implies by beginning his 'tragedies' with Adam's story, and by declaring: 'Had never worldly man so heigh degree'. Adam's superlative status is presented as literally the case, and all hyperboles are true when spoken of him.

Perhaps, more radically, he is the hero to whom the tragic hero aspires. In his superlative position, the latter is sometimes 'master of the world', as Shakespeare's Caesar, Corneille's Auguste (in *Cinna*), Racine's Néron *(Britannicus)* and Titus *(Bérénice)*. The 'French' Roman emperors are explicitly responsible for the world – for *l'univers* – like Adam. The turns of their personal drama determine the course of history and the moral health or sickness of humanity: the world is cursed through the unloosing of Néron's 'monstrosity', it is saved by the propagation of Auguste's and Titus' 'virtue'. (That tragedy should on occasion imagine a paramount man *not* failing, we shall need to consider when discussing the third moment of the dialectic.)

The hyperbolic process also endows tragic kings with a touch of the divine, and so raises them in another way close to the Adam of Genesis, formed directly by the hand of God. It is true that the hero of ancient tragedy derives, seemingly, from a ritual figure who may already be some kind of divine man; the imagination at work here is not that of the dramatist only but that of the society which produced him. One can still speculate on what, in such societies, prompted the conception of superhumans. In modern tragedy (Renaissance and neoclassical) the king holds his position by divine right. Shakespeare seems to go further than the doctrine requires, however, when making Claudius claim that divinity 'hedges' a king; and one ought presumably to view Racine's monarchs in the light of the doctrine as extended even more hyperbolically by his contemporary Bossuet, who asserted that 'God has placed in princes something divine'.

Tragedy projects its hero beyond the limits of the human as we know them. He is unnecessarily eminent and implausibly special. We think of him, significantly, as representative. The whole process is present, in all its strangeness, when Cleopatra addresses Antony as 'the crown o'the earth'. In ancient tragedy as well as the tragedy of 'Christian' Europe, the hero seems a bid, more or less obscure, to conceive Adam, the uniquely eminent and special, representative man, the pitch and lord of creation.

Naturally, the conception may not be in any other way Christian. The qualities of the hero (inside and also outside tragedy) to which we respond need not be those affirmed in the Bible. On the contrary, they are often, from a Christian point of view, an 'appeal to unregenerate man',[1] and they may even lie in the superior dimension of the hero's capacity for evil. But that is to be expected. In a fallen world we can assume that greatness will be ambiguous and contradictory, and that there will be, as La

Rochefoucauld observed, 'heroes of evil' as well as 'heroes of good'.

I am aware that my suggestion of an Adamic reference is perhaps itself hyperbolic and unacceptable; and it is not, of course, necessary to the argument. Whether it be Adamic or not, the meaning of tragic *grandeur* – that is, of the specifically heroic perspective onto *grandeur* that tragedy affords – will derive from the tragic dialectic as a whole. The important thing is to focus on it; and also to note that it elicits an appropriate response in the spectator. This might be termed wonder or, in the older meaning of the word, admiration. It is surely as essential as Aristotle's pity and fear, and it does, as a matter of fact, have a history, both in tragedies and in discussions of tragedy. As Polyxena is sacrificed in Seneca's *Troades,* the crowd 'admire and commiserate'. Sidney was presumably recalling this passage when he claimed, in *An Apology for Poetry,* that tragedy teaches the uncertainty of this world 'with stirring the affects of admiration and commiseration'. Corneille argued famously for 'admiration' when describing the emotion aroused by his own theatre (and contrasting it, in his case, with Greek pity); Dryden considered that heroic tragedy 'moves admiration' and that the action of tragedy in general should be 'admirable' and 'wonderful'. Milton's Samson has been at 'the top of wondrous glory'. The emotion is named frequently, and unexpectedly, in Racine.

The 'wretchedness' of tragedy is, if anything, even more of a commonplace than its 'greatness'. The understanding of it in any particular play will naturally depend on the individual writer and his culture, and may be far from Christian. A few of its general features are, however, from a Christian point of view, suggestive.

There is the fact that it often centres on discord within the family, not only in the 'Christian' tragedy of Shakespeare or Webster, say, or Corneille, or especially Racine, but also, and indeed most famously, in ancient tragedy, with the families of Laius and Atreus, with Theseus and Medea. Aristotle's explanation was that a 'deed of horror' committed inside the family is the most conducive to fear and pity, and he is doubtless right. The predilection for family killing, however, can also remind one that the first intra-human wrongdoing in Genesis after the expulsion from Eden was Cain's slaying of his brother Abel. The stories on which tragedy is frequently based may be expressions, along with the Cain and Abel story, of a fundamental anxiety about blood relations, as anthropology and psychoanalogy might now propose; or otherwise, Cain and Abel is, in one way or another, the true tale, and tragedy constantly rehearses that primary rift.

There is also, on occasion, the suggestion of something like original sin. In tragedies drawing on the misfortunes of the house of Atreus, successive generations are brought down by a series of crimes whose cause moves further and further away in time. The rivalry of the Montagues and Capulets in the generation of Romeo and Juliet reaches back, not to their fathers but, as the Prologue is careful to point out, well beyond them, to an 'ancient grudge'. Tragic writers, like biblical writers (though not necessarily in the same terms), in contemplating *misère* explore the obscure perplexities of origin.

In one of those explorations a character in ancient tragedy, not the least famous, even undergoes a process that resembles most strangely and compellingly that of discovering original sin and one's own implication in it. Oedipus sees suffering all around him and desires to know its cause. His inquiry takes him gradually backwards in time, and eventually he pins the guilt for the act from which all suffering has issued on the inquirer. His investigation leads him to himself. He learns simultaneously who he is, and that he is wretched; he encounters his contaminated origin; the day brings him, in the words of Teiresias, 'birth and death'.

And the *misère* of tragedy is indeed the *misère* of a fallen world. Rather than being incompatible with a Christian reading of evil, in a wide sense of the word, tragedy disallows superficial readings that purport to be Christian and obliges the Christian to read more radically. Characteristically, it refuses the demand, typical of neoclassicism, that only the guilty should suffer. In play after play, the women of Troy endure bereavement and exile as unwilling victims of war. Iphigenia, Cordelia and Britannicus die not through their own but through someone else's wrong choice. They suffer because of the way of the world, or, in a Christian perspective, they undergo the moral evil of a fallen humanity, comparable to the physical evil (earthquakes, floods, etc.) of a fallen matter.

Suffering may also be caused by an error or even a sheer misunderstanding. Although Greek notions of guilt come into play when Oedipus kills his father and marries his mother, from another point of view he becomes parricidal and incestuous through ignorance. Romeo, even more incongruously, brings about his own and Juliet's death through not realising that she is merely drugged. Their mistakes – the possibility of such mistakes – are as sure a sign, for the Christian, that the world is fallen as, say, Macbeth's desire for the throne.

So, I believe, is the determinism that sometimes moves, in various guises, over and through the characters of tragedy. Here above all tragedy is likely to be pronounced unchristian, on the grounds that any determinism – fate, fortune, necessity, gods, or even a predestinating God – by denying the hero free will absolves him from responsibility for his actions. The question is, of course, extremely delicate. The commonsense view, that a man is only guilty when, in full possession of the facts and of his own freedom, he makes a choice that he knows to be wrong, is surely, however, not Christian, and is excluded by two elements in biblical teaching that one might well call tragic. The first is the original sin just referred to. According to this, a man suffers the consequences of someone else's wrong choice, and enters a world terribly altered because of it; when he himself chooses he exercises a will that, far from being free, is inherited from his fallen race and is biased towards evil. The second is the determin-ing of events by God, most strikingly in the Crucifixion. What is there in tragedy more awesome than Jesus' words about Judas? – 'truly the Son of man goeth, as it was determined: but woe unto that man by whom he is betrayed!'[2] The fact that the Crucifixion was necessary in no way removes, or even lessens, the guilt of the human agent whose action occasioned it. And the words were spoken, one remembers, in Judas' presence. The coexistence of necessity and guilt appears with the same clarity in Peter's sermon at Pentecost, when having said that Jesus was 'delivered by the determinate counsel and foreknowledge of God', without a pause he accuses his hearers (numerous ordinary people now, not the 'heroic' Judas) of having him crucified.[3]

Presumably it can be said of Judas that he 'freely' willed to betray, in the sense that he wanted to. Like the crowd, he did what he wanted. The same combination of destiny and choice recurs, of course, in tragedy. The witches in *Macbeth* foretell the future as it will necessarily unfold; Macbeth consents to that future. Original sin, however, can produce a situation of even greater moral complexity, in which the will is alienated. Nowhere in tragedy is this more extremely and disturbingly explored than in Racine's

Phèdre. Phèdre's incestuous love for Hippolyte is the effect of
Venus's revenge on her family, rather than, in the words of the
preface, a 'movement of her will'. Nevertheless, while she arraigns
the invincible power that impels her, she also, and fervently,
acknowledges her own guilt. Indeed, when her nurse Oenone
protests (with the weight of the whole Pelagian tradition behind
her) that Phèdre's lack of freedom in her crime relieves her of
responsibility, she dismisses her in indignation and calls on 'just
heaven' to punish her.

Phèdre knows that she is guilty because of what she is; and that
what she is is beyond her control. She has descended, figuratively,
into that labyrinth of the Minotaur which continually draws the
play's imagination. Although its first meaning is doubtless the
lethal involvement of sexuality, it also signifies, I take it, something like the inner abyss of the self, which contemporaries of
Racine were investigating (and which the Jansenist Pierre Nicole
placed 'below' the consciousness).[4] Phèdre is 'Christian' in that,
while she succumbs to an overwhelming force beyond and deeply
inside her, she protests her guilt.

Original sin is not, of course, referred to in the play, and yet one
is bound to make the connection. And curiously, the metaphor
that Pascal had recently chosen to describe original sin and its
'incomprehensible mystery' had also been labyrinthine. 'The knot
of our condition', he wrote in a now famous fragment (131) that
Racine presumably knew, 'is twisted and turned in that abyss'.

One might say, in fact, that Phèdre repeats an exemplary and
explicit engagement with sin – an engagement pitiable, terrible
and thoroughly tragic – by Paul, as recounted in the seventh
chapter of his letter to the Romans. He also finds himself acting
against his will: 'For the good that I would I do not: but the evil
which I would not, that I do.' Like Phèdre he is solicited
imperiously by goodness: 'If then I do that which I would not, I
consent unto the law that it is good.' Like her also, he discovers in
himself a total inability to pursue it: 'For I know that in me (that is,
in my flesh) dwelleth no good thing: for to will is present with me;
but how to perform that which is good I find not.' And in a
moment of overwhelming dramatic concentration, he too stares
at an irresistible invading power that has alienated him from
himself: 'Now if I do that I would not, it is no more I that do it, but
sin that dwelleth in me.' Isn't this last verse even the underlying

source (deeper than another source in Ovid) of the most cele-brated line of Phèdre, and of all Racinian tragedy? –

> Ce n'est plus une ardeur dans mes veines cachée:
> C'est Vénus tout entière à sa proie attachée.

(It is no longer an ardour hidden in my veins: it is Venus in all her fulness grappled to her prey.)

Paul concludes, before going beyond what is available to Phèdre and turning to God through Jesus: 'O wretched man that I am! who shall deliver me from this body of death?' *(AV* margin). His experience – of seeing the 'greatness' of the law while being irremediably bound to his own 'wretchedness'; of knowing himself both powerless and guilty – is surely a profound, fundamental version of the experience of certain heroes of tragedy. And below Paul there is the most fundamental of all experiences, that of Jesus on the Cross. Isn't this the ground, displaced by the absence of wrongdoing, of all puzzlement over determinism and freedom, over guilt and innocence? Christ on the cross suffers because he chooses to, but also by the 'determinate counsel' of God. At the exact centre of paradox, he is perfectly innocent and totally undeserving of death and yet, having willingly assumed the sins of the whole race, he is at the same time perfectly guilty – more guilty than anyone else, and the most guilty that it is possible to be.

Tragedy is the confrontation, in the first instance, of these radical extremes of the human condition. It is founded on what one might call in this context, using the term with its sense in rhetoric rather than dialectic, the tragic antithesis of greatness and wretchedness. Although its heroes may fall through one act of *hamartia* or the possession of one 'tragic flaw', as Adam and Eve fell through a great error concerning the words of the serpent and a forbidden desire to know good and evil, they are more properly seen as divided antithetically, in the manner of fallen Adam. Oedipus is a 'double subject', in Pascalian parlance, at once 'the greatest man' and 'the most cursed ... the most abhorred by the gods'. Philoctetes' bow never misses its mark, but his wound (for the time being) is incurable. Mecaenas says of Shakespeare's Antony: 'His taints and honours/Wag'd equal with him'; in Dryden's version in *All for Love,* to Ventidius' eulogy: 'You're all that's good, and god-like', Antony himself replies: 'All that's

wretched'. Racine's Thésée is both a universal purifier in succession to Hercules and a wreaker of sexual havoc; his son Hippolyte
gives a mathematical strictness to that division when he calls the
recounting of his erotic adventures 'Cette indigne moitié d'une si
belle histoire', 'that unworthy half of so fine a story'.

   Phèdre as a whole, in fact, exemplifies the tragic collision of
contraries. With almost her first words Phèdre addresses the sun –
'Noble et brillant auteur d'une triste famille', 'Noble and brillant
founder of a woeful family' – in a line that has a perfect tragic
shape, the celebration falling in the same breath to lamentation:
Racine often focuses the structure of tragedy in the structure of
the alexandrine. Phèdre and her world, and even seemingly the
stage, are bathed in that polysemic light, but are also invaded by
numerous figures of darkness; they are pulled between vision and
blindness, good and evil, life and death, heaven and Hades.
'Hyperbolically', Phèdre descends on the one hand from Jupiter,
master of the gods, and from the sun, the crown of nature, and on
the other from Minos, judge in the underworld. Her mother was
Pasiphaë, 'the lustrous'; her father inhabits 'infernal night'. Her
divided being – her reverence for purity, her criminal passion – is
not a peculiarity of the heroine but manifests and intensifies the
tragic division of the universe.

   The tragic hero is at once great and wretched. But greatness
and wretchedness do not, of course, merely occur: there is, first, a
fall from one to the other. Curiously, in the most famous description of that fall in English, if you can bear with me quoting the
prologue to Chaucer's 'Monk's Tale' after so many others, the
Pascalian vocabulary actually appears:

> Tragedie is to seyn a certeyn storie,
> As olde bokes maken us memorie,
> Of him that stood in greet prosperitee
> And is y-fallen out of heigh degree
> Into miserie, and endeth wrecchedly.[5]

The fall, like the prosperity, is often pushed to an extreme, tragedy
forcing the two faces of our condition to their 'superlative' limit.
The Persian empire in Aeschylus' *The Persians,* for instance, is
frequently celebrated in its culmination under Darius; after the
defeat at Salamis Xerxes is said to have inflicted more evils upon it
than would be possible for all its previous rulers combined, and in

the judgement of a messenger such a large number of men had never before perished in a single day. Oedipus the greatest man becomes similarly, according to an array of separate lamentations, the worst man, the most cursed, the most crushed by fate, the man on whom an Immortal has made a more powerful leap than has ever before been made, and who enters 'an evil beyond evil'.

At the same time, tragedy characteristically concentrates that double vision in a single perception, as in several of the passages just quoted. One also recalls Philo's description of Antony as 'The triple pillar of the world transform'd/Into a strumpet's fool', and the fact that Samson has fallen in the same way 'from the top of wondrous glory ... To lowest pitch of abject fortune'. In the résumé of Samson offered by the Chorus, moreover: 'The glory late of Israel, now the grief!' one sees the antithetical perception expressing itself in the actual antithesis of 'glory' and 'grief' – supported in its turn by the temporal contrast of 'late' and 'now', and also by alliteration. Among the figures of words, alliteration in tragedy is particularly appropriate to reinforce antithesis, among the figures of thought, since, as meaning sunders the terms, sound binds them painfully together. (One might also note, in tragedy's drive towards linguistic finality in this strong neoclassical line, the clinching chiasmus, *glory, late/now, grief,* and the placing of 'Israel' at the centre of the two-way awareness.)

The single perception is perhaps most telling when it is situated within the hero's consciousness. In Racine's *Andromaque*, Pyrrhus recalls in anguish the sacking of Troy:

> La victoire et la nuit, plus cruelles que nous,
> Nous excitaient au meurtre, et confondaient nos coups.

(Victory and night, more cruel than we, roused us to murder and confused our blows.)

He recognises that, at the accomplishing of his greatness, not only night but victory itself turned cruelly against him, to unite his military exploit with savagery. He achieved in a single action his heroic plenitude and his fall. More typically, however, it is the process rather than the instantaneity of the fall that tortures the hero's thought, for all the world as if he were representative man considering the Fall itself. It is in these terms that Richard II laments the coming loss of his crown:

O! that I were as great
As is my grief, or lesser than my name,
Or that I could forget what I have been,
Or not remember what I must be now.

(Antony, again, complains of Octavius, 'harping on what I am,/Not what he knew I was'. Restless thoughts present Samson with 'Times past, what once I was, and what am now'.) Because greatness in tragedy is associated with something already lost or being lost, tragedy seems to deplore or re-enact the dispossession of Adam, the forfeiture of his 'first nature', as it assumes or creates an alienated past in the present. So striking, indeed, is the comparison with the expulsion from Eden that the explicit or near-explicit Christianising of the hero's misadventure, the assimilating of the tragic fall to the Fall, is in no way fanciful. I am thinking, say, of Garnier's *Troade,* which (taking occasion from a line in Euripedes) traces the sufferings of Troy to the culpable act of Paris in such a way as to recall Adam's: 'Ainsi par la faute d'un seul/ Nous sommes en pleurs continues', 'Thus by the fault of one we are continually in tears'; or of Chaucer's bold placing of the falls of Lucifer and Adam as prelude to all other tragic falls and, by implication, as their source.

The contradictory vision of tragedy surely demands another way of considering the response of the spectator – if it is true that the response can be defined. I. A. Richards has suggested that in the most famous and tenacious definition, that of Aristotle, pity and fear are opposites. Isn't the opposition rather between wonder on the one hand and both pity and fear on the other? The idea is not in fact novel: in passages quoted above, Sidney proposes 'admiration and commiseration', while in an actual tragedy, Seneca's *Troades,* the spectators of Polyxena's death who 'admire and commiserate' are also seized with 'terror'. (The three emotions are likewise in play at the end of another sixteenth-century French tragedy, Montchrétien's *La Reine d'Écosse.)* Whether named or not, these would seem to be the antithetical emotions that correspond to the antithetical nature of tragedy, and indeed of life: we experience something like wonder because of *grandeur,* something like pity and fear because of *misère.*

The emotions do not, however, exist in separation: the strange power of tragedy is to cause them to combine. This is the lesson of Racine's most famous theoretical statement, contained in the preface of *Bérénice,* when he demands as one of the indispensable requirements of a tragic work, 'que tout s'y ressente de cette tristesse majestueuse qui fait tout le plaisir de la tragédie', 'that all should be suffused with that majestic sadness wherein lies all the pleasure of tragedy'. The perception of majesty is tragic when it merges with sadness; sadness is tragic when it merges with a perception of majesty.

What is true of the feelings of the audience is also true of the play. Greatness and wretchedness are themselves interdependent. Greatness is tragic, rather than epic, if it is also wretched; wretchedness is tragic, rather than pathetic, if it is also great. Tragedy, indeed, is the place in literature where the interaction of the two truths of our double condition is most clearly operative. As one increases in intensity, moreover, so does the other. In a marginal note, Racine writes of Hector's farewell to Andromache in the *Iliad* that, because their conversation 'takes place at the gate of the city, through which Hector will go out never to return', it 'becomes more tragic and more noble'.[6]

The relation is so close, in fact, that it tightens into paradox. The audience enters paradox through enduring a pain which, as innumerable writers have noted and puzzled over, is also a pleasure. (Racine, in the statement quoted above, refers to a 'pleasure' constituted by a 'sadness'.) Within the play, characters enter paradox in a variety of forms. Romeo and Juliet are ripe for it, through the rhetorical cast of their minds: Romeo expects a 'fearful' consequence to emerge from the 'revels'; before she knows his name, Juliet foresees by indirection that her 'grave' will be her 'wedding bed'. Appropriately, therefore, the truth when it is known turns out to be paradoxical, and Juliet learns that her 'only love' has sprung from her 'only hate'. They experience great-ness and wretchedness in a paradoxical bond. The perception of that bond culminates in Capulet, when the news of Juliet's (apparent) death interrupts the preparations for her wedding:

> All things that we ordained festival,
> Turn from their office to black funeral;
> Our instruments to melancholy bells,
> Our wedding cheer to a sad burial feast,
> Our solemn hymns to sullen dirges change,
> Our bridal flowers serve for a buried corse,
> And all things change them to the contrary.

Greatness not only gives way to wretchedness, as in the Fall and in the tragic fall: the one 'changes' into the other, and the same trappings serve for both. And as a ground to the play of this dark wit, there is the homely theology of Friar Laurence. In the soliloquy by which he enters the play, Laurence notes the dawn as an opposition – 'The grey-ey'd morn smiles on the frowning night' – and ponders the division of nature, in which the same flower contains poison and medicine, and the underlying division, 'in man as well as herbs', of 'grace and rude will'. Antithesis modulates into paradox when he reflects that 'Virtue itself turns vice, being misapplied,/And vice sometime's by action dignified'; and most profoundly in his equally conventional meditation on the earth:

> The earth that's nature's mother is her tomb;
> What is her burying grave that is her womb.

The Friar's commonplace reaches down through the play to the deep paradox of life and death, which, in a fallen world, meet.

Paradox functions even more tensely when greatness actually causes wretchedness. Victory, the accomplishment of Pyrrhus' status as a hero, also produced, as we saw, his barbarism. Flavius considers in the same vein the fall of Timon:

> My dearest lord, bless'd, to be most accurs'd,
> Rich, only to be wretched, thy great fortunes
> Are made thy chief afflictions.

In the most famous of all such instances, Oedipus has to learn from Teiresias that it was precisely his ability to solve the Sphinx's riddle which led, through his consequent marrying of Jocasta, to his downfall, and that not failure, but his 'success', has 'undone' him.[7]

One notes, finally, that the family strife as discussed above, recurrent in tragedy, is also governed by paradox. The paradox is sometimes underlined, as when the murders of the *Oresteia* culminate in Orestes' killing of the woman who gave him life, or in the tangle of relationships – mother–wife, father–brother, etc. – produced by the union of Oedipus and Jocasta. Cain confirmed paradox by the slaying of Abel, hating where he should have loved; Donalbain in *Macbeth* expresses the tragic truth both paradoxically and punningly: 'The near in blood, the nearer bloody'.

Because of this dialectical interaction of the two contraries, greatness, when wretchedness is at its most intense, also culminates.
Extreme greatness, to adapt Pascal, is deducible from the quality
of the extreme wretchedness. Either the sight of the hero dead
inspires superlative and exclusive celebrations of his worth, as
with Coriolanus: 'Let him be regarded/As the most noble corse
that ever herald/Did follow to his urn', or with Antony and Cleopatra: 'No grave upon the earth shall clip in it/A pair so famous';
or the imminence of death lifts the hero or heroine to a new
height, as when Polyxena's beauty, in Seneca's account of her
sacrifice, 'splendours more than ever at its final moment'. In
tragedy's contention with a fallen world, this greatness that
survives death and even grows through death is the hint of a third
movement of the dialectic.

That third movement, beyond the collision of greatness and
wretchedness, is, moreover, often attained. One of the hasty
opinions about tragedy (shared, it is true, by Dante and Chaucer) is
that it 'ends badly'. Yet tragedy may be the quest for a world
renewed, and the quest may be accomplished. There is avoidance
of tragedy when a joyful conclusion merely dismisses the antece-
dent conflict and suffering: one recognises here the plot of
innumerable popular works, and of many serious ones. There is
tragedy, simply, when the *misère,* universal and permanent in man
and in the human condition, remains, while being at the same
time dialectically reversed.

The renewal occurs at times in the domain of history and
politics, through the coming to a city, kingdom or empire of a
prosperity of an entirely new order. The *Oresteia* works painfully
downwards, confronting its aggrandised characters with an
accumulation of miseries, until, having reached its nadir in
Orestes' killing of his mother, it veers again dialectically, to issue in
Athena's prophecy of a new and glorious future for Athens. Its
long misery, without in any way being nullified, is eventually
opportune.

Similar renewal occurs in plays of Racine, who is of particular
moment here, given the stress in criticism on the darkness, the
'tragic' finality, of his endings. At the conclusion of *Andromaque* the
heroic Pyrrhus is killed, and indeed all the Greek characters are
soon dead or mad; but the news from the distance is that the boy

Astyanax is to be king and that his mother Andromaque has been proclaimed queen. Justice presides even, allowing Andromaque personally to succeed beyond her hope – she saves the life of her son, remains faithful to the dead Hector and avoids the necessity of suicide – and causing the Trojans, defeated militarily in the recent war but celebrated throughout as morally superior, to over-come the Greeks. Most significantly, the passing of the sceptre from Pyrrhus to Astyanax renews the kingdom: it replaces the 'old' and ambivalent king by another king, younger and purer, and a fallen nation by a better one.

It is true that there are few Trojans left for Astyanax to rule; but his true role extends beyond the play, and consists in founding, as it were, the French monarchy. In his second preface Racine refers, as to an object of common knowledge, to the fact that 'ancient chronicles' and also Ronsard in his national epic *La Franciade* had traced the royal line of France back to the Trojan prince. In the triumph of Astyanax, therefore, lies the possibility, for the audience, of the prestigious reign of Louis XIV.

Bérénice issues in a new prosperity for the Roman empire and thereby for the whole world. In a way it is a continuation of the previous play, *Britannicus,* in which Néron's fall from 'virtue' to crime is said to reverse Augustus' rise from crime to virtue, and in which the universal doom initiated at the close is revealed to be doubly impermanent by a sudden prospect of the Immortals, into whose number Augustus, because of his virtue, has been received. In *Bérénice,* the new emperor Titus retraces the ascent of Augustus, by escaping from his wasted youth – spent, as Racine has him specify, at Néron's court – and by renouncing his love for a foreigner unacceptable to Rome. It is not simply that he acquiesces in a sad duty, to an abstract concept of the state or to his own personal reputation or self-esteem. The rational morality in whose terms the characters conduct themselves opens on to a mythic process: death, which has progressively infiltrated the play to culminate in the intended suicide of each of the three princi-pals, is repulsed, so that the emperor may offer his 'virtues' to the universe.

The Adamic 'master of the world' makes, indeed, the right choice – or the woman makes it for him, since it is actually Bérénice who takes the initiative. Because the choice has to be made not in Eden but in a fallen world, he joins many other tragic heroes in less resembling Adam than the 'last Adam', and is involved, like him, in a total dialectic. The superlatively great love of himself and Bérénice has to become superlatively wretched: it is both 'l'amour la plus tendre et la plus malheureuse', 'the most tender love and the most unhappy'; the sacrifice is then reversed in its turn into the well-being of the world. The *misère* remains, in the suffering of the lovers, and produces the famous last word of the tragedy: 'Hélas!'

In Shakespearian tragedy the kingdom or city is likely to be healed rather than renewed, by a Fortinbras, a Malcolm, an Albany or an Alcibiades. Nevertheless, at the end of *Antony and Cleopatra* there is the promise, beyond the tragic deaths, of a 'universal peace', which the spectators are invited to recognise as no less than the peace of Augustus. A peace on a smaller scale, though patriotically more appealing to the audience (like the victory of Astyanax), also concludes *Richard III*. The *grandeur* in which the tragedy opens is already a peace – that procured by the accession of King Edward and presented not directly but by way of Richard's irony: 'Now is the winter of our discontent / Made glorious summer by this sun of York', etc. – which is ruined as the tragedy descends to the *misère* of another war. With Richmond the tragedy rises again, and it is remarkable that he cures more than the misery contained within the play. His victory at Bosworth ends a dynastic 'division' and a trail of Aristotelian and biblical family killings –

> The brother [hath] blindly shed the brother's blood,
> The father rashly slaughter'd his own son,
> The son, compell'd, been butcher to the sire –

that stretches far back into the English past. By removing Richard, the 'minister of hell', he brings to England not only 'smiling plenty, and fair prosperous days', but also a greater peace than before – indeed, a 'perpetual peace', guaranteed by the founding of a correspondingly greater dynasty.

Romeo and Juliet also cures an ancient grudge older than the play, and issues in peace for Verona, though a 'glooming' one: the conclusion, in the manner of *Bérénice,* stresses the 'woe' of the continuing *misère.* The play also exemplifies the change of sign operated by tragedy in its quest for renewal. Everything combines for wretchedness, from the initial falling in love of a Montague and a Capulet to the accidents leading to Romeo's mistake and his own and Juliet's death. Romeo is not wrong to see himself as Fortune's Fool. Yet everything also combines to terminate the feud between the two families, by calming the parents' rage, 'Which', as the Prologue declares, 'but [for] their children's end, nought could remove'. Greatness meets wretchedness paradoxically in this play, as I suggested above; likewise, whatever tends to wretchedness also tends, paradoxically, to a new and unlooked-for harmony. The person, moreover, whose stratagem brings about both the evil and the larger good that results from it is again Friar Laurence, the holy man. Laurence is another and more significant kind of Fool, and the first of many to figure in this study – the Fool being an essential agent of the dialectic.

Tragedy is sometimes a quest for the re-creation of history, for the securing of a future beyond the conditions of the present, in which 'all shall be well'. It can also be a quest for personal renewal. We might expect this in an explicitly Christian, or at least biblical, tragedy like *Samson Agonistes*. And indeed: having lost his former greatness in a present wretchedness of blindness, captivity and apparent abandonment by God, Samson takes his misery to the extreme of death, but the death is at the same time a victory of a different order (he slaughters more foes in this one action than in all his previous life), and a sign of his inward regeneration and reacceptance by God. Via the Chorus's simile of the phoenix, his victory is also related to the definitive victory of the resurrecting Christ; while his freeing of the nation of Israel is correspondingly related to the freeing, at the Resurrection, of the higher nation of the Church – to the freeing, that is, of all men from spiritual bondage, 'let but them / Find courage to lay hold on this occasion'. Yet, as one knows, in ancient tragedy too the hero may be changed. Philoctetes, for instance. For years he has been stretched between the *grandeur* of his divine bow and the *misère* of the wound which seems necessarily and appropriately to accompany it. The work of the tragedy is to complete his misery, by having him lose the bow, as a prelude to his being told, once the weapon is recovered, that he will not only be healed but will achieve glory, by being transformed into the victor of Troy. The transformation is largely a matter, I take it, of personal heroic prestige. He also learns, nevertheless, that all will occur under the direction of Zeus; and there is surely a deeper suggestion in the fact that when over-coming Troy he will kill Paris, the most radical enemy, and the man who, in the perspective of the Trojan war, is 'the author of all woes'.

The Hercules of Seneca's *Hercules on Oeta* is also transformed, and on an entirely different scale. He begins as a hero whose superlative and hyperbolic status is both prodigious and, within the fiction, true. As 'the glory of the world and its unique protec-tor, he whom the fates [have] given to the earth to replace Jupiter', he has already brought universal peace, by conquering all monsters and all evils engendered by earth, sea, air or under-world. (One senses again behind the tragic hero, despite the huge and obvious contrasts, less Adam than the last Adam.) His wretchedness is his death, and for a while the whole human race laments. As soon as he accepts death, however, and chooses a funeral pyre, his wretchedness is reversed into his final victory, for in overcoming fire he also overcomes, as an onlooker perceives, 'the only evil that he had left unvanquished'. At the beginning of the tragedy he had complained that, although Jupiter's son, he was still refused a place among the gods; having accomplished what can now be called the last of his 'labours', he sees his father opening the heavens to receive him. His transformation is manifested, moreover, by his reappearance as a god.

And so (returning to Sophocles) to the most enigmatic and perhaps the most appealing of all transformations of a tragic hero, that of Oedipus at Colonus. Oedipus is again the hero perceived antithetically, in this case as the king dispossessed, or as the old blind man who is consecrated and pious, a bearer of benefits. Around him the play as a whole is stretched antithetically, its two tendencies concentrating in two of the most famous of choruses, the one celebrating life in a celebration of Colonus ('Come praise Colonus' horses, and come praise / The wine-dark of the wood's intricacies . . .', in Yeats's version), the other lamenting life ('Never to have lived is best . . .'). At the conclusion, without any of Seneca's emphasis Oedipus also voyages beyond himself, when, having led the way sightlessly to his tomb, he is mysteriously translated, in a passing 'more wonderful than that of any other man'. Behind his personal renewal, moreover, he too becomes a 'saviour' (a *sótér*), promising Theseus that, provided the Athenians 'remember' him, their city will be forever 'closed to sorrows'.

The tragic hero at times accomplishes a quest, as it were for us, by emerging from some kind of fallen condition into a state of something like grace. His renewal may be accompanied by a reversal in his favour of the attentions of a god or gods. In two trilogies of Aeschylus, the *Prometheia* and the *Oresteia,* the divine world itself changes. In *Prometheus Bound,* Zeus the master of the gods is hostile to the human race and to Prometheus its divine champion, who has not only given to men 'all the arts' but has saved them from Zeus' desire to destroy them. At the end of the play Prometheus' sufferings begin to spiral downwards in inten-sity, but the signs are that in the later parts of the trilogy (which have, of course, been lost) the wrath of Zeus is to be turned aside, and a reconciliation effected. Zeus himself will have become newly just and forgiving.

The *Oresteia,* equally clearly, achieves out of its pain a similar reconciliation of extreme parties in the divine world, singing in its final lines the accord of Zeus and Moira. This time it is the Erinyes who change, accepting the new justice of Athena and becoming, as the Kindly Ones, propitious towards Athens. The prosperous civic future is guaranteed by a prosperity in the relations among gods and humans; and even the natural world is to respond perfectly to human desire. Athena averts the Erinyes' curse; they reverse it into a blessing, on the mineral, vegetable, animal and also the human realms, promising abundance rather than sterility to mines, to trees and harvests, to sheep, and to marriages. It may be that a fertility ritual is allusively present; the ending certainly seems to meet the more radical desires of such rituals – that a ground which is cursed should be transformed, by the removal of that curse, into a paradise.

2

When tragedy achieves its movement-beyond (which is far, of course, from always being the case), it travels the whole dialectic. It drives towards transformation, towards a possibility greater than the greatness of the beginning. It operates on history and civilisation, on the personal life, on heaven, even occasionally in pagan works imagining a revolution in the divine world, a change, if not from wrath to love, at least from wrath to blessing. It traces, at various stages of displacement, the dialectic of the Bible.

One should expect the existence, therefore (to adopt a term of Northrop Frye's), of a demonic parody of the process – the devil's version of the dialectic, as it were, in which all the values are systematically countered. The most complete instance of this that I know is the *Sejanus* of Ben Jonson. The play is steadied by tragic commonplaces, as hubris, the wheel of Fortune, the inordinate rise that makes the 'fall more steep and grievous'; and it leads to the drawing of a conventional lesson in its final lines:

> Let this example move the insolent man,
> Not to grow proud and careless of the gods. . .
> For, whom the morning saw so great and high,
> Thus low and little, 'fore the even doth lie.

Sejanus' story, however, enacts a far more wayward process, to which these traditional wisdoms are inadequate. His heroism, to begin with, is a travesty both of superlative greatness –

> Great and high,
> The world knows only two, that's Rome and I

and of hyperbolic greatness –

> My roof receives me not; 'tis air I tread;
> And, at each step, I feel my advanced head
> Knock out a star in heaven!

Fortune knows herself likewise 'the lesser deity', and merely Sejanus' servant; Jove is only his 'equal'. In his way, therefore, he inspires wonder, as a 'prodigy of men'.

He is, of course, a 'héros en mal'. But he also takes the heroic villain's villainy to such a pitch that, demonically, wretchedness becomes greatness. In celebrating himself he celebrates not Adam but fallen Adam. And again in keeping with the villain, he relishes rather than laments wretchedness, so turning the Fall into a triumph:

> A race of wicked acts
> Shall flow out of my anger, and o'erspread
> The world's wide face, which no posterity
> Shall e'er approve, nor yet keep silent. . .
> On, then, my soul, and start not in thy course;
> Though heaven drop sulphur, and hell belch out fire,
> Laugh at the idle terrors. . .

A more subtle reversal of wretchedness into an object of desire occurs in Shakespeare's *Timon of Athens,* when Timon's liberality has itself been reversed into hate:

> Matrons, turn incontinent!
> Obedience fail in children! slaves and fools,
> Pluck the grave wrinkled senate from the bench,
> And minister in their steads! To general filths
> Convert, o' the instant, green virginity!
> . . . Piety, and fear,
> Religion to the gods, peace, justice, truth . . .
> Decline to your confounding contraries,
> And let confusion live!

Capulet had sadly observed all things 'turn' and 'change' and become their 'contrary'; Timon uses the same dialectical and tragic vocabulary to summon that fall. And Shakespeare, while we are in this parenthesis, also explores, beyond the contradiction by which wretchedness is declared greatness, the ambiguity by which they are entangled one with the other – bedevilled, in fact – in the chorus 'Fair is foul, and foul is fair', which launches *Macbeth,* and which is spoken appropriately by the weird sisters.

The most radical parody in *Sejanus,* however, lies not in its dealings with the tragic contraries but in the third movement of its dialectic – the removal of Sejanus and his replacement by a successor – which, far from renewing *grandeur,* deepens *misère.* There is parody of social renewal when, in punishing Sejanus by dismembering him and hanging both his children, the Roman multitude indulge in cruelties greater than those of the criminal; they are said to perform, even more emphatically, 'Deeds done by men, beyond the acts of furies'. There is further parody of social renewal and also of the renewal of individual heroism when Sejanus is succeeded by 'the wittily and strangely cruel Macro', who circumvents the law against executing virgins by having the hangman rape Sejanus' daughter before killing her, and about whom it is prophesied that he will become 'a greater prodigy' than his predecessor. And there is parody of the renewal of divine favour when Arruntius demands:

> Dost thou hope, Fortune, to redeem thy crimes,
> To make amend for thy ill-placed favours,
> With these strange punishments?

'Punishments' is the disturbing word. The concluding actions of
Sejanus differ from the revenges in, say, *The Duchess of Malfi* or *'Tis
Pity She's a Whore,* which intensify the horror of a fallen world.
Here, the intensifying of horror poses as a purging. The nightmare is not in the fallen world merely but in the movement
beyond, in the process of the world's cleansing. It expresses our
terror, I presume, that punishment should be in the hands not of a
just and loving God but of devils. The play suggests as much, when
Macro's killing of Sejanus' children is called an 'act most worthy
hell'.

And there is more: the tragedy opens to the possibility of
demonic apocalypse. If divine apocalypse is the definitive 'movement beyond', the perfect re-creation of ourselves and the world,
demonic apocalypse would be a final reign of destruction and
terror. At the beginning of the play Arruntius and others are
convinced that they live in a time of decadence:

> The men are not the same: 'tis we are base,
> Poor, and degenerate from the exalted strain
> Of our great fathers . . .

At the end, the decadence slides giddily forward via the intuition
of an unnamed messenger reporting the invective of Sejanus'
widow:

> Her drowned voice gat up above her woes,
> And with such black and bitter execrations,
> As might affront the gods, and force the sun
> Run backward to the east; nay, make the old
> Deformed chaos rise again, to o'erwhelm
> Them, us, and all the world . . .

Jonson has taken the suggestion of 'wretchedness' as far, perhaps,
as it is possible to go, by conceiving a tragedy that functions

perfectly, but parodically, as the accomplishment of a kind of diabolical quest.

3

I have been claiming that tragedy articulates, for a variety of its own purposes, the Christian dialectic. The reverse also seems true: Christianity, in a certain light, is tragic. It is often argued that the Christian belief in an order that comprehends suffering and death and a grace that is able to overcome evil – a belief in paradise, resurrection, a redeeming God – removes from *misère* its tragic sting. Yet Jesus himself wept, on two famous and significant occasions.[8] His tears on the way to the grave of Lazarus seem to have had many causes; among them were presumably his friend's death and the suffering of Lazarus' sisters. He wept, remarkably, despite the fact that he was about to raise Lazarus from the dead and turn the suffering into joy. The pain of a fallen world cannot be discounted, even if one has a Messiah's knowledge of the future, because of its present reality. He also wept over Jerusalem, seeing the city's blindness, which was causing it to refuse him and would soon lead to its own destruction. The present reality of sin is likewise a reason for pity, and, to ordinary humans, for fear as well. Its persistence even more so. Hell (except in those theologies that avoid it and that usually are untragic) even seems to carry something of tragic darkness into the final splendour of glory.

Christianity is also tragic because its dialectic continues. As I suggested in the previous chapter, renewal becomes the source of a further conflict, since wretchedness reasserts itself and the definitive renewal is reserved for the future. And there is at least one tragedy whose dialectic is similarly continued, and which is also Christian: Racine's Old Testament play *Athalie*.

Here, in terms of social quest, the favoured people of God and their city Jerusalem, having fallen into the *misère* of being ruled by the pagan and partly foreign Athalie, are renewed by her despatch and by the unhoped-for victory of her grandson Joas, who has been presumed dead. The old queen is replaced by a king who is young and innocent – who is, in fact, like Astyanax, a child. In terms of personal quest, the greatness of Joas, the boy who should be king, confronts the wretchedness of his concealment and of the new threat to his life, to be renewed in his recovery of the throne. As the latest of the royal line, moreover, from whom the Messiah should be born, he is no less than the supreme figure of his generation, the focus of human hope. His triumph is therefore religious as well as national: his return, as it were from the dead, is described as a 'resurrection'. In terms of religious quest, God, who has seemed to most of his people to have abandoned them, reveals himself at the close.

Even without the further rebounding of the dialectic, the play is already fully a tragedy, mainly because of Athalie herself. Athalie also is a divided heroine: a 'great queen', a 'great soul', she has involved herself in family bloodshed, through murdering her grandchildren, and is herself involved in a kind of family determinism, being the daughter of Jezabel. Above all she is excluded from the kingdom of grace, and after a final confrontation with God – 'Impitoyable Dieu, toi seul as tout conduit!', 'Pitiless God, you manoeuvred it all!' – she is literally exterminated. Athalie is the pitiable heroine who exposes a fearful world and a lasting misery, that of the reprobate. The experience of the audience in the dénouement, however joyful, is bound to include sorrow at life, the awareness of a world out of joint.

The play could well finish with the exulting of the victorious Jews; but, as I suggested, the ternary pattern of tragedy is continued here into a fourth movement. The transformation in the ending becomes the thesis (the *grandeur*) of a new dialectical action, whose antithesis (or *misère*) is announced in a prophecy of the High Priest. Beyond the action of the play itself, the renewed Jerusalem will fall captive to Babylon, the renewed Joas will murder the High Priest's son and successor, and the renewed favour of God will be withdrawn when he 'casts off his love'. Even Athalie on the point of dying is allowed to add her curse, and to involve Joas in her own necessity. She traces through successive generations of her family, all of them the enemies of God, the 'original sin' that will finally overwhelm him.

In the future that is projected beyond its joyful conclusion, the tragedy places the audience back within the process of an unfinished dialectic. Even more strikingly, however, it also enters a fifth movement, as the dialectic is once again, in the even more distant future, resolved and exceeded. According to the same prophecy, while the 'ancient blessings' of God return, Jerusalem will be 'reborn more splendid and more beautiful' as the Church, and the child-hero Joas will be assimilated into the Hero of heroes,

when the earth 'gives birth to its Saviour'. It is as if the ending of
Athalie were the beginning of a new tragedy, whose quest leads,
through a worse *misère* of captivity, apostacy and godlessness, to
the ultimate accomplishment.

With this large imaginative stroke, Racine has definitively
situated tragedy within the terms of Christian belief. He has set
the tragic triumph in a world still fallen and still falling, and he has
interpreted that triumph as a version of the triumph to come.

4

And what of language? Does it too enter the tragic process? We
have already seen tragedy drawing on linguistic forms to convey
its dialectic; and by combining what in individual plays occurs
discretely we might array elements of rhetoric and grammar in a
total tragic design. The superlative and hyperbole figure *grandeur*.
Antithesis figures the collision of *grandeur* and *misère*. Paradox
also figures their strange relation, as does oxymoron: Antonio's
luck in being loved by the Duchess of Malfi, which will lead to his
death, is an 'unfortunate fortune', and Phèdre's incestuous desire a
'black flame'. Oxymoron may also figure the new world that
emerges beyond. In Racine's *Bérénice,* the funeral by night of the
late emperor has been the occasion of his apotheosis, with the
nocturnal ceremony also revealing the 'lustre' of his successor,
Titus; in words that look to the end of the play, when another
triumph is achieved out of Titus' own metaphorical death,
Bérénice refers to the funeral and remembers the 'splendour' of
that 'night'. (The order of the French: 'De cette nuit, Phénice, as-tu
vu la splendeur?', along with the grammatical indirection, the
pausing, through the name of an interchangeable *confidente,* and
the interrogative enthusiasm, are beautifully accurate.)

Language is tragic, however, not when it conveys the dialectic
of tragedy in its forms but when it is itself involved in that dialectic. The characters of tragedy may encounter, in various ways, the
misère of a language bedevilled. This occurs most simply when
other characters mislead them with the language of the serpent,
as Goneril and Regan mislead their father in the opening scene of
King Lear. Goneril's lying is especially diabolical, since she claims
that language – 'word', 'breath' and 'speech' – is inadequate to her
love, whereas it is her non-existent love that is inadequate to her

entirely able eloquence; and the lies of both Goneril and Regan have the further diabolical effect of preventing the language of Cordelia. Iago's language to Othello is closer to the serpent's in strategy, being insinuative; and when, in Sophocles' *The Women of Trachis,* the centaur Nessos tells Dejanira that his blood will act as a charm to prevent her husband Heracles from preferring any other woman – that is, that it will kill him – he deceives her in a pagan work with precisely the ambiguity, the lie concealed in a truth, that ruined Eve.

Lies are not, of course, exclusive to tragedy. It is nevertheless in tragedy, which sounds the wretchedness of the human condition with a peculiar perseverance, that all enactments of the corruption of language are most appropriately sited. Another such enactment is the curse, like that by which Oedipus, prior to Aeschylus' *Seven Against Thebes,* has vowed his sons to mortal combat. Since the curse has a constraining power over the future, Eteocles wrestles in the course of the play with a language that partly causes his fratricidal passion and that finally kills him. Another is the oracle, a version of which confounds Macbeth. The language of the witches and of their 'masters' is actually seen to be that of the serpent, both by Banquo: 'And oftentimes, to win us to our harm, / The instruments of darkness tell us truths', and, too late, by Macbeth himself, who begins to doubt 'th'equivocation of the fiend, / That lies like truth'. It is founded on confusion: 'Fair is foul, and foul is fair', works by ambiguity, 'paltering' with Macbeth 'in a double sense', and even taunts its victim with apparently meaningless reference, to someone not born of woman and to a wood moving. Groping in the semantic obscurity of a world in which the devil has spoken, the tragic hero goes to his death.

There are other ways in which tragedy explores what I am calling a fallen language. Thésée in Racine's *Phèdre,* for instance, experiences wretchedness in his own speech. Fooled into believing that his son is guilty of attempted rape, he launches towards Neptune words asking for Hippolyte to be killed, to discover, when he changes his mind, that they can no longer be withdrawn. What he receives back from the god – 'funestes bienfaits', 'funeste bonté', 'faveurs meurtrières' (deadly benefits, deadly kindness, murderous favours) is revelation of the state of things conveyed in a series of oxymorons. Yet there is surely a deeper and more inward involvement in tragedy of the *misère* of language, an involvement that does not show itself in the matter of the play, and which is the affair in any case not of the spectator and reader but of the writer. I am thinking of the constraints to which the writer submits, for the making of his language, as for the making of his play as a whole. Doesn't he by his labour, by his toiling 'in the sweat of his face', undergo language after the Fall, and work language outside Eden? Again, the labouring of a language fallen from the ease and efficacy which the writer glimpses and desires is not in any way confined to tragedy: it is perhaps the most universal sign of linguistic wretchedness, and is equally discover-able in epigrams or pastoral. It too, however, has in tragedy its most sharply focused significance. One might think, indeed, that the rigour through which the tragic writer passes – not necessarily entailing anything dramatic, like wasting his life-energies for the sake of his art, or even burning the midnight oil, but simply strug-gling hard to make it right – re-enacts, in this context, the rigour of tragic experience; and that by his toil the writer of tragedy enters the fallen world of his heroes, and suffers something of the tragic process.

By taking on the *misère* of that world he also transfigures it, achieving from his labour a perfection, maybe, of language (as of theatrical craft, and of various kinds of vision) that corresponds, within the tragedy, to the final renewal. For language participates also in the third movement of the dialectic. Language too is accomplished; and it is once again in tragedy that its accomplish-ing acquires special moment. Hence, to quote someone who knew from the inside, another, and surprising, passage in the preface to Racine's *Bérénice,* where, listing the elements necessary to sustain-ing a tragedy, he passes from the violence of the passions and the beauty of the feelings to 'the elegance of the expression'. 'Elegance' is not a term that would have occurred to us, and finding it in Racine we may be tempted, if we are English, to echo Dryden on the French and their insipid good breeding. I take *élégance* more seriously, however, to be Racine's version of that linguistic achievement in a tragic work that parallels the achieve-ment of its action in the domain of the personal, the historical or the religious.

Isn't the achievement of language also one of the means by which tragedy actually copes with *misère* and carries through beyond it? Guilt, suffering, the exactions of a fallen world, all the distressing events and implications of tragedy, are gradually absorbed, while remaining themselves, into a renewing language, as into the many renewing forms of the drama. It happens at the level of the work as a whole, and also detail by detail. To stay with Racine, there is a moment in Théramène's recital of the death of his pupil Hippolyte when he pauses:

> Excusez ma douleur. Cette image cruelle
> Sera pour moi de pleurs une source eternelle.

(Excuse my grief. That cruel image will be to me of tears an eternal source.)

The simple inversion of 'de pleurs une source éternelle' (along with the use of metaphor, among other things, and the placing of the expression in a continuous sonority, in a pattern of rhyme and in the configuration of the alexandrine) gathers 'grief' and 'tears' and the 'cruel image' which causes them into a new eloquence. This is, of course, the familiar alchemy in which the disagreeable, by virtue of art, becomes agreeable; but here too, in tragedy the process culminates. The excitement of language does not, or should not, remove the evil or cause us to forget it: it transforms evil, turning a potential pain, as Hume saw, into a certain pleasure; and it constitutes in itself one of the successes – in fact, the most secure success – of tragedy's dialectic.

The emergence of language as a value often occurs most pointedly, as here, at the moment of the hero's death, that is, at the climax of wretchedness. The language is sometimes spoken by a fluent messenger, who may begin his account in such a way that we expect an oration, perhaps with an introduction deliberately quiet. Théramène had begun: 'A peine nous sortions des portes de Trézène . . .', 'We were just passing out through the gates of Troezen . . .'; while the opening of the Message in *Samson Agonistes* is even more understated: 'Occasions drew me early to this city'. Whatever the reasons for the convention by which death occurs off-stage, its result is that the death is mediated to the audience through language, and that in language it is intensified, heightened, ordered, phrased. When the convention is not operative, the hero himself may deliver the crowning utterance. Part of our delight is again in a perfection of language, as that of Racine's Phèdre or Seneca's Hercules, which is consummated at death and which survives beyond it. The hero may even be aware of his linguistic role. Othello is, when on the point of transforming

death, and his own life, into particularly self-conscious artistry, he
asks for 'a word or two'. However we respond to that self-regard,
and whatever the problems in general of a word that effects a
redemption which is only aesthetic, the move is surely right. At
the extreme moments we desire language (or silence); and we are
always glad when the hero achieves his final aria, as if touched on
the arrival of death by the gift of Pentecost.

3 Comedy and Possibility

The other kind of literary work most clearly dialectical, I suggested, is comedy; and I should now like to explore, after the tragic, the comic way of engaging with a fallen world and of creating a new world of possibility. In particular, I shall be concerned with farce and with the Fool, and, more centrally than in the previous chapter, with language. The focus will be narrower – I shall be looking at Molière, Shakespeare, Sheridan and Dickens – but I believe that the type of comedy considered is fundamental enough to involve comedy as a whole. (From another point of view the scope is actually wider, since it includes the novel as well as drama, and also, passingly, film.) The collocation of those writers may appear odd: I trust that it will explain itself as we advance; and if I begin with a French dramatist rather than say, Ben Jonson, and fail even to mention a number of his more familiar plays, it is because the plays that I do concentrate on in some detail are the most perfect examples I know of the comic process as I understand it.

1

Molière and Lully's *Le Bourgeois gentilhomme* opens with music and ends in song and dance. It is sustained throughout by airs and ballets, and culminates in a mock ceremony in which the title character believes he is being received into a Turkish order of knighthood. Jourdain is the centre of a copious theatricality, and he gives himself to it ludicrously but wholly. He spends his day arranging for artistic entertainments in his house, showing off his clothes, extravagantly bowing, mouthing vowels and consonants as instructed by his philosophy teacher, singing, fencing, performing a minuet. When he is made a 'Mamamouchi', someone says of him that 'if he had learnt his part by heart, he couldn't play it better'.

43

Is this a work about a bourgeois who wants to become a gentleman, or a man who wants to play? Jourdain surely sees life in the
aristocratic world as a marvellous and inexhaustible game.
Mimicking a gentleman allows him to enter a gorgeous vision. His
courtship of Dorimène is a fantasy of serenades, diamond rings,
bouquets, banquets, fireworks on the water. He wants to act, and
the Play is his occasion. It provides him, in the climax at the end of
Act 4, with the Turkish ceremony, when he dresses up and
becomes the star actor in a solemn ritual.

The play is, in one perspective, a satire, a comedy of psychological and social observation and judgement, based, one assumes, on
actual conditions in seventeenth-century France. It would be
wrong, however, to consider it fundamentally a satire, with
various entertainments added (perhaps only to please Louis XIV),
rather than what it calls itself, a comedy-ballet. Lully's music and
also Beauchamp's dances are as integral as Molière's text, and are
necessary to the effect of the whole.

The work's 'serious' concerns are absorbed into another kind of
gravity, that of play. Its underlying patterns are, most immediately,
those of the *commedia dell'arte* and of farce. (Not, of course, that
these are lacking in realistic wit.) There are the male and female
servant roles, the two pairs of *amorosi,* the philosophy teacher who
recalls both the doctor of the *commedia* and the pedant of French
farce, and the fencing-master who bears some resemblance to the
braggart Captain; while Covielle, the intriguing valet who organ-
ises the Turkish plot, is actually named after his Italian counterpart
Coviello. Jourdain himself is, partly, the 'old man in love who is
hoodwinked', and, since Dorante cheats him of both Dorimène
and his money, he also plays the 'dupe' to Dorante's 'rogue'. As
well as the music and the dance, the disguises and the masquer-
ade, the final ballet uses provincial dialects, in the manner of farce
and the *commedia,* and even includes a mime by Scaramouches,
Trivellinos and Harlequin.

The play is animated largely by traditional characters and situations (many of which go even further back, to Latin and Greek
comedy) and what Jourdain wishes to acquire for himself, by
becoming a gentleman, is another role. Convention combines
with dance and music and ceremony to create the play as an
abundant theatrical artifice. They lift it out of reality into an
inspired unreality. Even language is left behind. In its fantastic
journey towards elsewhere, the comedy of manners and of charac-

ter loses its French. Not only does the final ballet move through the patois of Gascony and Switzerland into Italian and Spanish: the climactic ceremony and its preparation whirl into mock Turkish and the dog Italian of *lingua franca.*

The play projects a world of glory, to be entered by laughter. That world is quite other and perfectly fictive; it is not, however, merely an evasion. In the privileged space of the stage it transforms our world into itself. At one moment, Jourdain is disrobed and robed anew by four balletic tailors to the accompaniment of the orchestra, so as to be dressed, as the text describes it, 'rhythmically' ('en cadence') and 'with ceremony'. Music and dance descend with exact artifice to transfigure the hero's changing of his clothes.

The symbolic suggestion of the scene is crowned in the Turkish ceremony. This is, after all, the burlesque of a ritual specifically of transformation. Jourdain is a clown, but his desire is a deep one: to be raised and remade. The ceremony is a doubly artificial event, a play within a play, and the rank to which it promotes Jourdain, being non-existent, is doubly fictive. Secure in its unreality, the ritual changes him, in the comic mode, granting him a new status in excess even of what he aspired to.

A ritual also closes Molière and Charpentier's *Le Malade imaginaire,* another comedy-ballet and the last of Molière's works. The play moves even more pointedly from social and psychological reality into the empire of artifice. It emerges from a prologue in a pastoral setting and concludes with a burlesque in which all of the characters take a role; while in one of its long interludes, written partly in Italian, Punch of the *commedia* transposes the fundamental patterns of the play, in music and ballet, and in a different fiction altogether. In the burlesque, Argan the hypochondriac, who desires to heal his corrupted body, and who stands in religious awe of the medical profession, is received as a doctor in hilarious macaronic Latin. Like Jourdain, he is transformed beyond, as it were, his wildest dreams.

The ceremonies are gifts to Jourdain and Argan, but they are also, naturally, devices at their expense. Jourdain is fooled into marrying his daughter to a man he has egotistically refused as a bourgeois, but who is now disguised as the son of the Sultan of Turkey; Argan is fooled into thinking he is being made a doctor, so that he will consent to a son-in-law who isn't one. The comedy re-creates the world in hilarity, and it does so by overcoming the world's evil.

This is the strategy of Molière's comedy-ballets, and all their
details further it. Like (and unlike) tragedies, they resolve conflict
and suffering into art. In *Les Amants magnifiques,* Eriphile silently
meditates the loss of the man she loves while four mimes 'adapt
their gestures and their steps to the uneasy sorrowings of the
young Princess'. The audience sees her 'real', though already
fictive, emotions and also their redemption in the artistry of the
mime. At the end of the 'Overture' to *Monsieur de Pourceaugnac,*
four passers-by quarrel and unsheath their swords. Then, 'after a
most pleasing engagement, they are separated by two Swiss
guards who, having reconciled them, dance with them, to the
sound of all the instruments'. The vigorous patterning of scene
and dialogue likewise gathers harsh emotions into aesthetic play.
This can be very complex in the great works; a simplified version
is the double lovers' quarrel that opens *Mélicerte:*

Acante: Ah! charmante Daphné!
Tyrène: Trop aimable Eroxène.
Daphné: Acante, laisse-moi.
Eroxène: Ne me suis point, Tyrène.
Acante: Pourquoi me chasses-tu?
Tyrène: Pourquoi fuis-tu mes pas?
Daphné: Tu me plais loin de moi.
Eroxène: Je m'aime où tu n'es pas. *etc.*

Pastoral intervenes to the same end. It opens the stage to
another place, Arcadia, where problems exist but are resolved
with ease. In *Le Bourgeois gentilhomme,* the happy solution of the
play is mirrored in a musical dialogue in the first act, an entertainment for Jourdain presented by the music master. A shepherd who rails against love because of the infidelity of woman
is persuaded to join in a final chorus in praise of love by a shepherdess who, renouncing her desire for independence with
implausible speed, offers him her heart. The original prologue
to *Le Malade imaginaire* is another 'eclogue', even longer and
more elaborate. In a 'highly pleasing rural scene', complete with
dancing Zephyrs and Fauns, Pan and Flora preside over a competi-
tion in which two love-sick shepherds vie with each other in songs
to the glory of the king. Their sickness is cured when both receive
the prize and their shepherdesses consent to marry them. In the
action of the play itself, Argan's daughter and her lover, during a

music lesson at which Argan is present, contrive to declare their love by transposing it, detail by detail, into a 'little impromptu opera' about a shepherd and shepherdess. It is as if their love, thwarted for the time being but sure of success at the end of the play, really does occur in the charmed world of pastoral.

The marriage of the lovers is, in fact, the clearest and most traditional sign of the comic intention. Here, as is so often the case, the function of comedy is partly to allow young lovers to triumph by ruse over an older man, either the girl's father or an unwanted rival. One usually reads, under this comic cliché, an archaic symbolism: the victory of spring over winter, of youth over age. Isn't the process, however, more than seasonal and cyclic? The ruse and the triumph represent a comic overcoming of the way of the world. This basic plot of comedy is also a plot against a fallen condition.

A specifically Christian interpretation of the marriage would relate it, I believe, rather ambitiously: to 'Edenic' marriage, and to the Church. When Adam sees the woman whom God has fashioned from his rib, he declares, 'This is now bone of my bones, and flesh of my flesh', and the writer comments: 'Therefore shall a man leave his father and his mother, and shall cleave unto his wife: and they shall be one flesh.' To marry, it seems, is to recover something of that primal unity that preceded the Fall. At the other end of history, as Northrop Frye observes in *Anatomy of Criticism* (p. 185), the young man's winning of his bride can be seen as corresponding, at a certain depth, to Jesus acquiring a bride in the form of the Church. Indeed, the analogical bond between marriage and salvation is startlingly close. In the course of a famous exposition of marriage in the fifth chapter of his letter to the Ephesians, Paul re-applies Adam's statement concerning himself and the woman to the relation between Christ and Christians: 'we are', he says, 'members of his body, of his flesh, and of his bones'. (That he has Genesis in mind is certain: he continues by quoting the other passage about 'one flesh'.) In this perspective, the marriage of the lovers, which is the success of the comedy, looks towards the supreme success, the end of the dialectic, in so far as that too is a marriage, both spiritual and eternal. One notices, moreover, that, as in the events that followed the Fall – and also as in tragedy – the *misère* against which the lovers achieve their marriage is often family discord.

The ceremonies are similarly dialectical. There is a moment in the Turkish ceremony of *Le Bourgeois gentilhomme* where the actors pretend to strike Jourdain with sabres and then really strike him with sticks. He rejoices, and is beaten. Doesn't this small piece of stage business focus the whole play? Jourdain's folly, which creates the play but which remains a folly nevertheless, is derided; he pays for it, and for the bliss it brings him. The payment is comic, and almost painless. It is also aesthetic, for the blows strike him 'en cadence'.

All the forces that have been brought into the play meet here. There is the glorious folly of Jourdain, and also the violence inherent in the play's egoisms: in Jourdain's uniquely selfish obsession and his dangerous 'bile', in Dorante's financial and erotic knavery, and in the vanity of the various masters, which has already led to their fighting. Covielle's actors express this violence; Jourdain submits to it. As the violence is expended and absorbed, so the transformation of Jourdain into a Mamamouchi can occur, and so the hilarity can be achieved.

There is something disturbingly unsophisticated in a man being beaten with a stick. A certain kind of response to literature disparages it. It was the similar moment in *Les Fourberies de Scapin,* when Géronte hides in a sack and is belaboured by a valet, that Boileau chose for disapproval, when making the characteristic neoclassical distinction between Molière's high comedies and his low. The distinction is often made, in favour of comedy that 'pleases and instructs', or that constitutes a 'criticism of life' – comedy that is an achievement of high civilisation. Yet farce can be at the very centre. Simple, basic, primitive, profound, it enacts not problems of civilisation but underlying realities of the human condition. It can be deadly serious, showing and fictively purging the Fall; it can be gloriously re-creative, intimating in the liberation of its laughter a new world and a new man.

The ceremony of *Le Malade imaginaire* concludes a play openly concerned with purgation. Argan is appalled by the corruption of the body, and longs for cleansing and renewal. (He is the Fool set apart for his wise daftness, his awareness of death and of the need to be cured.) Alone on the stage in the first scene, he reckons up the month's bills from his apothecary. They detail with persuasive particularity the actions of innumerable medicines and enemas on the various inner parts of his person:

> ... un petit clystère insinuatif, préparatif et rémollient, pour amollir, humecter et rafraîchir les entrailles de monsieur ... un

bon clystère détersif ... pour balayer, laver et nettoyer le bas-
ventre de monsieur ... une bonne médecine purgative et corro-
borative ... pour expulser et évacuer la bile de monsieur ...

*(a small, insinuative, preparative, easing clyster, to soften, moisten and
refresh the Gentleman's entrails ... a good detersive clyster ... to scour,
wash and clean the Gentleman's lower abdomen ... a goodly physic, purgative and corroborant ... to expel and evacuate the Gentleman's bile ...)*

The nicety of the jargon, which descends into Argan's nether
regions and raises them to decorum and poetry, effects, in
language and in the comic mode, a redemption of the body. (This
delicate scatology follows immediately from the opening eclogue.
The unclassical range of tone and experience, as throughout
Molière's writing, is extensive: from Arcady to arse.)

Argan's doctor, appropriately 'Monsieur Purgon', suggests the
moral, metaphysical dimension to the hypochondriac's terror. On
Argan's refusal of yet another rectal injection, Purgon renounces
him in the manner of a priest excommunicating a 'rebellious'
penitent (from enema to anathema), refusing to 'clean' him, giving
him over to the 'sickness' of his constitution, the 'intemperance' of
his entrails, the 'corruption' of his blood, and abandoning him to
the seven deadly illnesses: bradypepsia, dyspepsia, apepsy,
lientery, dysentery, dropsy, and privation of life.

The young lovers triumph also over a more sinister corruption
than the lovers of *Le Bourgeois gentilhomme*. As well as Argan's
egoism, and the doctors who bleed their patient both literally and
metaphorically, there is Argan's second wife, Béline – the stepmother of fairy tale – who schemes for his inheritance and gloats
over what she believes to be his corpse.

In the final ceremony, Argan rises above the sickness of his
body by becoming a doctor, though, unlike Jourdain, he is not at
the same time symbolically punished. The play does include farcical violence, and at one point Argan's servant stuffs a pillow in his
face while pretending to make him comfortable. But it is Punch
who pays in his stead. Punch is another foolish old man, and, since
he is described as a usurer, he also represents the rapacity of
Béline and the doctors. During a nocturnal interlude, he is continually frustrated in his attempts to serenade his mistress. He is
mocked, when a railing old woman sings in reply, and then beaten
with sticks, 'en cadence'.

On the other hand, neither is Argan as much transformed as
Jourdain. The title of Doctor, rather than Mamamouchi, retains

him, almost, in our world; and the ceremony, unreal in its make-
believe and its dog Latin, is nevertheless satirical, and concerned
with the reality of the medical profession. Yet the satire itself lifts
into fantasy. The statements of the mock doctors become more
and more outlandish, until the President of the Faculty grants
Argan power

> Medicandi,
> Purgandi,
> Seignandi,
> Perçandi,
> Taillandi,
> Coupandi,
> Et occidendi
> Impune per totam terram.

*(to Physic, /Purge, /Bleed, /Pierce, /Cleave, /Cut /And kill / With impunity
throughout the world.)*

Comedy here deals with corruption by making it worse, by
exaggerating it to the point where it passes beyond the real, and
becomes hilarious.

There is also a suggestion of festivity. As soon as she enters the
strange world of the play, Madame Jourdain complains that her
house is given over to endless 'Shrovetide revels'. At the close, she
wonders if Jourdain is marrying their daughter to a 'Shrovetide
mask'. Similarly, Argan's brother Béralde claims that the burlesque he has prepared is authorised by 'the carnival', meaning
Shrovetide again, or else the whole carnival season from Twelfth
Night to Lent. The rapid references place the entertainments,
interludes, dances, songs, disguises, masquerades, the impromptu
playlet in *Le Malade imaginaire* and the wild abuse of its finale in a
context of festivity. Even the dressing-up and mocking of Jourdain
and Argan resonates with folklore. The plays are related, like
many of Shakespeare's, to the audience's experience of revelry,
and in particular the revelry of spring.

In these two plays, a character wants to rise above his condition,
foolishly (rather than heroically); his wish is granted, burlesquely,
and we rejoice in the vision he opens of a world new-made. In
confronting evil, however, the comedy exposes its fool; and one
can imagine that, to achieve its ends, it might expose him far
more, while still remaining comic. The fool would experience, in a
comic perspective, the terror of evil and, instead of escaping

virtually scot-free, he would really suffer, for us. As a victim only, he would not be transformed, and the unreality that he entered would be not euphoric dream but nightmare.

Precisely this occurs in *Monsieur de Pourceaugnac,* another comedy-ballet in which Molière collaborated with Lully. The work is even closer to the *commedia,* being based on two Neapolitan Punch plays; it leads to a final masque, in praise of folly, laughter and pleasure, in which the characters other than Pourceaugnac 'enjoy the seasonal entertainment'; and it is another ruse in favour of young lovers. The whole play, in fact, is a series of ruses by which Pourceaugnac, a rival for the girl's hand, is discredited with her father and forced to flee the town. The angle of vision changes, however, with respect to *Le Bourgeois gentilhomme* and *Le Malade imaginaire,* when the play discloses that the ruse which fools the Fool is itself potentially evil. The 'man of intrigue' who abets the lovers congratulates his accomplice on her previous escapades, when she cheated a young foreigner out of twelve thousand crowns, drew up a false contract that ruined a whole family, and gave evidence that hanged two innocent people.

Pourceaugnac sinks into a world of unreason. He is incessantly accosted by strangers, two of whom claim to be his wives. Children claim him for their father. Doctors oblige him to listen to speeches of inordinate length in which he is diagnosed as insane. Musicians and dancers emerge from one of the entertainments to pursue him with enema-syringes. He is completely reduced – 'What the devil is going on? Is everybody here mad? I've never seen anything like this, and I don't understand a thing of what's happening' – and then made to dress up. But this is no holiday disguising, as a doctor or a Mamamouchi: to avoid being hanged as a polygamist, he puts on women's clothes, and gets himself handled by two Swiss guards.

Violence falls on Pourceaugnac, without his receiving a reward; he is fooled so that youth and love can triumph, without a triumph of his own. He is, of course, a scapegoat, and more starkly so than Jourdain and Argan. Ludicrously attired, as soon as he comes on to the stage he is made to expose himself to our ridicule. His entrance is that of a clown; and although he speaks into the wings, it is as if he addresses the delighted audience:

Hé bien, quoi? qu'est-ce? qu'y a-t-il? Au diantre soit la sotte ville, et les sottes gens qui y sont! ne pouvoir faire un pas sans trouver

des nigauds qui vous regardent, et se mettent à rire! Eh!
Messieurs les badauds, faites vos affaires, et laissez passer les
personnes sans leur rire au nez. Je me donne au diable, si je ne
baille un coup de poing au premier que je verrai rire.

*(What's up, then? Mm? What's the matter? Tarnation on the stupid town,
and on the stupid people in it! One can't take a step without coming on
boobies who stare at one, and start laughing! You there – don't gawp. Go
about your business, and let people pass without laughing in their faces. The
devil take me if I don't strike the first one I catch laughing.)*

He then goes through a comic hell, in which he is – significantly –
judged and condemned.

By the finish, he has been laughed out of the play. Like Jourdain
and Argan, however, he is more than the scapegoat of social
satire. Even here, Bergson's notion, in *Laughter,* that 'the comic
expresses, above all else, a special lack of adaptability to society', is
scarcely adequate, because of the demonic suggestion in what
Pourceaugnac undergoes, and because of the ambivalence of the
society he quits. In the case of the other two plays, it is even
clearer that the comedy does not call back to a norm, by expelling
a character of threatening extravagance. The plays are occupied
not with confirming the world but with hinting a better world,
through a liberating mirth that centres precisely on the Fool. It is
through Jourdain that the creativity of *Le Bourgeois gentilhomme*
passes, and in opposing his joyful folly the 'normal' Madame
Jourdain seems a kill-joy, a spoil-sport.

There can be no allegiance to normality when the plays see the
normal world as corrupt. Hence, to move outside the comedy-
ballets, the ambiguity of a character like Philinte, in *Le Misanthrope.*
He may seem to speak for the golden mean against the inadapt-
able idealism of the misanthropic Alceste; and he does pronounce
the famous maxim apparently defining the viewpoint of Molière's
'raisonneurs': 'La parfaite raison fuit toute extrémité', 'Perfect
reason shuns all extremes'. Yet it is arguable that Philinte is more
deeply, more seriously, careless of others than Alceste – suavely
contemptuous of humanity:

> Et mon esprit enfin n'est pas plus offensé
> De voir un homme fourbe, injuste, intéressé,
> Que de voir des vautours affamés de carnage,
> Des singes malfaisants et des loups pleins de rage,

(And my mind in short is no more offended to see a man sly, unjust, self-seeking, than to see vultures hungry for carrion, monkeys malefic and wolves furious)

and wittily self-satisfied with things as they are:

> Tous ces défauts humains nous donnent, dans la vie,
> Des moyens d'exercer notre philosphie;
> C'est le plus bel emploi que trouve la vertu.

(All these human defects give us in life the occasion to exercise philosophy; virtue cannot be better employed.)

The society that mocks Alceste – and that disappears itself at the end, leaving an empty stage – holds little reassurance for the 'normal' spectator.[1]

The scapegoat has a more elemental role. He assumes our condition, and may offer a glimpse of rising above it. He parades our failings or experiences our fears; he suffers ridicule and perhaps violence in our place; and he enables us to enter an aesthetic world of hilarious possibility. He is both a diminished and an enlarged image of ourselves.[2]

Isn't this true of the Fool or Clown generally? A man disfigures himself with a funny face, puts on a coxcomb or a fox-tail or asses' ears, mocking his pretention to manhood. He exhibits his dwarf body or the hump on his back. He performs before us, wearing inane clothes. He fails to cope. He suffers banana skins, buckets of water, collapsing chairs. He abases himself, and thrusts at us our profound foolishness, degrading us by his wit, like Jonson's Carlo Buffone – 'a public, scurrilous and profane jester, that more swift than Circe, with absurd similes, will transform any person into deformity' – or by his simple presence.

(Should the butt on the other hand refuse to see himself as comic, he commits a comic version of tragic *hubris;* we laugh at the catching-out of a man claiming not to be a sinner. 'The joke of life is the fall of dignity' – Mack Sennett.)

He also raises us: in the custard pie routine, for example – that favourite unloosing of farcical violence. It abuses by daubing the face, the place of personality and consciousness; yet at the same time it redeems violence in comedy and convention. As it inexorably gathers momentum, involving more and more participants in a total frenzy, it also takes off into festive play. Perhaps the effect is even more powerful when the violence is accepted willingly and, in practical terms, unnecessarily: as when Laurel waits without moving for Hardy to pour the whitewash over his head.

The Fool or Clown sets up a total dynamic, from our degradation to our possibility of redemption. It is surely in part the fact that he descends, comically, into our fears about ourselves and the world and, comically, lifts us, that draws us to him so powerfully. In Chaplin's dress, the baggy trousers, overtight jacket and oversize boots are countered by bowler, bow tie, walking stick and moustache. The tramp is also a dandy. A circus clown almost fails to climb the steps up to it, then walks across a rope with a show of panic clumsiness that belies a thrilling virtuosity. Suddenly terrified, Harlequin turns a backward somersault, without spilling a drop from the wineglass in his hand.

In particular, the Fool's routine is often a mastering of time and space. Laurel and Hardy jest with time, elongating it beyond the plausible by their infinitely slow playing. Time seems to dissolve, as they enter another time, free from the constraints of this one. Others speed up time, in the whirl of their gags. Space is mocked in a celebrated scene in *The Great Dictator,* where Charlie as Hitler performs an enthralled ballet with a balloon globe of the world. At the most charged moment he nonchalantly sends it up again with his backside. In this beautiful farce, the menace of a will to world domination is not only ridiculed: it is transformed into a dance that lifts beyond the hold of gravity.

Of course, our feelings towards the Fool can be more ambivalent, according to the light in which he is imagined. It is not only that he threatens us, with a disclosure of our and the world's foolishness. At times he exists in a dangerous other dimension, which he half reveals. He may have strange knowledge, that we can only guess at. His being is different. One wonders if he is blessed or damned. The gay Harlequin probably originated, after all, as the nocturnal leader of a troop of demon riders. Is he the messenger of a desirable, radiant world, or an envoy of darkness, like the medieval clown devils who try to drag spectators into Hell-Mouth – cousins to the sinister forces that harry Pourceaugnac? Is the topsy-turvy world into which he calls us a salvation from our own fallen, inverted world, or a worse confusion, a fool's paradise?

The ambiguity of the Fool results, no doubt, from his closeness to heaven and hell, and from our bafflement before those depths of our condition. In his profundity, he is a grotesque, a mockery, to use a Pascalian expression of René Char, of our 'hallucinated order', and either, I suppose, a holy fool or a devil.[3]

2

The new world into which comedy leads us involves at times a burlesque renewing of language. The ceremony of *Le Bourgeois gentilhomme* passes through mock Turkish into Mediterranean pidgin; that of *Le Malade imaginaire* leaves the audience in a prodigious macaroni of gallicised Latin.

Why should a comic writer abuse language, in this way? And why do we laugh? Surely part of the answer is that, within the comedy, language itself is entering a dynamic of play and of transformation. As bewildering foreign tongues pass before us, a re-creative imagination mocks and works them. They are changed, into an artifice cognate with that of Mamamouchi and false doctor, and suggest another world where language too is remade. Isn't this a comic triumph over the fall of language into multiplicity – a delighted derision of Babel? We laugh as the comedy contends with Babel and, for a moment, lifts the curse. Maybe that is what comedy is: the temporary lifting of a curse.[4]

Once again, a shift in perspective would show Babel as horrific, as a teeming nightmare; and Molière has again made the move. Part of Pourceaugnac's ordeal is to enter the malaise of language. The musicians threatening him with syringes sing at him in Italian. The false wives rail volubly in the dialects of Languedoc and Picardy. The Swiss guards molest him in Swiss. Even Oronte, the girl's father, is duped by the intriguer in the disguise, and with the patois, of a Flemish merchant.

Perhaps Sganarelle, in an earlier comedy-ballet, *Le Mariage forcé*, suffers language more radically. He repeatedly asks the same question as Rabelais' Panurge: 'if I marry, shall I be cuckolded?', but the words he wants to hear never arrive. Pancrace (a pedant from the *commedia*) is concerned for verbal precision – shouldn't an Aristotelian say the 'shape' rather than the 'form' of a hat? – and for language as 'communication', yet talks endlessly without listening. His desire to know in what language Sganarelle will address him suggests a Babylonian confusion – 'Italian? ... Spanish? ... German? ... English? ... Latin? ... Greek? ...

Hebrew? . . . Syriac? . . . Turkish? . . . Arabic? . . .' – and Sganarelle dismisses him pointedly as 'a devil of a babbler'. The Sceptic Marphurius, who doubts everything, causes Sganarelle's words and meanings to dissolve: 'you shouldn't say, "I have come", but, "It seems to me that I have come" '; while gipsies avoid answering his question by singing 'la, la, la, la . . .' each time he asks it. Language takes on a hostile life of its own, and continually slips from Sganarelle's grasp.

Pourceaugnac and Sganarelle undergo the dark side of language, as scapegoats; but in the first play at least, as in *Le Bourgeois gentilhomme* and *Le Malade imaginaire,* the audience also experiences, as it were, an emerging radiance. As Molière comically purges and raises the world, so he comically purges and raises language.

In the language of tragedy we observed mainly contradiction and ambiguity, associated with the fall of language as provoked by the serpent; and also the general 'confusion' associated with the further fall of language at Babel. Here, we have witnessed for the first time the confusion of Babel itself. Such an explicit Babylonian focus is, however, rare in literature, and the linguistic confusion of comedy takes many other forms. These too, one realises, while enacting the *misère* of language are also a means to its transformation.

They are especially abundant in Shakespeare; and, most significantly, they occur in the midst of plays which, otherwise, far from abusing language strive most evidently for its perfection. Shakespeare renews language both by procuring in it change after change – in the 'Conclusion' to *The Use of Poetry and the Use of Criticism,* Eliot refers in particular to his 're-creation of word and image', his production 'again and again' of a 'reborn image or word' – and also by joyfully distorting it: as if, in renewing language, he wanted to acknowledge and to counter its fall; and as if the surest remaking of language could only pass by its unmaking. Here as elsewhere Shakespeare's practice is radical and exemplary.

Characters who damage language and exhibit its mangled condition are present from the beginning. Already in *Love's Labour's Lost* and *The Two Gentlemen of Verona,* under the genteel, lordly and royal wit comes the wrenched patois of Dull and Costard and Launce. They invert meaning: 'welcome the sour cup of prosperity! Affliction may one day smile again', substitute mean-ing by what we should now call malapropism: 'I have received my proportion, like the prodigious son', and displace meaning along the sentence: 'my mother weeping, my father wailing, my sister crying, our maid howling, our cat wringing her hands . . .' Launce even undermines the language of his interlocutors –

> Speed: . . . But, Launce, how sayest thou, that my master is become a notable lover?
> Launce: I never knew him otherwise.
> Speed: Than how?
> Launce: A notable lubber, as thou reportest him to be

– so spreading his linguistic anarchy.

The double manoeuvre continues into *Much Ado About Nothing,* where Dogberry commits perpetual crime on English, by the same processes, while Beatrice and Benedick are expending their wit famously and explicitly; having culminated in *A Midsummer Night's Dream,* which I shall be considering in a later chapter, in the contrast between the courtiers and the even more variously illegal mechanicals, with their extensive repertory of disruption. Simi-larly, the eloquence of Portia in *The Merchant of Venice* and of the Duke in *Measure for Measure* has to contend with the gabble of Lancelot Gobbo, Old Gobbo and Elbow. Speeches such as 'The quality of mercy is not strain'd' or 'Be absolute for death' are only allowed, as it were, when accompanied by 'my true-begotten father', 'My wife, sir, whom I detest before heaven . . .', or 'two notorious benefactors'.

With great accuracy, Dull, Dogberry and Elbow are all con-stables. It is in part through burlesque representatives of the law – mock defenders of the 'hallucinated order' of language – that the lawless language is propagated.

Even in the tragedy of *Antony and Cleopatra,* moreover, an oratory of gorgeous exaggeration that reaches down to Enobar-bus ('The barge she sat in . . .') meets, when about to attain its climax in Cleopatra's final speech, the language of the Clown who brings the asps. The Clown's babble is especially appropriate. He jumbles sense, informing Cleopatra that those who die of the snake 'do seldom or never recover', but his inversions of meaning also propose possible new meanings that bear profoundly on the situation. The snake's bite may indeed be 'immortal' as well as mortal, since Cleopatra (who will shortly declare her 'immortal longings') intends it to usher her into immortality. On the other hand, when he claims the statement 'the worm's an odd worm' to be 'fallible' rather than infallible, the intimations are not only that the asp will cause Cleopatra to *fall* (like Iras – 'Dost fall?') but also, more pointedly and poignantly, that Cleopatra is perhaps *deceived* in her epic dream. Language is derided into an extra semantic suggestiveness – abused and raised – as the complex ending of the tragedy is being realised.

We are more familiar with the notion that Shakespeare re-creates language than with the notion that he was conscious of any linguistic *misère;* and it may be thought that I am reading my own concerns into his plays. Yet there is one passage – an admittedly difficult one – where he seems actually to be considering the fall of language. I am thinking of an exchange about words in *Twelfth Night,* between the Clown, once again, and Viola disguised as Cesario, whose culminating point has puzzled all the editors:

> Viola: Save thee, friend, and thy music. Dost thou live by thy tabor?
> Clown: No, sir, I live by the church.
> Viola: Art thou a churchman?
> Clown: No such matter, sir: I do live by the church; for I do live at my house, and my house doth stand by the church.
> Viola: So thou mayst say, the king lies by a beggar, if a beggar dwell near him; or, the church stands by thy tabor, if thy tabor stand by the church.
> Clown: You have said, sir. To see this age! A sentence is but a cheveril glove to a good wit: how quickly the wrong side may be turned outward!
> Viola: Nay, that's certain: they that dally nicely with words may quickly make them wanton.
> Clown: I would therefore my sister had had no name, sir.
> Viola: Why, man?
> Clown: Why, sir, her name's a word; and to dally with that word might make my sister wanton. But indeed, words are very rascals since bonds disgraced them.
> Viola: Thy reason, man?
> Clown: Troth, sir, I can yield you none without words; and words are grown so false, I am loath to prove reason with them.

(Act 3, scene 1)

The problem is the sentence: 'But indeed, words are very rascals since bonds disgraced them'. Explanations have included an order of the Privy Council which, by placing severe restrictions on the theatre, might be said to have placed words in bonds, or to have disgraced them since the penalty for flouting the restrictions was bonds in the sense of imprisonment; the Jesuit doctrine of equivocation, which allowed a Catholic under oath to say one thing to a Protestant magistrate while meaning another, and which was much in the news after the Gunpowder Plot, when Feste, provided the play was written or revised at the time, might declare even more specifically that words had been disgraced by the bonds or oaths of the conspirators; the use of words in money bonds, such involvement in the trickeries of business somehow disgracing them; and this passage from Bacon, suggested by Morton Luce in the old Arden Shakespeare not as a source but as a 'kindred thought': 'Let us consider the false appearances that are imposed upon us by words, which are framed and applied according to the conceit and capacities of the vulgar sort; and although we think we govern our words . . . yet certain it is that words, as a Tartar's bow, do shoot back upon the understanding of the wisest and mightily entangle and pervert the judgement' *(The Advancement of Learning,* II xiv 11).

What if, going along with Bacon's more general mistrust of language, the expression 'disgraced them' is a way of saying 'caused them to fall from grace' – to be dis-graced, or un-graced? 'Bonds' would still not be completely clear, but it might then imply quite naturally, and by a familiar metaphor, the bondage of sin, which has dis-graced words by turning them, along with ourselves, into 'rascals'. (Since Posthumus in *Cymbeline,* with more word-play, describes both his prison and life itself as 'these cold bonds', Feste could also be suggesting, possibly, that words have been dis-graced by being involved in the bonds of our mortal, suffering life. He may even be alluding, though this is perhaps to strain ingenuity, to the bonds or binding engagements of the serpent, at the very moment of the dis-grace, when he promised Eve that Adam and she would not, by eating the fruit, 'surely die', and that they would be as gods, knowing good and evil. The serpent's bonds also disgraced words, of course, in the usual sense of the term, by employing them for a disgraceful purpose.)

That words are rascals since the bonds of sin made them fall from grace certainly assorts well with the passage as a whole. The dense and multiple word-play reaches a first climax in Viola's 'wanton', which, in a single term, gives to the *playfulness* and hence equivocation of words an evidently moral colouring, by dubbing it a *licentiousness*. (The moral, or immoral, colouring is, of course, specifically sexual, and picks up not only the general hint of moral reproach in 'how quickly the *wrong* side may be turned outward!' but also the particular sexual innuendo in 'the king lies by a beggar'. We shall meet a similar combination of illicit language and illicit sex in the poetry of Eliot.) Feste confirms the point, and then moves to his enigmatic remark.

If the remark has puzzled editors, one notices that it also puzzles Viola: she too asks the Clown what he means. She gives him thereby the opportunity of making the perfect answer: 'Troth, sir, I can yield you [no reason] without words; and words are grown so false, I am loath to prove reason with them.' Feste may not be the richest of Shakespeare's clowns, but he is granted this insight. Called on to explain, so to speak, the fall of language, he can only reply that any explanation which he might give, being itself expressed in words, would be involved in that fall. It is the Clown who has discovered, should this reading be correct, the disturbing and absolutely fundamental fact that we cannot 'reasonably' discuss fallen language, because the only language available for the discussion is a fallen one. (I have not been unaware of the fact in the writing of this book.)

Hence, perhaps, the deliberate failure in the linguistic sally by which he exits. He tells Viola that he will inform those in the house where she comes from but not who she is nor what she wants, because 'who you are and what you would are out of my welkin; I might say "element", but the word is overworn'. Since *welkin* qualifies as a synonym for *element* when it means the sky but not when it means, as here, one's sphere of concern, he voluntarily fluffs the word. Hence also his function in Olivia's household, which he describes in the course of this same scene: to be her 'corrupter of words'. By continually corrupting words, both his own and those he is offered by others, he makes manifest language's corrupt instability.

Which returns us to our point of departure: Feste's enigma. Isn't it precisely because the Clown believes that language is disgraced that his statement to that effect is a puzzle? Had it been clear it would have implicitly denied what it said, whereas part of its significance lies in the very fact that it *is* puzzling. The muffling of 'disgraced', the deviousness of 'bonds', along with the imprecision of 'since', is a highly concentrated corrupting of words, which dallies wantonly with them and with us, and sets commentators composing gloss after gloss. My own gloss, if it is accurate, is also of course, by the same token, somewhat ironical. One can at least say in its favour that it explains why an explanation is needed.

The re-creative abuse of language that we have been considering also occurs in two related female characters of later English writing: Sheridan's Mrs Malaprop and Dickens's Mrs Gamp. They too are 'corrupters of words' who assist language to fall while simultaneously (and paradoxically) raising it above itself. Both seem to derive ultimately from Shakespeare, though more immediately from Mrs Slipslop, the 'waiting-gentlewoman' of *Joseph Andrews*, who constantly speaks like this:

> ... is it not a pity such a graceless young man should die a virulent death? I hope the judge will take commensuration on his youth. As for Fanny . . . if poor Joseph hath done anything, I could venture to swear she traduced him to it: few men ever come to a fragrant punishment, but by those nasty creatures, who are a scandal to our sect.

The play with language extends to other characters. Mr Adams, the curate, is given to lacing his English with Latin and Greek: 'What would it avail me, to tarry in the great city, unless I had my discourses with me, which are *ut ita dicam,* the sole cause, the *aitia monotate* of my peregrination?' Bellarmine decorates his letters with what purports to be French: 'my surgeon gives me hopes of being soon able to attend your *ruelle;* till when, unless you would do me an honour which I have scarce the *hardiesse* to think of, your absence will be the greatest anguish which can be felt by, Madam, *Avec toute le respecte* in the world, Your most obedient, most absolute *Dévoté,* Bellarmine.' Even an episodic coach traveller makes a similar motley with Italian: 'here had been only a little boxing, which he said, to their *disgracia,* the English were *accustomata* to'.

Curiously, however, Fielding's comedy is the reverse of Molière's, as I have been describing it. The attitude to language at work here is that its norm is healthy and its misuse ridiculous. This is clear in the lampooning of the poet laureate, when the power of love to metamorphose and distort the human senses is compared to Cibber's distortion of English, his confounding of number and gender and his breaking through every rule of grammar at will. The motive of the comedy seems to be not delight in the imagina-tive possibility of language, in a fantasticating voyage beyond the normal, but sturdy fun at the expense of affectation.

Sheridan too is concerned, in Mrs Malaprop of *The Rivals,* with affectation and the ridiculous that results from it; but he also elevates her prattle into a prodigious neology.

She again represents the older generation that has to be fooled so that lovers can marry: 'there is an old tough aunt in the way'. As Jourdain and Argan are violent towards their daughters, so she is violent towards her niece – breathtakingly so:

> Lydia: Madam, I thought you once –
> Mrs Malaprop: You thought, miss! I don't know any business you have to think at all – thought does not become a young woman.

There is the same outrageousness in her illustration of the ease of forgetting – 'I'm sure I have as much forgot your poor dear uncle as if he had never existed' – and of the need for a little aversion at the beginning of matrimony – 'I am sure I hated your poor dear uncle before marriage as if he'd been a blackamoor'. As with Sir Anthony Absolute's suggestion that Mrs Malaprop should per-suade her niece into an unwanted marriage by locking her up and letting the servants forget to bring her dinner for three or four days, the violence in the world that the young lovers overcome becomes hilarious by sudden inflation.

She is likewise a Clown. Ludicrously ugly (an 'old weather-beaten she-dragon'), she is also unable to cope, not with ladders or music-stands but with words. Yet her bungling is transformed into an unconscious wizardry, and it is through her that the play lifts into euphoria. She is, moreover, supremely aware of language:

> There, sir, an attack upon my language! what do you think of that? – an aspersion upon my parts of speech! was ever such a brute! Sure, if I reprehend any thing in this world it is the use of my oracular tongue, and a nice derangement of epitaphs!

Linguistic delicacy even extends beyond her, since it appears in the play's other Clown, Bob Acres (whose rustic name announces that he is the Clown as country bumpkin, and the name of whose seat, Clod Hall, takes one back to the possible origin of the word 'clown'). In his concern that his oaths, like his hair and his dress, should be in fashion – 'Damns have had their day!' – he comes by a new method of swearing: 'odds triggers and flints!', 'Odds bullets and blades!'

Mrs Malaprop's blissful absorption in language serves partly to make her comic. But one notices also that her language is pervaded by the vocabulary of language-study:

> ... long ago I laid my positive conjunctions on her, never to think on the fellow again; – I have since laid Sir Anthony's preposition before her, but, I am sorry to say, she seems resolved to decline every particle that I enjoin her.

When she begins an avowal of love to Sir Lucius O'Trigger, it is 'female punctuation' that forbids her to continue. Other words that slip in sideways include 'illegible' (eligible) and 'to illiterate' (obliterate); while literary idiom surfaces in the replacement of catastrophe by 'antistrophe' and alligator by 'allegory'. Not only does Mrs Malaprop talk about language: language becomes, as it were, self-aware, and talks about itself.

A language-world is created, in which anything could happen. Even the writ of a great classic is put into a condition of instability: 'I protest, when I saw him, I thought of what Hamlet says in the play:

> Hesperian curls – the front of Job himself! –
> An eye, like March, to threaten at command! –
> A station, like Harry Mercury, new –

Something about kissing – on a hill . . .' In this giddy atmosphere, Mrs. Malaprop's language takes wing. At times it seizes on another meaning, and sets a possible world alongside the actual:

> No caparisons, miss, if you please. Caparisons don't become a young woman.

> Why, thou barbarous vandyke.

Or it outshines the phrase it muffs:

Sir, you overpower me with good-breeding. – He is the very
pineapple of politeness!

Or it runs close to a cliché which it then transfigures in nonsense:

Oh, there's nothing to be hoped for from her! she's as headstrong as an allegory on the banks of Nile.

Instead of being an ordinary 'nice arrangement of epigrams', her
language really is a nice derangement: a delicate convulsing of
English, a linguistic folly – hilarious 'epitaphs' to a reality destroyed but also made new. Hers is a kind of 'oracular tongue', that
announces another world perceived through nonsense.

To attain her, the play quits plausibility. Hence the bafflement
of a commonsense critic writing in 1792: 'it is not to be supposed
that a woman who could make use of such language as she does,
could misapply her words'. No, it isn't; but then she misapplies
them in accordance with a kind of art to which the plausible is
foreign.[5]

Of that art, Dickens is one of the great masters, as we know.
Martin Chuzzlewit's Mrs Gamp is a caricature pressed close to the
centre of comedy, a grotesque who reaches from the Fall to the
possibility of re-creation.

The novel occurs explicitly in a fallen world. The point is made
in the opening chapter, which traces the ancestry of the Chuzzle-
wits to Adam and Eve, and notes, as a matter of sociological
interest, that the first family contained a murderer. Jonas Chuzzlewit, in killing Tigg, proves the continuing burden of that ancestry;
while the excursion of Martin Chuzzlewit and Mark Tapley to
America deflates the Americans' claim to have rediscovered Eden.
Comedy takes on this fallen world, and it is chiefly in Mrs Gamp
that it does so. She is introduced as just having attended 'a
ceremony to which the usage of gossips had given that name
which expresses, in two syllables, the curse pronounced on Adam'.
She is involved in the 'labour' of a lapsed world, where the ease of
Eden is no longer possible. She moves, not through an earthly
paradise but, as she puts it in the various guises of her favourite
expression, 'this walley of the shadder', 'this Piljian's Projiss of a
mortal wale'.

Delightfully fat and ugly, Mrs Gamp is again a Clown: her nose
is 'somewhat red and swollen', her dress is absurd, her umbrella is

a Clown's prop, forever prodding, entangling or throttling other people, and she is unable to manage words. She is again violent, with the extravagance of comedy:

> 'Bite a person's thumbs, or turn their fingers the wrong way,' said Mrs Gamp, smiling with the consciousness of imparting pleasure and instruction to her auditors, 'and they comes to, wonderful, Lord bless you!'
> 'Betsey Prig has nussed a many lunacies, and well she knows their ways, which puttin' 'em right close afore the fire, when fractious, is the certainest and most compoging.'

She does not, however, play a traditional role in the novel, by opposing the marriages of the hero and his valet. Nor is she the centre of power, as are Jourdain, Argan and Mrs Malaprop. She is 'unnecessary', and apparently peripheral. Yet from the first she gathers around herself intriguing possibilities of significance. Her profession is both midwife and watcher, and in her first chapter she comes from a confinement, attends the dead Anthony Chuzzlewit, and is then called out again for twins. A comic 'guardian of the mysteries',[6] she nurses a fallen humanity at the extreme moments of birth and death. Since she profits from both, moreover, she declines to discriminate emotionally between them – 'she went to a lying-in or a laying-out with equal zest and relish' – and it is in fact death that claims her the more powerfully. Death is around her – she lodges at a bird-fancier's, two doors away from a mutton-pie shop and opposite a cats'-meat warehouse – and on her, since she goes from one suit of mourning to the next. It also holds her imagination. Surveying Lewsome's sleeping body, she finds herself pinning his wandering arms against his sides, and murmurs: 'he'd make a lovely corpse!' Her appraisal of the *cadavre exquis* shifts the Romantic fascination with beauty-in-death into her own ambiguous comedy.

Mrs Gamp is, in fact, an eerie figure, funny and frightening at the same time. One of her functions, described in a tone at once jocular and supernaturally menacing, is to be a 'performer of nameless offices about the persons of the dead'. Her discarded weeds become her 'ghost', to be seen hanging in a dozen or so second-hand shops in Holborn. Her clothes hooked up over the bed retain her shape, and convince several impatient husbands rushing into her room that she has hanged herself. The Clown's garb is no longer quite harmless. The weirdest moments occur when she nurses Lewsome. The room becomes 'ghostly', the house is as quiet as a 'sepulchre', and the night so chilly she reckons 'the devil's in it'. Lewsome's terror of death and judge-ment, for having connived at murder, is then set off by her singu-lar clowning. She counterpoints his ravings with replies of her own:

> 'That makes five hundred and twenty-one men, all dressed alike, and with the same distortion on their faces, that have passed in at the window, and out at the door,' he cried, anxiously. 'Look there! Five hundred and twenty-two – twenty-three – twenty-four. Do you see them?'
> 'Ah! *I* see 'em,' said Mrs Gamp; 'all the whole kit of 'em num-bered like hackney-coaches . . .'

A moment before, when his delirium had woken her, she had sat up in bed with a watchman's coat tied around her neck by the sleeves, 'presenting on the wall the shadow of a gigantic night constable, struggling with a prisoner'.

The being of Mrs Gamp is elusively suggestive. There is a world involved in her, just beyond grasp. Here, in the 'dead of night', she becomes double and enormous, the projection, in the same instant, of Policeman and Criminal. One remembers that she has the power of multiplying herself, through her sets of clothes; and that she is equally paradoxical as a cruel nurse. Even her ugliness stirs profoundly, recalling an observation of Victor Hugo: 'what we call the ugly . . . is a detail in a great whole that escapes us'.[7]

In terms of comedy, she is also a scapegoat Fool. Near to death, and parading human corruption, she is another means by which laughter confronts evil. The perspective now, however, is that of a kind of grotesque, in which evil, in becoming comic, does not quite lose its terror.[8]

It is through Mrs Gamp, the character most immersed in a fallen world, that language is both abused and re-created. She distorts words, so that they 'slip, slide, perish' comically in her mouth; but she also transforms them. Whenever she intervenes, language is mocked and made unstable. By the mangling of writ, for example, and holy writ at that: 'Rich folks may ride on camels, but it ain't so easy for 'em to see out of a needle's eye.' By the dis-ruption of a time-honoured phrase with a pun:

'Where's the patient goin?' asked Sweedlepipe.

'Into Har'fordshire, which is his native air. But native airs nor native graces neither,' Mrs Gamp observed, 'won't bring *him* round.'

And above all by the constant wrenching of English vocabulary, to produce 'owldacious', or 'cowcumber', the occasional malapropism: 'the torters of the Imposition', and words graced with the famous soft g's, substituted – 'dispoged' – or added – 'denige'. She is abetted in the work by Pecksniff's habit of using 'any word that occurred to him as having a good sound, and rounding a sentence well, without much care for its meaning'.

Out of this derision, this ubiquitous play, come strange new objects and existential possibilities. Instead of, and alongside, 'half-a-dozen fresh young lively leeches' there appears 'half-a-dudgeon'. A reference to Young Bailey's 'Bragian boldness' (for 'brazen') calls into being another nation of foreigners as barbarous as the 'Rooshans' and the 'Prooshans'. At the end of the tale of Mrs Harris's first confinement, we hear that, her husband having been taken with a fit, collared by the doctor and 'laid ... on his back upon the airy stones', she was told to ease her mind, 'his owls was organs'.

The language realises itself mainly, however, in long set pieces:

'Why, goodness me!' she said, 'Mrs Chuzzlewit! To think as I should see beneath this blessed ouse, which well I know it, Miss Pecksniff, my sweet young lady, to be a ouse as there is not a many like, worse luck and wishin' it ware not so, which then this tearful walley would be changed into a flowerin' guardian, Mr Chuffey; to think as I should see beneath this indiwidge roof, identically comin', Mr Pinch (I take the liberty, though almost unbeknown), and do assure you of it, Sir, the smilinest and sweetest face as ever, Mrs Chuzzlewit, I see, exceptin' yourn, my dear good lady, and *your* good lady's too, Sir, Mr Moddle, if I may make so bold as speak so plain of what is plain enough to them as needn't look through millstones, Mrs Todgers, to find out wot is wrote upon the wall behind. Which no offence is meant, ladies and gentlemen; none bein' took, I hope. To think as I should see the smilinest and sweetest face which me and another friend of mine, took notige of among the packages down London Bridge, in this promiscous place, is a surprige indeed!'

This 'extemporaneous concerto' is the virtuosity of the clumsy clown. The language falls apart, through the indulgent use of the notorious 'which' as the weakest of conjunctions, only to be gathered, through the continuous inventiveness of its rhythms, into the glorious whole of a new syntax. In the act of transforming language, moreover, Mrs Gamp evokes the transformation of all things, by referring to 'this tearful walley' of a fallen world being changed into a paradise, a 'flowerin' guardian'.

A layer-out of the dead and also a midwife, Mrs Gamp kills and gives birth to language. And her greatest linguistic feat is the invention of Mrs Harris. There are psychological motives behind this, of course; but doesn't she also create 'Mrs Harris' in the way that Dickens creates 'Mrs Gamp'? She even describes her with all of Dickens's own implausible and 'unnecessary' particularity:

> I knows a lady, which her name, I'll not deceive you, Mrs Chuzzlewit, is Harris, her husband's brother bein' six foot three, and marked with a mad bull in Wellington boots upon his left arm, on account of his precious mother havin' been worrited by one into a shoemaker's shop . . .

> Mrs Harris . . . has one sweet infant (though she *do* not wish it known) in her own family by the mother's side, kep in spirits in a bottle; and that sweet babe she see at Greenwich Fair, a travelling in company with the pink-eyed lady, Prooshan dwarf, and livin' skelinton, which judge her feelins wen the barrel organ played, and she was showed her own dear sister's child, the same not bein' expected from the outside picter, where it was painted quite contrairy in a livin' state, a many sizes larger, and performing beautiful upon the Arp, which never did that dear child know or do: since breathe it never did, to speak on, in this wale!

Mrs Gamp, a character functioning as a novelist – and a sign that the novel we are reading *is* a novel – brings Mrs Harris into being by the power of the word. With Mrs Harris, the reader moves one dimension further into the domain of the possible – into an exuberant superfluity, an overplus of imagination. And Mrs

Gamp's inexhaustible, immediate, exhilarating flow is an insight, perhaps, into Dickens's own creative speed.

So comedy is a response to the human condition. It exposes and contends with a corrupted world. Its material is egoism, violence, conflict, suffering, sickness, death, nightmare, judgement. It exaggerates evil so that it becomes unreal, and we can manage it. It deflects our profounder dismays, by directing laughter towards deformities and failures that are other than moral and spiritual. It looks from the outside, from a distance, turning nightmare into the routine of the Clown who can't cope, and making even death trivial or odd. It disrupts an hallucinated order, by unstabilising the norms of character, and event, and language.

Comedy also redeems. It transforms labour into play. It purges evil in artifice and ceremony. It outwits it by ruse. And above all it opens to miracle – to the raising of Argan, the elevation of Jourdain into a Mamamouchi, the glimpsing of a marvellous language. It may be that, if we could move beyond this world, we should no longer need to laugh; but in our present condition laughter is one of the means by which we seem to make that move. Laughter is the perception of possibility.[9]

Perhaps comedy sometimes redeems laughter itself. Our laughter at the comic hero begins as ridicule, as a glorying in our own superiority. By mocking someone who falls foul of an evil world, we share in the evil. But we may come to realise that the hero has a special excellence, to which we cannot aspire. Neither dismissed nor merely integrated, he may be the point at which the Fool-comedy reaches beyond itself. He may elicit the kind of response conveyed in Dorante's hyperbolic description of Jourdain: 'I don't think that in the whole world you could find another man as mad as he.' Isn't this a comic version of the lauding of the hero in tragedy – the exaltation of Oedipus as 'the first of men', or of Heracles as 'the best of all men who have appeared on the earth'? Our Hobbesian, Baudelairean, contempt is changed into a sympathetic wonder.

A Christian version of such a theory of comedy might be grounded on the laughter of Abraham and Sarah, as described in chapters 17 to 21 of Genesis. At first, when told by God that they are to have a son, they react with scorn:

Abraham fell upon his face, and laughed, and said in his heart,

> Shall a child be born unto him that is an hundred years old? and shall Sarah, that is ninety years old, bear?

> Sarah laughed within herself, saying, After I am waxed old shall I have pleasure, my lord being old also?

This is the laughter of a fallen world, perceiving what might have been. It sees a ridiculous, hurtful cleavage in things, an antithesis of profusion of life and old age, of birth and death. (It is also a laughter that isn't comic – which doesn't contain, that is, any pleasure; the Bible not coming at evil through protective indirections.)

The son is nevertheless born, and Sarah laughs again:

> And Sarah said, God hath made me to laugh . . . all that hear will laugh with me.

The passage arrives out of the blue, producing in the reader the same surprise that, in Sarah, touches off laughter. Hers is now the laughter that encounters miracle, that leaps beyond the plausible into a world of joyful possibility. The son, moreover, is a 'child of promise', born 'after the Spirit' rather than 'after the flesh', and therefore a sign of Christian regeneration, and a type of Christ Himself, the true 'seed of Abraham'.[10] He takes comedy into the furthest reaches of the theology of salvation; and even his name, Isaac, comes from a word meaning 'to laugh'.

But comedy is not religion, and the kind of comedy we have analysed offers only metaphors of religious events. It sets up a fictive world, as the place where a dynamic – of destroying and re-creating, purging and transforming – can be fulfilled. It draws the spectator or reader into its process. But it also sends him away; it subverts itself.

The Fool-hero is ambiguous: it is right that a certain ridicule should remain in our wonder. In particular, his characteristic childishness, which enables him to 'play', also unfits him for adult living. He is ahead of us, but also behind us. He does not lead us, moreover, into a real new world, but into revelry, which as well as being a glimpse of that newness is also an appeal to delightful irresponsibility. A cold light may even fall on his transformation. Jourdain attends the final ballet in continuing ignorance of the tricks that are being played on him; Argan's hypochondria is to be cured by a doctorate conferred by actors.

Similarly with language. Jourdain, Argan, their revellers, Mrs Malaprop and Mrs Gamp make a fresh language-world for us, imaginatively exhilarating and humanly warm. As a triumph of nonsense over sense, however, their fool's babble hangs between an unprecedented order and chaos, between Pentecostal speech and a clownish gibber.

And we are, after all, experiencing a fiction. Towards the end of *Martin Chuzzlewit,* Betsey Prig says of Mrs Harris, to an aghast Mrs Gamp: 'I don't believe there's no sich a person.' The 'memorable and tremendous words' point up the precariousness of the fantastication by which Mrs Harris has been brought into being. (It is true that the double negative also expresses a nice ambiguity, since we both believe and disbelieve her non-existence.) They also suggest the unreality of Mrs Gamp, and even of Betsey Prig; and so, since the latter is speaking them, they expose Dickens himself. Our consciousness meets his in an ironic awareness, an awareness of the craft of fiction. We know that the comic vision is realising itself in a fictive character's fictive character.

4 Story

1

It is to this craft that I now want to turn. I have suggested that tragedy and comedy, major literary kinds with a discernible shape (which different critics describe, of course, in different ways), carry the dialectic in the process of their plots; they are dialectical in terms of the events they enact. Story, which may choose any shape imaginable and enact any sort of event, including tragic and comic ones, is, I believe, dialectical in itself. The mere fact of story arises from the dialectic, and in turn illuminates it.

Story, indeed, is quite mysterious, and certainly not to be taken for granted. We might, rather, be surprised that we tell each other tales, and write them down, obsessively, from country to country and from generation to generation; that we delight in engaging our minds with hypothetical situations and fictitious persons, with happenings that didn't happen, in a world not exactly ours. And to sound story is again to ask the basic question: what does it mean? The question goes deeper than the more familiar ones, about the nature of epic, of romance, of the novel, or of fairy tale. It leaves aside the forms that narrative takes, to focus on narrative itself. It also extends beyond narrative as a genre, since it can be referred to drama, or to poetry, or, for that matter, to jokes.

The answer to it lies, I suggest, in the fact that we cannot imagine stories in Eden. There could certainly be the recounting of events, so as to pass on information or communicate a response; but the events would be received as in no way different from reality, and if the recounting was felt as having a form, the form would be that which reality continually displayed – a small instance of the Cosmos. There would be no need for stories in which event is imagined and form is created. Nor would there be any need for invented characters, or for invented place or time. Since evil and death would be unknown, one presumes that being

72

would be undivided, the present would be presence, and the real would be enough. According to the old adage, a happy people has no history; it also has no story.

The need for story comes with the exile from Eden. And this is so whether or not Eden actually existed. It suffices that we know that, in either case, we are not living there now. Whatever our beliefs or lack of them, a flaming sword 'turns every way' between our notion of what a garden of perfection would be and our experience of what the world is. The oneness of Eden excludes story; when evil enters to corrupt that oneness – whether as an event in history or an event in our consciousness – story is born, as another world to be reached for out of this fallen one. Necessity is the mother of invention, as they say, and need is the mother of story.[1]

We tell stories in a fallen world. By their matter they may lament and counter that fall, as they often do via the tragedy and comedy that we have already discussed. The strange power of story, however, is also to achieve those ends simply by being itself. Whatever its 'content', it opens a story-world, where everything coheres infrangibly and is impeccably. That world may well be as fallen as the one we inhabit daily; it may even be more terrifying or more grotesque. Yet as a narrated world it represents a desirable otherness. Story quits a world that does not, seemingly, have a story – or whose only story: 'There was a fall from Eden', may be repeated but cannot be finished – for a world that, within the consciousness of the tale, does. We tell stories because we desire a world with a story.

Story offers an otherness, of unity and purposive sequence. It also offers, in particular, beginnings and ends.[2] The search for beginnings is, naturally, a fundamental enterprise, in cosmogonies, genealogies, histories. The specific of story is that it appeals to the desire for a new beginning. We may come to story with any version of the idea that a first beginning, if there was one, has gone deeply wrong, that universal, individual or social Creation has been succeeded by Fall, and that evil needs to be removed in a fresh start. The start of story is so fresh that it occurs in another dimension, which replaces ours in the twinkling of an opening sentence. Into the dead present of Ecclesiastes: 'The thing that hath been, it is that which shall be; and that which is done is that which shall be done: and there is no new thing under the sun' (1:9), it intrudes the magic departure of 'Once upon a time'; it responds to the preacher's question: 'Is there any thing whereof it may be said, See, this is new?' (1:10) by presenting itself. It provides, in the seeming safety of narrative, an aesthetic version of St Paul's *kainé ktisis* (2 Corinthians 5:17), a 'new creation' that promises an irresistibly unfolding story ahead.

An end is equally a form of salvation, substituting, for mere addition, finality and climax, and concentrating time into a shape. It may also be another kind of beginning. It is so, though irresponsibly, in popular narratives – which are likely to manifest more clearly than others the latent design of story – whenever any version of the formula 'And they lived happily ever after' inaugurates a future of undemanding and quasi-infinite hope. The characters do not so much 'quit the story', as Raymond Queneau phrases it, as enter a further dimension of the story-world so secure that it doesn't even need to be told.

As story is a response to fallen history, so it responds to a fallen physical universe. Again, this need not imply that it transforms the latter's 'vanity' and 'corruption' (in St Paul's words) into order and newness, since the change operates in terms not of the universe to which story alludes but of the manner of existence of that universe. The most chaotic, alien physicality will inevitably be a locus of narrative, a story-place, invulnerable before the forces by which real place is undermined.

The time of story also is different from our time. One sign of this, among many, is that while story-time is usually articulated by the past tense of the verb, the pastness of the tense has been strangely removed. The verb does not refer to the past of the writer or of the reader, nor does it refer to the past of the world – even in stories located in history. Within the tale, their past is no more historical than that of stories occurring in the present, or even in the future: if we discover in Scott that Edward Waverley took leave of his family sixty years ago, we also learn, on opening Orwell's most famous book, that 'It was a bright cold day in April', 1984. The function of the tense is to proclaim itself the tense of narrative: it is less the past historic than the past storic. It 'signals an art' (according to Roland Barthes in *Writing Degree Zero*), and eases our passage into the story-world.

Most importantly, personae in story live charmed lives in comparison with persons in reality. As we want the world to have a story, so we should like our life to be a tale, its moments caught up into significance and its whole governed by the logic of final causes. The characters of fiction (I use the word 'characters' for want of a less loaded term), even if they see themselves as amorphous, and even if they are presented as such, have already achieved that privilege. However 'true to life' they may be, and however they may suffer within the tale, their salvation lies in the fact that they are narrated. Although they may, referentially, be denizens of our own, fallen world, they also inhabit the glory of form. Their story may be read over and over again, and can never be damaged.

Modern narrative and reflection on narrative have familiarised us to a certain extent with the notion of the possible otherness of the story-world. This otherness, however, this fictionality of fiction, is not a feature of one type of story only, to the exclusion of others. In *Le livre à venir,* Maurice Blanchot describes what he calls the *récit* as treating of 'an exceptional event which escapes the forms of quotidian time and the world of habitual truth', so as to distinguish it from the *roman,* which is 'an entirely human story', founded on human time and human passions (pp. 11–13). Yet, no matter how far a narrative may be from a concern with the exceptional and the inhabitual, no matter how meticulously it may set about a plausible and exact rendering of what it assumes to be the real, by the very nature of story its events happen elsewhere, in another time, and differently. The world of the most dogged *roman,* of the most realist of Victorian novels, is a world essentially narrated.

The same is true of what seems to be the natural conclusion of the foregoing: that the navigation of story is supremely towards itself. Again, Blanchot says of the *récit* that it 'is not the relation of the event but the event itself, the approach to the event, the place where the event is called on to occur: an event still to come and through whose drawing power the *récit* also can hope to materialize' (p.13). Yet here too, even when narrative pretends, as it usually does, that its events have occurred already, prior to their being written about, it is nevertheless the story that produces them – they can only occur, in fact, as they are narrated, and even real events change in narration and occur in a new guise – and that, by the same act, produces itself. What story recounts is its own recounting; it tells its own possibility. It is naturally reflexive, not only within the scope of modernism but under any historical conditions.

Not all stories, of course, are aware of themselves in these

terms. Very many are, however: in a surprising array of major
works, the self-telling is essential and explicit. I should like briefly
to consider several such works, not for the purpose of illustrating a
theory but so as to meditate it from a number of different points
of view, and in a way to allow the writers – all great story-tellers
– to speak for themselves.

Consider, first, Boccaccio's *Decameron.* It begins by describing the
Black Death of 1348 at a length and with an insistence that have
been found puzzling. Why does Boccaccio dwell so much on the
plague when he only needs to indicate, apparently, that it was the
reason why the ten young people left the city together? Is he
merely taking the opportunity of expressing compassion, horror,
indignation at the cruelty and foolishness of the citizens? Or is he
establishing the plague as the source of the subsequent hundred
stories? In terms of mimesis, seven young women and three
young men escape from plague-ridden Florence to a carefree
estate on the slopes of a nearby hill; in terms of narrative self-
reflexion, future story-tellers flee from a fallen world, 'in quest of
health', to a world of stories.

    Through the particulars on which the narrative focuses, more-
over, the Black Death resembles original sin. It spreads from the
East, passes from person to person through far slighter contact
than contagious diseases usually demand, and affects not only
humans but all living creatures. There is also a suggestion that the
story-tellers escape from the wrath to come: the narrator specu-
lates that although the pestilence may have been disseminated by
the influence of the celestial bodies, it may also have been 'sent
upon us mortals by God in His just wrath by way of retribution for
our iniquities'. And the place where the story-tellers assemble to
tell their stories is paradise. There are strong hints of this in the
description of the domain in which they spend the first two days; it
becomes explicit when they move to another domain. They enter
a walled garden, are 'wonder-struck', smell odours of 'all the spices
that ever grew in the East', and conclude that no beauty could be
added to it and that no 'other form could be given to Paradise, if it
were to be planted on earth'.

    Their journey to this further story-world is also carefully plotted
in terms of the dialectic. They leave one place of health, travel
over a Friday and Saturday during which they remain silent and
storyless, in memory of Easter Friday on which 'He who died for

us bore His passion', and enter a more splendid paradise on a
Sunday of resurrection.

The *Decameron* is exemplary in that it causes the significance of
story to declare itself. It tells the story of characters whose main
occupation is to tell stories, thereby suggesting that story's intrinsic
concern is itself. It places story-telling in the context of death and a
fallen world on the one hand and paradise on the other. It defines
the site where narrative occurs. If that site is paradisiac and resur-
rectional, moreover, one also realises that the plague is still
raging, a mere few miles away. The memory of the plague brings
the narrative domain back, as it were, to earth. It qualifies the
paradise of story, as being not an achieved salvation from *misère*
but a glimpse, a metaphor of that salvation.[3]

Chaucer's *Canterbury Tales* also tells of people telling stories, and
indicates the narrative status of its world. It is a kind of voyage
through tales: the characters travel both towards Canterbury and
towards heaven – towards St Thomas the 'holy blisful martir' –
and they do so by making their way along a road of stories. The
first line of the very first tale: 'Whylom, as olde stories tellen us',
even declares that one is about to enter, not a tale but the tale of a
tale; it draws its hearers, and also its reader, into more than one
narrative depth. The *Tales* are themselves a pilgrimage, and where
they lead is into a story-world.

They refer to the fact that they are being related; and they also
refer, on one brief occasion, to the person who is relating them. I
am thinking of the Prologue to Sir Thopas, whose function is not
only (if at all) to provide a now famous description of the real-life
Chaucer, but to summon the author out of hiding:

> And than at erst [our hoste] loked up-on me,
> And seyde thus, 'what man artow?' quod he;
> 'Thou lokest as thou woldest finde an hare,
> For ever up-on the ground I see thee stare'.

It is not merely that the Host turns for a story to 'Chaucer' the
pilgrim. The person staring intently downwards may well be
Chaucer the pilgrim taking notes, but he is also Chaucer the
writer, who is scrutinising the page on which he is in the process
of writing those very lines. The Host looks both within the poem
and out from the poem, to detect his author and to mock him. He
even calls him a 'popet', as if punning on 'poet'. As the author's

master of the tale-telling, he addresses the only actual tale-teller, by piercing his disguise as narrator–pilgrim, and asks him for a tale. It is a vertiginous moment, and an extremely sophisticated one.

The sudden shift from the story-world to the room of the story-teller, by occurring in the middle of the book, brings to our attention the fact that the entire work through which we are making our way, however prolifically, pleasurably and instructively 'real', is a huge and single Tale, the invention of a particular writer. It invites the reader not to lose himself in the story but to find himself there, by measuring one against the other the fiction and his sense of fact. The Host may even be addressing the reader directly, since he too is looking down. In that case, the work springs him out of the story-world even more drastically, makes him aware of the activity in which he is engaged, and forces him to relate to the story-world before returning to it.[4]

Furthermore, as it discloses the writer behind the narrator, so the Host's gaze puts Chaucer himself on the spot. I suggested that we should like our lives to be tales and ourselves to be characters; Chaucer has achieved that ambition, by placing 'Chaucer' among the pilgrims and so entering his own tale thinly camouflaged. He is aware, however, of the problematic nature of that move. By causing his Host – a real character – to banter him back into his study, he makes clear the merely fictive, ludic status of himself-as-character. And by having the Host pose that most searching of questions: 'What man artow?' he reveals even more of a deep personal exploration in the *Tales,* and acknowledges, in a marvellously swift piece of comedy, that if the writer sounds himself and the world through his work, the work also sounds him. I take it that only as the *Tales* come to an end is the question beginning to be answered.

Malory's *Tale of the Sankgreal* also refers to itself as narrative, and is in some ways even more unexpected. It tells the story of a story-world – not simply in the sense that its medieval knight-errantry is romance, but in the sense that the events of the story are described, over and over again, as 'adventures'. What happens in the story is story. It also moves forward to a point from which it can look back on itself, and exhibit its own concluding:

And whan they had etyn, the kynge made grete clerkes to com

before hym, for cause they shulde cronycle of the hyghe adventures of the good knyghtes. So whan sir Bors had tolde hym of
the hyghe aventures of the Sankgreall, such as had befalle hym
and his three felowes, which were sir Launcelot, Percivale and
sir Galahad and hymselff, than sir Launcelot tolde the adventures of the Sangreall that he had sene. And all thys was made
in grete bookes and put up in almeryes at Salysbury.[5]

The adventures attain their end by being told; and they are
gathered finally into a book, which, at a number of removes, is the
book that we have just been reading.

One thinks of Proust. The most celebrated of modern quest
narratives, his *A la recherche du temps perdu,* is also a search for
story, as much as for lost time, since Marcel turns his experience
of involuntary memory, and the adventurous moments of pure
time which it procures, into the possibility of writing. He is only
about to begin writing as the novel closes, but, as in Malory and
Malory's source, the book to which he refers at the end is
nevertheless the book that we have already read. *A la recherche* is
another story questing for itself. Its modernity lies partly in the
fact that it is now the narrator who searches for narrative, partly
in the extra degree of explicitness – indeed, in the obviousness –
of the reference to that search.[6]

The Tale of the Sankgreal recounts the means by which it became
itself. The special interest of the tale, however, from the point of
view adopted here, is that its characters are also endeavouring to
become, precisely, characters in a tale. In seeking the Grail they
seek 'adventures', which, as the etymology suggests, will come to
them, and take control of them in real life (as it were) just as stories
control characters in a book. Accordingly, a voice says to Galahad,
Perceval and Bors: 'Lordis, tomorow, at the owre of pryme, ye
three shall departe everych frome other, tylle the aventure brynge
you unto the Maymed Kynge' (*Sir Galahad,* 11); while the white
knight tells Galahad, in what is both a command and a promise:
'go where the aventures shall lede you' (*The Castle of Corbenic,* 14).
Whereas Boccaccio's characters recount stories in paradise,
Malory's characters desire actually to enter the paradise of story.

Malory also isolates, however, a higher level of story and
declares it alone to be genuinely paradisiac. Not all knights, nor
even all 'adventures', have access to it. Before being adopted by
the higher level, Galahad and Lancelot find 'many straunge

adventures and peryllous', but since they do not concern the Grail
they remain unrecounted: 'the tale makith here no mencyon
therof' *(The Castle of Corbenic,* 13). Other knights, refused entry, find
that even ordinary adventures have abandoned them. Gawain
rides 'longe withoute ony adventure', and meets the equally luck-
less Ector, who tells of twenty other knights in the same distress
(Sir Gawain, 1). They ask a hermit why they no longer meet with
adventures as before, and are told that they are unfit for the story
which has superseded all others, for it is 'the adventure of the
Sankgreall whych be in shewynge now' (section 5). This is partly a
matter of self-explaining literary choice: certain knights and
certain events are required for the particular story to be written,
while others are not. Relations are also established, however,
between the story-world and our world. It is because of real,
human failures that knights are excluded from the Grail story:
Gawain and Ector for their 'evyll fayth' and 'poore beleve' (section
2), Lancelot for his 'olde synne', *(The Miracles,* 19). Those who
succeed do so because of real qualities.

The *Tale* is again placing story, like *The Decameron,* in terms of
Fall and Paradise. The knights travel through this 'unsyker' or
unstable world, compounded of a variety of evils, and what they
seek is simultaneously the Grail and adventures, as if the heavenly
vision, or the road towards it, were to be understood as a narrative – as if, story being a kind of paradise, paradise were also a
kind of story. Some knights fail both of the Grail and of adventure;
their lot is not only sorrow but, more pointedly, 'disadventure' or
'mysadventure'. Some become the heroes of ordinary adventures,
and enter the fiction of a redeemed world; they enjoy finality,
significance, looming eventfulness. Some few are accepted for the
adventure of the Grail, and are, simply, redeemed.

Each of these works, as it happens, is a compilation of tales, and
two indicate as much by their title. This type of narrative seems
particularly significant: it attests a desire for story after story, and
for story within story, and suggests that we can never have
enough stories. *The Thousand and One Nights* also belongs here, and
Ovid's *Metamorphoses,* as do numerous and various works of
episodic fiction from the *Odyssey* to picaresque novels.[7] So, tell-
ingly, does a short and tightly organised narrative like Madame de
La Fayette's *La Princesse de Clèves,* with its several 'digressions'.

In their showing of the need for story and of the ease with

which story becomes self-aware, however, works that are not
overtly tales at all are even more suggestive. Take, for example,
the plays of Shakespeare, considered not as dramas or dramatic
poems but as dramatic narratives. Many realise their status as
stories at the moment of their completion. In the final scene of
Romeo and Juliet, Friar Laurence resumes the events for the benefit
of the Prince in a long and circumstantial 'tale', whose technical
purpose seems to be to reiterate as story what the audience has
been experiencing as theatre. The audience perceives the whole
play now as a single narrated sequence, and is even invited by the
Prince in the concluding couplet to compare it with others of a
similar nature: 'For never was a story of more woe / Than this of
Juliet and her Romeo'. There is a kind of literary withdrawal from
the events of the play, comparable to the moment when the
stories in Malory are chronicled and 'made into books'. A similar
effect is produced when plays finish by having their characters
retire, perhaps to an abbey or a cell and with a circle of listeners,
to recount and to hear the 'story' or 'discourse' of all that has been
performed;[8] or when they are prolonged into a fictive future by
the promise of a good tale of more limited scope.[9]

The writer may also be revealed. The Chorus at the end of
Henry V, in the lines, 'Thus far, with rough and all-unable pen, / Our
bending author hath pursu'd the story', replaces play, players and
playhouse by story, writer and study. (Interestingly, the expression,
'bending author', reminds one both of Chaucer's sudden appearance and of his physical posture.) Characters too may become
literarily self-aware, at the end of the play and of their life, by
perceiving their life as narrative. Hamlet, for instance, appeals to
Horatio to tell his 'story', and much is made of the fact, with
Horatio giving Fortinbras a kind of foretaste of the tale ('carnal,
bloody, and unnatural acts . . .' etc.), and Fortinbras responding by
gathering a circle of hearers and calling 'the noblest to the
audience'.

The most remarkable of such cases is Othello's. About to kill
himself, he tells Lodovico what to write about him:

> I pray you, in your letters,
> When you shall these unlucky deeds relate,
> Speak of me as I am . . .
> Of one that lov'd not wisely but too well;
> > . . . of one whose hand,

> Like the base Indian, threw a pearl away
> Richer than all his tribe; of one whose subdu'd eyes
> Albeit unused to the melting mood,
> Drop tears as fast as the Arabian trees
> Their med'cinable gum.

Not only does Othello foresee his life become narrative at some future date: he himself transforms it into narrative by recounting it with the conventional signs of the past tense and the third person. The sudden move into the present tense – 'Drop' – shows, moreover, that he is also apprehending the present as story; and with almost his last words and his last action he causes the two temporal dimensions to merge:

> Set you down this;
> And say besides, that in Aleppo once,
> Where a malignant and a turban'd Turk
> Beat a Venetian and traduc'd the state,
> I took by the throat the circumcised dog,
> And smote him thus.

He returns to the narrative past, but he continues to live the narration in the present. His stabbing himself may be 'a superb *coup de théâtre*' (Leavis) – it also brings the time of story into the time of his life (at the stroke of death). In the dizzy time-shift between 'smote' and 'thus' Othello becomes, even more self-consciously than the Grail knights, the hero of a story. It is left to Lodovico, in the final lines, to distance himself from the play and from the place, and to gather the deed into more customary narrative: 'Myself will straight aboard, and to the state/This heavy act with heavy heart relate.'

When they have run their course, Shakespeare's plays achieve various ends, as tragic fulfilment, or comic marriage. They also achieve story. A happy train of events is likely to brim over into tale; an unhappy one, by being perceived as a tale, may transpose its *misère* into the otherness of story. Characters may even be aware of that otherness. Once again, works uninfluenced by modern theories of fiction bring to their surface their quest for narrative. One wonders, indeed, if the idea of 'story' was not as important for Shakespeare as the more familiar idea of 'theatre'.

And then consider Dante, whom I have held over to this point despite chronology because of the extensive importance of the *Commedia*. As well as being dialectical in the self-reflexion of its story, the *Commedia* is dialectical in its plot – perhaps more perfectly so than any other work. It begins in a 'wild wood', where the *grandeur* of an original garden is no more than a memory, a 'straight way' that has been lost; it moves through the *misère* of a deepening hell; it ends in a paradise. Indeed, its reach is so all-embracing that it combines both the major dialectical forms, comedy and tragedy; and our insistence on its being one rather than the other can limit our response to it, as it certainly limits our general understanding of tragedy as a kind.[10] The *Commedia* is comedy in that it achieves a marriage – the spiritual marriage of Dante with Beatrice; but it is tragedy in that it effects, by its last movement, a vast renewal: of the character 'Dante', of the whole world, and of the relation of all things to God. It is comic and not tragic, certainly, in its expansive exploration of the joy which it enters (whereas the *Oresteia,* say, or *Samson Agonistes,* close almost as soon as the joy is secured). Yet in at least two of its features it is actually tragic and not comic. It approaches evil and suffering directly rather than indirectly, the *Inferno* descending deeper and deeper into the grounds of pity and fear; and its *misère* which is unredeemable, eternal and literally hellish, is in no way set aside in the rejoicing, but is maintained within the complex, final vision. The *Commedia* is a paramount text for many reasons, and one of them is that it is comprehensively dialectical, before the divergence of the dialectic into tragedy and comedy.

It also enacts more consummately than any other work the change of sign by which wretchedness is reversed into triumph. Dante in hell spirals down through the earth towards Satan. He falls as far as it is possible to fall, both figuratively and literally. Suddenly, however, in the last canto of the *Inferno,* he finds that Virgil, on whose back he is being carried, is no longer clambering down Satan but climbing upwards towards the feet. Having negotiated the mid-point at the centre of the earth, Dante passes from the demonic downward spiral of hell, which has been gradually closing in on him, to its reverse image, the divine upward spiral of Mount Purgatory. He locates paradox, changes direction while continuing along the same line, and learns that the way down is the way up. He traverses zero, the infinitesimal point from which possibility springs, and from then on is aiming straight towards Paradise.

Exemplary by the shaping of its plot, the *Commedia* is also exemplary as a self-conscious narrative. Like *The Decameron,* and in the same terms, it defines the fundamental project of story. It emerges from fear, from the *paura* to which it refers repeatedly in the first few lines, and ends in paradise. The way to paradise is itself a path of tales. Dante voyages as a pilgrim through an infernal and purgatorial earth and through the heavens, but he also voyages as a listener through stories, advancing by way of them and past them even more evidently than Chaucer's pilgrims. Those stories, moreover, are placed, almost literally. As Dante the writer tells tale after tale, embracing all narrative possibilities (and composing, incidentally, yet another compendium), he gives every kind of tale its location – in terms of reality, in terms of the single story uniting all the others: the journey of Dante the character, and in terms of the higher, divine Story which is enacted both by reality as a whole and by the *Commedia* itself: the story of a world purged of evil and raised to bliss.

The journey (another basic paradigm of story) is once more a quest, and once more a quest for a book. When Dante achieves his final vision, and gazes into 'the supreme light', what he sees, according to a celebrated stanza, is a volume:

> Nel suo profondo vidi che s'interna,
> legato con amore in un volume,
> ciò che per l'universo si squaderna . . .

(Within its depths I saw that there is gathered, bound with love into one volume, what through the universe is scattered in quires.)

That the end – or very nearly the end – of the whole of Dante's long peregrination should be a book, is actually quite startling. Certainly, the book is not his own, as in the case of the *Sankgreal* or *A la recherche*: it is God's book, the universe, and derives from the medieval notion of the 'Book of the World'. It might seem, there-fore, that Dante's concern is entirely outward and that the *Commedia* itself is not in question. As he looks into the vision, however, his own book becomes one of two which the divine book judges.

The other is Virgil's. Virgil represents for Dante, as we know, a multiple threshold – to the Christian era, to the empire of the Roman Church, to grace, to Italian, to Dante's own 'good style'. In the same way that Virgil can no longer be Dante's guide when he enters Paradise, so Virgil's book pales before the book of God. The contrast is made implicitly, by the unstated parallels between the vision of the book in the very last canto of the *Paradiso* and the meeting with Virgil in the very first canto of the *Inferno*. Here are Dante's words to him:

> Or se' tu quel Virgilio, e quella fonte,
> che spande di parlar si largo fiume? . . .
>
> O degli altri poeti onore e lume,
> vagliami il lungo studio e il grande amore,
> che m'ha fatto cercar lo tuo volume.
>
> Tu se' lo mio maestro, e il mio autore.

(Are you then that Virgil, and that spring, which pours such a broad river of speech? . . . O glory and light of other poets, may the long study avail me, and the great love, that made me search your volume. You are my master, and my author.)

Dante had searched Virgil's volume as he has sought, through a hundred cantos, the volume of God. As a kind of mnemonic to recall the earlier passage, both volumes rhyme with 'lume' (which in the later instance is a rhymic pun, since God's 'volume' is stated to be, and also sounds and looks like, a 'lume'); and 'amore' is also present in both cases, gaining hugely in significance from one to the other. Whereas Virgil is a source of rich 'parlare', however, human 'parlare' fails, says Dante, before the final vision (line 56). And whereas Virgil begins as 'mio autore', 'my author', God alone is described, in an earlier canto of the *Paradiso* (26, line 40) as the 'verace autore', the 'veracious author'.

Virgil's pagan quest-epic, which stands here presumably as the greatest human book, is overwhelmed by the book of God. It has already been superseded, however, by Dante's Christian quest-epic, and this too is measured by the divine volume. Its limits are established, and its adequacy defined: it is only the means to achieving a far more exalted book, but it does provide a model of that book. It bears a correct relationship, of analogy and discipline, to truth.[11] For beyond the vision of the volume is a vision of three circles that figure the Trinity, but that also suggest the three canticles of the poem which they crown. The trinity-in-unity of the poem leads to a God who is Three in One. Similarly, the mathematical shape, and even the material constitution, of the work are ordained. Alongside numerical exigencies like that which determines the $3 \times 33 + 1$ cantos, there is the specifying of the number of sheets for writing on, which obliges Dante, or is said to oblige him, to cut short the end of the Purgatorio, 'since all the pages devised for this second canticle are filled'.

Within the terms of Dante's beliefs, the relation here between story and reality is ideal. Given the nature of reality, the *Commedia* is the right work to compose – indeed, in a way it is the *only* work to compose, rather like Proust's one novel. As Dante is rewarded for passing through hell and purgatory with a vision of God's paradise, so he is rewarded for passing accurately through the *Commedia* with a vision of God's book. Then, his writing having transformed the 'wild wood' into a volume, it ceases when in sight of the greater Volume beyond.[12]

2

Dante, completing his book, refers to it, but he also refers his book to reality. There, of course, is the question: if story is a response to the Fall, an imagining, a fiction, of a world remade – a sign, perhaps, of paradise – what of the relation between that fiction and, shall we say, the other fiction that we call fact? To stress the otherness of story is clearly to risk de-valuing the fallen world; and I should like, in the remaining sections of this chapter, to explore the two most extreme and most opposed reactions to that risk.

The first would welcome it: it would choose story in place of the world, making of it an ersatz of salvation, in another kind of demonic parody. Such a choice is made in Sartre's *La Nausée,* which enacts with great precision and complexity a flight from despair of the world to story for story's sake. Frank Kermode, in a brilliant chapter of *The Sense of an Ending,* has already drawn attention to the importance of this novel for any theory of narrative, and has discussed many of the features that I shall be mentioning. Since he reads it, however, in the light of concerns that Sartre only developed in his later writings, he seems to me seriously to dulcify its desperate extremity.

The source of the novel, or more strictly, of the diary it pretends to be, is the narrator Roquentin's experience of nausea, provoked by contact with an uncreated world, where no 'être nécessaire et cause de soi', no necessary and self-causing being, guarantees the

ultimate stability of a giddy contingence. As fear impelled Dante,
so nausea impels Roquentin to write, in the same absence of God
and in a world similarly closed to his desire. His writing activity is
likewise foregrounded, in the opening sentences: 'The best thing
would be to write down events day by day. Keep a diary so as to
see clearly', and also after the climactic illumination, the revelation of contingence, in the Public Gardens: 'The word "Absurdity"
is emerging under my pen ... How am I going to be able to fix
that with words? ... I didn't formulate my discoveries. But I think
it would be easy for me to put them into words now ... I left, I
came back to the hotel, and there it is, I have written.'

One of the events that Roquentin writes about is coming across
a narrative and finding that the world has no power over it. While
lunching in a certain brasserie he reads a page, not from a
medieval tale or a modern anti-novel, but from Balzac's *Eugénie
Grandet,* the epitome of a realist *roman.* The day is Sunday, as in
Boccaccio, and the page opens miraculously on to the domain of
story. It is ordered, utterly self-sufficient, and untouchable by
Roquentin's surroundings, which include the edges of another
client's plate decorated with 'the gobbits of grey meat that she has
spat out'. Roquentin reverts to those surroundings, which turn out
to be a detailed burlesque of the scene in Balzac; yet, while one
imagines him ironising about the emotions, the social attitudes, of
the scene, it does bring him the vision of a world blessed by being
narrated. Placed in the text of *La Nausée,* which at the moment we
are receiving not as Sartre's novel but as the worldly, random
experiences of Roquentin, it also brings that vision to the reader.
In terms of a comparison used by Valéry (in his 1939 Zaharoff
Lecture), it intrudes into Roquentin's 'noise' like the 'sound' of a
tuning-fork or musical instrument.

At first Roquentin endeavours to enter that narrated world, by
becoming himself 'the hero of a novel', and for the rest of Sunday
he seems to succeed. He contrives to experience the successive
moments of his journey – he walks the streets – not as contingent
and random but as necessary and fatal, by supposing that some
powerful event is waiting for him round the next corner, on the
far side of the next square. He transforms living into an
'adventure' – the word is his own – and, like Malory's Grail
knights, is caught up into a vivid significance ministered from
beyond him. Nor is he alone in his quest: two other characters, the
Autodidact and Anny his former mistress, have also sought

'adventures' or dream of seeking them. (The Autodidact is even called Ogier, presumably after Ogier the Dane, the hero of medieval romances.) Like them he fails, concluding that, since an adventure must be told, it cannot be lived, and that 'adventures are in books'.

At the end of the novel, therefore, he chooses telling. It is the 'sound' of music that determines his choice, the hearing of a ragtime song, 'Some of These Days', on the phonograph of another café. Against a world of soft contingencies the song appears 'hard' and 'necessary'; it exists 'in another time' and in another place, 'outside'. It too emerges from *misère,* transforming the pain of loss ('you'll miss me honey') into 'measure', and super-seding what Roquentin imagines to have been the vexations of its composer. The otherness of its 'inflexible order' and its inhuman 'metallic transparency' were even achieved in spite of the composer, who in the very act of writing belonged to the soft, unnecessary world, and held his pencil 'mollement', 'slackly'. So Roquentin's decision in the final pages, which mimes that of Marcel in *A la recherche* while significantly altering it, is to write a novel likewise situated 'above existence' and 'hard as steel'.

What he hopes for thereby is expressly his own version of Christian salvation. He sees the work of art as a process of death and rebirth: the notes of the song 'die' so that the singer's voice may be 'born', while new combinations are 'born' in a card game by successive cards 'disappearing'; and he believes similarly that when he himself dies to be reborn in his future novel he will be cleansed of the 'sin' of existence, 'justified' and 'saved'. He is in fact on the same quest as the Grail knights – like them he is looking simultaneously for story and for salvation; and he is on the same pilgrimage as Dante, but with no world to measure his writing and no God to authenticate his redemption.[13] A belief in the Book of the World had enabled Dante to situate human books, including his own, with respect to it. The decline of that belief, as Gabriel Josipovici has shown, has led to the exploration of many possible relationships between story and reality; it has also led to the imagining of books so ambitious that it is they which situate the world. Friedrich Schlegel evoked 'an infinite book . . . the absolute book'. Novalis contemplated the writing of a Bible. Mallarmé, whose *Livre* is the focus of the most drastic thinking on the subject, quipped in all earnestness that 'the world is made so as to end in a beautiful book'. In *La Nausée,* Roquentin conceives of a book so alien that it could save him from the world by turning its back on it.

Yet where is that book? There is no suggestion, as at the end of *A la recherche,* that the novel he is about to write is the one we have been reading. Equally: where after the close is Roquentin himself? A Publisher's Foreword at the front of *La Nausée* states that the notebooks that follow 'were found among Antoine Roquentin's papers', as though Roquentin, presumably without having written his novel, had in some way or another disappeared. And of course he *has* disappeared, but for the simple reason that he only ever existed for the duration of *La Nausée,* and that he is precisely the 'hero of a novel' that he desired to become – not of his own novel, which is never written, but of Sartre's novel, of which he was unaware. *La Nausée* is just the kind of book that he leaves with the intention of composing, 'a story ... of the sort that can't happen, an adventure'. It 'couldn't happen' because, while Roquentin's experiences are, for him, merely a series of occurrences, for us they constitute an adventure in the classic mould, with a begin-ning: there was once a man of thirty called Roquentin who picked up a pebble and had to drop it; a middle: the search for the cause of his nausea and for a solution; and an end: the decision to write a novel.

La Nausée, in fact, is two texts in one. Roquentin records contin-gence in a diary; Sartre contrives necessity, by writing out that same diary as a novel. The novel, which is quite different from the diary though verbally (almost) identical with it, does not, therefore, falsify its own philosophy (as Kermode maintains) – it doesn't, while attempting to remain faithful to the contingence of the real, find itself baulked by the fact that a novel, unless it collapse into chaos, has to impose patterns. It wants to impose patterns, and does so with elaborate strategy, since it not only refers, from the diary, to the saving necessity of art – it also enacts that necessity within itself. And if Roquentin expects to be 'saved' by writing a novel, so Sartre expected to be saved by writing *La Nausée.* Accord-ing to a passage in his autobiography, *Les Mots* (which Kermode quotes but dismisses as 'good fun' and not 'serious'), the function of *La Nausée* was to point up the 'unjustified' existence of his fellow men while exonerating his own existence. The ploy involved a doubling not only of the text but of the writer's consciousness: '*I was* Roquentin; I revealed in him, without complacency, the course of my life. At the same time I was *me,* the elect, the chronicler of Hades, a photomicroscope of glass and steel bent over my own protoplasmic syrups.' Roquentin suffers amorphously; Sartre suffers, like the 'little melody' of the jazz tune, 'en mesure'. Roquentin wants to live an adventure; Sartre does live an adventure, by narrating the storylessness of the world as a story and by telling his own life as a tale, and so becoming the hero of a novel. As both his character and his character's teller, it was Sartre and not Roquentin who supposedly rose above the sin of existence, and who justified himself by recounting his lack of justification. As demonic parody, therefore, *La Nausée* both proclaims story as redemption and ministers that redemption to its own author.

The relationship of Roquentin to Sartre is more wayward, one realises, than that of Marcel to Proust, or of 'Chaucer' to Chaucer. And it is far more than a question of ironic distance (though that too, of course, can be richly complex, as in the case of, say, Swift and his gullible traveller). Here, the relationship is defined within the very terms of story, in that Roquentin is precisely a novel-hero and Sartre precisely a novelist. One also realises that *La Nausée,* which opts for story at the expense of life, is an early work, different from the 'committed' works that follow from *Les Mouches.* Indeed, it became quite foreign to Sartre well before the time of his autobiography. When considering the French Symbolists in *Qu'est-ce que la littérature?* which appeared ten years after the novel, and denouncing their 'gratuitous' and 'inhuman' project, he might already have been denouncing Roquentin's.

3

Story, as the fiction of a fallen world remade, is in fact always in danger of losing the world by substituting itself, whatever its intention, of eventually dissatisfying its readers through its unreality. So there are many stories that, from age to age, parody story, deflating its pretensions and dismantling its artifices. They are particularly telling when they also mock the insidious inference that a story coheres immaculately because the world it represents is already an immaculate cohesion. Among such works, Voltaire's *Candide,* the other extreme from *La Nausée,* is of seminal importance.

Candide satirises the philosophy of Leibnitz, or of his followers, by demonstrating that the world denies all the major Leibnitzian postulates, to the discomfiture of their champion, Pangloss. Being a tale and not a treatise, however, it only operates in part through its surface argument: it also operates through the functioning – or rather, the dysfunctioning – of its narrative and its language. And this is doubly appropriate, since Leibnitzian logic is itself a kind of narrative, and a powerful narrative model. Presumably the same is true of any philosophy that argues a comprehensive order; yet the philosophy of Leibnitz seems especially akin to story, and possesses the added interest of having arisen at the very moment that the novel was rising. His 'concatenation of events' is what makes story possible, by relating events one to another in a sequence which goes beyond mere temporal succession. Candide's rendering of this, as instructed by Pangloss: 'everything is linked necessarily', even reminds one of Roquentin's perception of the 'necessity' that events enjoy in the story-world. His favouring of 'final causes' (which Bacon and Descartes had rejected) corres-ponds to the teleology of narrative, its purposive drive from a beginning through a middle towards an end. His 'cause and effect' and his 'sufficient reason' chime with narrative plausibility, and in particular with the plausibility of 'character' – the joining of actions to motives and external influences – which the novel especially has been concerned to explore. His 'pre-established harmony' would even be a fine way of describing the oneness, the wholeness, of story (or indeed of any art-work), all of whose elements, including those that are quite disparate and lack any apparent connection, combine within a point of view, or a mood, or a vision. Leibnitzian philosophy reads the world, in fact, as a book, and specifically as a story-book. It sees in the world those characteristics of story that make it a desirable otherness. It argues, in a phrase that receives the brunt of *Candide's* indignation, that this is 'the best of all possible worlds'; and in keeping with classical rationalism as a whole, in practice it denies the Fall.

Candide quotes all those expressions of Leibnitzian thought that suggest a world of story, and pits against Leibnitzian narrative another, that one might call Humean. Humean narrative would correspond to the relentless demolishing of the constructions of reason in the first book of the *Treatise of Human Nature* (before the appeal to experience, habit and imagination succeeds in recover-ing everything that was lost). It would forego narrative logic, from the belief that 'necessity ... exists in the mind, not in objects' (part

3, section 14). It would proceed without purposively drawing to a conclusion, through a lack of conviction regarding final causes. It would be weak on causality in general, supposing that 'all our reasonings concerning causes and effects are deriv'd from nothing but custom' (part 4, section 1), and no doubt little preoccupied with plausibility. It would be suspicious of character, on the grounds that 'what we call a *mind,* is nothing but a heap or collection of different perceptions, united together by certain relations, and suppos'd, tho' falsely, to be endow'd with a perfect simplicity and identity' (part 4, section 2); and, because of the merely suppositional coherence of the world as perceived by the mind, it would be suspicious of the coherence of its own story-world.

Actually, appearing when the novel was under way, the first book of the *Treatise* provides a complex though unintended rebuttal of its aspirations, and the material for possible reactions against it. Sterne's *Tristram Shandy* is already in many ways a Humean anti-novel; and in our own century, with the weakening or demise of the various logics of nineteenth-century fiction, 'Humean' narrative has become an established mode. As Hume's thinking is the ultimate origin of much of Roquentin's thought (the latter's terror that a tongue might become a centipede, for instance, is traceable to Hume's bland assertion that 'any thing may produce any thing', part 3, section 13), so the implications of his thinking for narrative are behind Roquentin's diary. (They are not, of course, behind Sartre's novel, which is 'Leibnitzian'.) They also surface in Camus's *L'Etranger,* where a Humean first part of discrete sensations and happenings is followed by a second in which lawyers, examining the 'character' of Meursault and the events 'leading up to' his murder of an Arab, attempt to rewrite the first part as a nineteenth-century novel, with a Leibnitzian coherence. They could be said above all to govern Eliot's *Waste Land* – which includes a figure who can 'connect/Nothing with nothing', which offers a 'heap of broken images', and which, though a poem and of no great length, presents itself firstly as a waste land of narrative.

So as to move, as it were, from Leibnitz to Hume, *Candide* begins in a Leibnitzian Eden. Its hero inhabits, in 'the best of possible worlds', 'the most beautiful of castles', whose chatelaine, for good measure, is 'the best of possible baronesses'. He is then cast out of the earthly paradise, and allowed gradually to discover that it was in fact no Eden, but part of the earth's universal *misère.*

Similarly, the tale sets itself up as a story-world. Its ingredients are transparently conventional: it tells of the unrecognised illegitimate son of a noblewoman who begins to lose his innocence through a sexual awakening and who, separated from his Lady, spends the tale questing for her; it sends its many heroes on 'adventures'; and it constitutes a narrative compendium, in which the heroes them-selves also recount and listen to a variety of tales, with two early chapters: 'Cunégonde's Story' and 'The Old Woman's Story', alerting one to the fact by their headings. Here too, however, there is an expulsion, and the paradise of story is subverted. Voltaire disrupts the hallucinated order of Leibnitzian logic, by substituting for the concatenation of events a cascade of hetero-geneous happenings, whose only relation within each separate story is that they follow one another, and whose only link from story to story is the one he furnishes by telling them. He also jostles them forward at a vertiginous pace with little show of direction. He leaps into the implausible, by killing off several of the characters only to have them reappear alive many chapters later, and perhaps on another continent, and by reuniting all the main figures after scattering them over the globe. (He even causes the implausibility to declare itself: Candide says to Martin, of their having supped with six dethroned kings, 'that was a highly improbable adventure', to which Martin replies, 'It was no more extraordinary ... than most of the things that have happened to us.') And he allows the tale to fall into a heap of discrete fragments, figured, possibly, in the *membra disiecta* that Candide sees after a battle: 'Brains were spilt out over the ground, by the side of amputated arms and legs.'

He is not satisfied, however, with this undoing of the tale, for in a second parodic assault the tale is connected up again, but wrongly, by a form of zeugma. Incongruous elements are yoked together in the events: 'They ... heard a most pathetic sermon, followed by some beautiful faux-bourdon music. Candide's but-tocks were flogged in time to the singing; the Biscayan and the two men who wouldn't eat fat were burned ...'; and also in the language: the old woman relates that she has 'grown old in misery and opprobrium, having only half a backside, always remember-ing that [she] was the daughter of a Pope', while Pangloss introduces into the recital of how he caught syphilis the reflection that the pox is peculiar to Europe, 'like religious controversy'. (The device derives from the rhetoric of satire, from the mismatching which also produces a battle's 'heroic butchery'.)

Similarly, the tale restores a powerful but parodic finality both to history and to its own telling. Again while waxing eloquent on the question of syphilis, Pangloss not only traces his own disease backwards through history to the very fountainhead, in this case one of Columbus's companions (thereby parodying biblical and other genealogies), he also reasons that 'if Columbus had not caught . . . this disease which poisons the source of generation, which often even prevents generation, and which is evidently opposed to the great purpose of nature, we should have neither chocolate nor cochineal'. He and other characters also tell, or even more pointedly, re-tell, great tracts of narrative, enabling the reader to play their teleological conviction against the jumble into which they are in fact forced, and perhaps against his own memory of the events as he has already received them. At her first reunion with Candide, Cunégonde recounts her story and then resumes it:

> . . . my mind was filled with the massacre of my father, of my mother, of my brother, the insolence of my horrid Bulgarian soldier, the stab he gave me, my slavery, my work as a cook, my Bulgarian captain, my horrid Don Issachar, my abominable Inquisitor, the hanging of Doctor Pangloss, that long faux-bourdon *Miserere* during which you were being flogged on the buttocks, and above all the kiss I had given you behind a screen the day I had seen you for the last time.

She concludes, without pausing for breath: 'I praised God who was bringing you back to me through so many trials.' At the close, Pangloss recapitulates, with customary bathos, the whole of *Candide*:

> All events are linked together in the best of possible worlds. For after all, if you hadn't been thrown out of a beautiful castle with hefty kicks up the backside for the love of Mademoiselle Cunégonde, if you hadn't been tried by the Inquisition, if you hadn't travelled across America on foot, if you hadn't thrust your sword roundly into the Baron, if you hadn't lost all your sheep from the good land of Eldorado, you wouldn't now be eating candied citrons and pistachios.

Candide confronts two types of narrative; it also confronts two languages. The 'Leibnitzian' language is, naturally, that of Pangloss, who, according to the etymology of his name, is on the simplest level 'all tongue' but more radically, I suggest, the ambition of a 'universal' or 'complete language' to be a 'language about everything'. He corresponds in general, therefore, to Leibnitzian logic, a language claiming to be adequate to the describing and gathering of a world; and in particular to Leibnitz's project of a *characteristica universalis,* a mathematical symbolism based on simple or indefinable terms capable of extending knowledge in all branches of study indefinitely and indisputably. The 'Humean' language is that of Voltaire himself. It is the language of the writer, or of a certain kind of writer – an unremitting subversion, a continuous disordering, appropriate to a fallen and disordered world.

And there is more: the language of *Candide* is also presented, in a note that follows the sub-title, as a translation, for the tale was allegedly 'translated from the German of Doctor Ralph'. The choice of a German for the original author is, to be sure, ironical, since it suggests that Leibnitz is being fleered by a compatriot; and the name 'Ralph', which has associations with 'wolf', would seem to be a punning reference to Christian Wolff, the most eminent of Leibnitz's followers. The deeply significant fact, however, is the obvious one: that Voltaire chose to feign the existence of a foreign author. The text that we are about to read, he says, is not the text of *Candide* but a translation of it; and we shall never read anything more than a translation, since the German original from which the translation was made does not exist. Even the German text, moreover, is disturbed, since the translation is said to include 'the additions that were found in the doctor's pocket, when he died'. It was still a text in process, which Ralph failed to establish definitively, and which has been completed, by a person or persons unknown, through the use of material discovered on his corpse. As the world is chaoticised in the text of *Candide,* so that text is itself offered not as the best of all possible texts but as a corrupt one.

The tale does not conclude, however, with that attempt by Pangloss to restore it to the dignity of final causality. It concludes with Candide responding, first, by a marvellously economical and accurate comment on Leibnitzian philosophy: 'Cela est bien dit', 'That is well said', and then by the famous last clause: 'mais il faut

cultiver notre jardin', 'but we must cultivate our garden'. Those
few words achieve a great deal. They join the end to the beginning, which also occurred in a 'paradise' or garden; and they
transform the beginning, not by changing the world but by
changing the understanding of the world. The false paradise
becomes a true garden, about which there is only one laconic
phrase to be said: 'il faut', to admit, whatever the absence of logic
and of story, the presence of moral obligation; 'cultiver', to
acknowledge the expression of that obligation in work; 'notre', to
recognise human community on the sad planet; and 'jardin', to
give the world back to the characters. Dismissing story ('mais'), the
ending, in the words of the candid hero, opens to the world
outside.

So the tale has been teleological after all. The purpose,
however, was that of the writer, and the final cause drawing it
towards its conclusion was located not in the tale but in the storyless world beyond it. The paradigmatic Voyage, having fractured
irremediably into a multiplicity of voyages, is reassembled at the
end with hilarious implausibility, in order to deposit the characters
near Constantinople.

Candide has numerous points of contact, one sees, with Dante's
Commedia, of which it could almost be a parody. (Even Cunégonde,
the Beatrice whom Candide finally attains in the 'garden' after
passing through numerous circles of hell and being purged of his
ignorance, turns out to have become 'dark, with bloodshot eyes,
scraggy throat, wrinkled cheeks, red, peeling arms'.) The two
works agree in pointing beyond themselves to a task to be
accomplished in the world (in the case of the *Commedia,* the
reader's own journey); they differ as to the nature of that task, and,
more to my purpose here, they differ in their reading of the world
and consequently in their idea of the book. Many will feel nostal-
gia for Dante's wholeness, as indeed for the supposed 'medieval
synthesis' from which it derives; while *Candide* will seem the
product of our own, unhappy and fragmented age. It is arguable,
however, that the medieval idea of the Book of the World was
itself nostalgic, an attempt to see the world as if it were still Eden.
That the universe, as the creation of God, is a revelation of his
nature is, of course, a biblical doctrine: the first chapter of Paul's
letter to the Romans, for example, declares that 'the invisible
things of [God] from the creation of the world are clearly seen,
being understood by the things that are made'. Yet this text, which

is fundamental, as Josipovici argues, to medieval thought and art, is not Paul's final word on the subject: in the eighth chapter of the same letter occurs that passage which I have already had occasion to quote, where he claims that 'the creation was subjected to vanity', and that it lies in 'the bondage of corruption' *(RV)*. We may read the world, and discover there specifically God's 'eternal power and Godhead', but we must also recognise, according to Paul, that the world as a sign of God is no longer untroubled – that one of the lessons it teaches is its own fall.

Besides, to see the world as a perfect order, perhaps with the book – another order – related to it by the order of analogy, is in effect to deny the need for the world to be re-created. Whereas again for Paul, in the same eighth chapter of Romans, 'the whole creation', rather than being an immaculate and definitive wonder-work, 'groaneth and travaileth in pain together'. This is another of Paul's immense metaphors, a sudden new vision of the cosmos. We see, in the things that are made, the invisible attributes of God; but what we hear are the groans, as it were, of a woman in labour, of a whole universe straining for the birth of new heavens and a new earth. Not surprisingly, therefore, in one of the few instances where the Bible itself refers to the world as a book – an eschatological text of Isaiah (34:4) which is reiterated in Revelation (6:14) – the book is being destroyed: 'all the host of heaven shall be dissolved, and the heavens shall be rolled together as a scroll: and all their host shall fall down'.

In a biblical perspective, the world with which story engages is at one and the same time 'this so marvellous book of all the universe',[14] where the 'heavens declare the glory of God; and the firmament sheweth his handy-work' (Psalm 19:1), a place of exile and death, and a labouring towards renewal. To read it correctly is to see the *grandeur* and the *misère,* and also the possibility – to decypher in it the story of a process, from world through fallen world to re-created world. Dante in the *Commedia* decyphers that story in spiritual terms, perhaps more powerfully than any other writer, whereas Voltaire in *Candide* does not. Nevertheless, Voltaire is exemplary in that, perceiving at least 'vanity' and 'corruption', and also the hallucinated wish-fulfilment of the various coherences that we impose on reality, he acknowledges the vanity and the hallucination in his form, and he allows a corrupt world to corrupt his book. Though almost explicitly anti-Christian in its purport, *Candide* establishes a relation between its own text and the text of the world which corresponds to one possible relation that a Christian writer might want to establish. His strategy is also important and suggestive, I take it, whatever one's point of view.

5 Eliot/Language

This is the moment, therefore, to consider in detail a writer who likewise acknowledged in the condition of his texts the fallen condition of the world, but who also produced them in accordance with the full process of the dialectic. In turning to Eliot we shall be exploring a writer who became a Christian, and for whom the question of writing Christianly was paramount; and who, through-out his career, actually worked with a theory that can be called dialectical, although the term itself was not part of his vocabulary. We shall be able to follow the conscious working of the dialectic in a writer's developing practice. We shall also concentrate for the first time on poetry; and the chapter will articulate the move, by and large, from a study of the wider manoeuvres of literature to a study of the engagement of writing with language.

At the same time, since I believe that Eliot's poetry is of radical importance for poetry today – indeed, for all writing – this is the chapter where the concern for contemporary relevance will, I hope, be evident.

I have also felt it necessary to write about Eliot in a manner appropriate to his own writing.

Q. Where do the women come and go, talking of Michelan-gelo?
A. In 'the room'.
Q. Where is the room?
A. In the poem.
Q. Yes; but why are those two lines in the poem?
A. Why indeed? The language is numb. There are neat iambics, there is rhythm, there is rhyme, but the verse floats self-absorbed, beamed from nowhere, without referents. The syntax is complete, and empty. For all its formal rightness, the writing alienates. It is a foreign language.
Q. Why do the women talk of *Michelangelo?*

A. They could be talking of anyone, or anything. The line signals that it is gratuitous. 'Michelangelo' fills the next language-space.

Q. Again, why Michelangelo?

A. Perhaps because the women reduce art-works to objects of cultivated conversation. Perhaps in the interest of mock-heroic. Perhaps because of his sexy nudes. Also because of his gorgeous name, full and varied in the mouth, profuse in syllables.

Q. Why do they *talk* of Michelangelo?

A. Because the poem is partly about language, its inevitability, its inadequacy.

Q. Is there any significance in the combination of a rich word and a drained sentence?

A. Yes.

Q. Are you as certain of all this as you sound?

A. No.

———————

'Prufrock' burlesques a particular type of poem, as we know. The 'love song' is veered towards bathos by a famous deflationary simile ('Like a patient etherised . . .'), learnt from Laforgue, by an inappropriate absence of lover's passion, and perhaps also by the wandering in a low-keyed city instead of, say, Petrarch's wild nature, and the comically expressed fear of ageing in place of the seriously expressed fear in, say, Ronsard.

But the mockery of ways of writing is also a mocking of poetry, of language. In *The Invisible Poet* (pp.5–6), Hugh Kenner points to the Tennysonian sonorities of:

> In the room the women come and go
> Talking of Michelangelo,

and:

> I grow old . . . I grow old . . .
> I shall wear the bottoms of my trousers rolled,

and it is true that the lines cleanse a style. However, doesn't the simultaneous creation and ruin of prestigious sounds in foolish meaning also signal a fundamental hiatus? Doesn't it enact a fall of language? The lines do not stand, essentially, in an assured, ironic relationship to Victorian mannerisms; deep down, they turn in on themselves, insecure, self-doubting. Their sounds and their senses slip apart. The mock-heroic disproportion within the language becomes the means to reveal a radical flaw.

Eliot's poetry moves from derision of types of literature to derision of literature itself.

'Shall I say, I have gone at dusk through narrow streets . . .?', etc. Prufrock's problem is that he can say anything, he is faced with enormous possibility; but he cannot *say* anything, he cannot attain truth and declare it, establish it, once and for all. In terms of the process of the poem, at this point Eliot could go anywhere, but nowhere is necessary, or right. The passage is only a possible sentence (its indicatives made ambiguous, moreover, by the continuing interrogation), a small poem from among the many that might have been.

So Prufrock, comic-despairingly, would like to reduce the noise he makes from articulate talk to the scratching of a pair of ragged claws scuttling across the floors of silent seas. A meaningless scratching in a vast silence. The lines have been seen (by Kenner) as 'a slight aesthetic error . . . too good a couplet to sacrifice, but not quite at home in the context of the poem' (p.31). Yet a crab moves sideways, like a writer's hand. And the image is not two pairs of claws but a single pair, the thumb and fingers of the poet gripping his pen. Attention does shift, but only to refocus start-lingly on the page, on the mindless hand scrawling its way across the silent sea of paper.

The world of 'Prufrock' has fallen, and so has the language. At the same time as having for its 'theme' the meaningfulness of basic questions about life, say, the poem doubts its own ability to deal with that theme. Eliot comprises the anguish of the poem in its writing-out, and 'Shall I say . . .?' interrupts the writing process to question it. What is outside the poem (concerns about life and language) and what is inside the poem (the functioning of its own language) are involved with one another.

Whereas the author of a desperate tragedy might see no paradox in looking for the most perfect language for it. (And selling it to a theatre — but that opens on to a more conventional puzzle.)

For Eliot, the problematic of life is intimately present in

the problematic of the poem.

The composing of 'Prufrock' by the collocation of fragments may derive from Eliot's reliance on what C. K. Stead sees, in *The New Poetic,* as the short-winded inspirations of his 'dark embryo'. It may also be a means of avoiding linearity, a beginning-middle-and-end, with its suggestion of purposiveness and necessity. Prufrock does not believe in either. But it may also relate to a sense in the poet of experience and language as shattered. The poem comes to us precisely as an accumulation of pieces; and the fact that one of them – 'No! I am not Prince Hamlet . . .' – maybe sticks out like a sore thumb, instead of damaging the work actually reinforces its effect. (A problem that this last notion throws up is, of course, that of deciding what could damage writing of this kind.)

The place in 'Prufrock', although a city, or the nerves of the speaker, or his mind, is essentially a nowhere, the space of the poem. It is no more a real place than Prufrock is a person. The work contains, strictly speaking, no narrative and no descriptions.

It is an assortment of possible poems. Prufrock tries out a number of moods, various ways of being ('Shall I say . . .?'). At one point, he has a go at writing about fog, slipping into the past tense.

In Canto 27 of the *Inferno* is the image of Guido da Montefeltro imprisoned in a flame. He attempts to speak to Dante, but at first his words are trapped in the fire and are changed into its 'language'. Only when they reach the tip do they give the flame the same vibration that Guido's tongue has given them, and so become audible.

It is a powerful moment, and it turns partly, I presume, on the problematic of language. Guido's words begin as unintelligible utterance, the mere roaring or crepitation of his hellish nature. They are language struggling in evil. (The extreme of this in the *Inferno* is the nonsense speech of Nimrod in Canto 31 – 'Rafel mai amech zabi almi' – a babble from the instigator of the Tower of Babel.) So the words have to force their way up and out of the flame, at which point the flame is mastered (?), and itself becomes a tongue. Guido is utterly concentrated, refined, as speech; and his speech is visibly that of a sinner.

A later passage from the canto provides the epigraph to 'Prufrock', and suggests, of course, that Prufrock too is speaking from hell. (There is no doubt also an involving of the reader, most sharply in the final words: 'ti rispondo', 'I answer you', which carry straight into the first words of the poem proper: 'Let us go then, *you and I* . . .' From the outset, Eliot is intent on sniggling the reader, the 'hypocrite lecteur'.) The epigraph also includes, however, another reference to the shaking flame, and so intimates that 'Prufrock' likewise is concerned with language. Prufrock's words struggle similarly from the flame which is the hell of his condition, as he tries, like Guido, to 'tell who he is'.

In his hell, he can imagine Paradise:

I have heard the mermaids singing, each to each.

Appropriately, it is a place where language is redeemed – where it becomes song, the 'love song' that Prufrock can only burlesque and that he dare not believe addressed to himself: 'I do not think that they will sing to me'. And what awakens him, or rather 'us', from the dream, and causes us to drown, is not human evil in general but specifically 'human voices'. (Which is not to deny that the dynamic of the poem is also erotic.)

———

(Dante continues his exploration of the fall of language, for beyond Guido in Canto 27 and Nimrod in Canto 31 are the shades of Canto 34, the last in the *Inferno*. They represent the deepest sin, the worst kind of treason, and they suffer the deepest failure of language. The unnamed sinners are packed in ice, and are incapable of speech. Of the three named sinners, who are champed in Satan's three mouths, Judas has his head inside, and although the heads of Brutus and Cassius are free it is pointedly said of the former that he 'does not say a word'. Satan's own mouths are absorbed in their silent munching. As Dante descends lower and lower into hell before rising towards paradise, so he descends in language to a hellish speechlessness, where for once no shade addresses him. He encounters a dumbness at the core of language, before mounting towards the redeemed language – the singing – of the *Paradiso*.)

All of Eliot's poetry is preoccupied with the 'overwhelming question', as much before he became a Christian as after. Prufrock cannot see his way to formulating it, preferring protective allusions, to John the Baptist, Lazarus, Hamlet.

All of his poetry is likewise concerned with conversion, with the problem of spitting out all the butt-ends of one's days and ways. Prufrock drowns because he cannot exist in a paradise.

Why is 'Prufrock' so funny? Why is the language so memorable?

If 'Prufrock' is a burlesque of the love song, 'Gerontion' is a subverted dramatic monologue, where speech has broken down. Another poem, in fact, about language.

In the lines:

> In the juvescence of the year
> Came Christ the tiger

> In depraved May, dogwood and chestnut, flowering judas,

at the unpunctuated blank is a religious and linguistic hiatus, corresponding to a hiatus in experience and in language.

So the language may confute itself:

> I was neither at the hot gates
> Nor fought in the warm rain
> Nor knee deep in the salt marsh, heaving a cutlass,
> Bitten by flies, fought.

The tough consonants, the spondees, the alliterative, syntactically vehement (though vulnerably odd) 'fought', lie stunned by the negative particles.

Or it is words that we are given, lists:

> Rocks, moss, stonecrop, iron, merds

> sight, smell, hearing, taste and touch

> De Bailhache, Fresca, Mrs. Cammel . . .

They accumulate not to compose but simply to accumulate. And they are loosened from referents, especially the row of proper names, which like the other proper names in the poem refer to nobody, and exist as mere words, additions of syllables;

though giddy with conjecture.

Yet the poem creates no less than three new words – Gerontion, juvescence, concitation.

'Gerontion' explores the 'echoes and recesses' of words (an expression of Empson quoted by Kenner). And the exploration leads time and again, as many have shown, to linguistically muffled sex. 'Knowledge' in the famous 'After such knowledge, what forgiveness?' carries no doubt the extra biblical connotation of sexual knowledge. Mr Silvero's hands may be 'caressing' Limoges porcelain or something else. The Muse of History resembles a courtesan. The 'wilderness of mirrors' could recall the voyeuristic glasses of Sir Epicure Mammon (in Jonson's *The Alchemist*). Another horn may be alluded to in Cape Horn, a bawdy trade in 'the Trades'. 'Since what is kept must be adulterated' reinforces by juxtaposing them hints of kept woman and adultery. Gerontion 'stiffens', it seems, both for death and for sex. The Bear is perhaps 'shuddering' in orgasm.

Towards the end especially, the poem is obsessed with sex. Furtive puns, double entendre, knowing allusions lead down 'contrived corridors' in language that end in the same darkness. The wealth of language turns out to be a rich corruption.

Language itself seems to have undergone a Fall, where it has put on knowledge, and in particular sexual knowledge. Its inevitable, multiple echoes and recesses constantly beckon there.

Part of the speaker's 'terror' is that he cannot escape from the maze of his fallen language. Corrupt, he writes a corrupt work. (Only in those terms can he claim: 'I would meet you upon this honestly'.) The concluding lines –

> Tenants of the house,
> Thoughts of a dry brain in a dry season

– are taken as a feeble explaining of the poem, a blurting-out of its method. They seem to me a despairing, curt dismissal of it, a recognition of its necessary inadequacy.

The paradox of 'Gerontion', as of 'Prufrock', is that Eliot has made great poetry which despairs of poetry. As language, his suggestions of the inadequacy of language are more than adequate.

From *Four Quartets* one will learn that he saw the contradiction as natural, and language as shot through with the paradox of its deficiency and its prodigious power.

'Gerontion' suggests loss of meaning, and also refers to where meaning is, or may be – in the unspeakable word. Note the suddenly vulnerable sounds:

> The word within a word, unable to speak a word,
> Swaddled with darkness.

Prufrock hears the mermaids singing, though only 'each to each'. Gerontion cannot even imagine the unspoken word; he can only refer, verblessly, to 'the word within a word'.

This alters Lancelot Andrews's formula: 'the Word without a word'. The change of preposition focuses perhaps on the freshly creative language waiting in a fallen language, the possible new word present within a word (in the manner of Mallarmé's 'fleur', the mere saying of which creates an amazing idea-flower 'absent from any bouquet'). The removal of the capital no doubt translates, on the contrary, a lack of religious and linguistic confidence, new speech being swaddled with the darkness of language and of the self.

For Gerontion as for Prufrock, salvation involves a new language. The poem can make small gestures towards it: 'concitation', 'juvescence' – 'Gerontion'.

The Waste Land is a poem with an epigraph and dedication in four languages.

Containing two (unspecified) quotations.

If we look up Petronius' *Satyricon,* under Eliot's mocking glance, we find that Trimalchio, the speaker of the epigraph, has 'three libraries, of which one is Greek, another Latin'; that, being a man who does not 'despise learning', he is capable of random and muddled allusions to various literary works; and that the narrator considers his story of the Sibyl to be one of his 'bits of nonsense'.

In *The Waste Land* we want to know what the passages in foreign languages mean – how they translate into English, where they come from, what they are doing in the poem. But their profoundest significance is surely the most superficial: that they *are* written out in other languages. (Eliot could have translated them, as a neoclassical poet would have done.)

Reading the work, we encounter lines that we do not understand, and that is the point. The text is impenetrable. We consult a dictionary or a crib, and think we are home; we can read through the German, the Italian, the Sanskrit, and so forth, to an English version. Yet the foreign languages are still foreign. We know how they might look in our own tongue, and we can appreciate many ways in which they feed and are fed by the whole poem; yet they are not in our tongue and, although in our desire for (a certain kind of) meaning we risk forgetting it, their first, immediate effect is sharply exact.

Eliot has led us into Babel, a babble of dissonant voices which registers the most intimate loss that the poem is concerned with, the loss of a single, just speech. There is cultural alienation, certainly, and psychological alienation, but above all – or below all – a linguistic alienation, climaxed in the headlong jostle of languages in the closing lines. The final subtlety, the last terror, is that in such a context English too reads like a foreign language. Which it is.

———

Less the meaning of the words in the text than the meaning implied in the way the text is composed.

———

Possible hints of Babel:

Its 'abolished tower' seems to be evoked, appropriately, amid the confusion of languages at the end of the poem.

Earlier in 'What the Thunder said', the 'towers' of various linguistic capitals 'fall', are seen 'upside down in air', and, like the scattered languages which bear etymologically the traces of other tongues, they 'toll reminiscent bells'.

———

By the time we reach the twelfth line of the poem: 'Bin gar keine Russin . . .', we realise that the opening paragraph should perhaps be read with a German accent, and not that of a German but of a Lithuanian.

———————

Like much Symbolist poetry, *The Waste Land* is a great deal concerned with itself, of course. Its self-regard sometimes takes the form of involving the reader in remembering a passage he has already seen. The 'reminiscent bells' tolled by 'towers' upside down in air are reminiscent within the poem, since they remind one of an earlier 'peal of bells' and 'white towers'. Asked by the woman what he remembers, the man in 'A Game of Chess' recalls a line from a few pages back, 'Those are pearls that were his eyes'. The reader becomes in a way the speaker (the 'hypocrite lecteur' becomes, perhaps, Tiresias); and the fact that he is in the process of working through a poem is forcibly set before him.

The reason, surely, is that part of the anxiety of the poem is an anxiety about language, and this is not merely talked about but is incorporated in the text. The reader cannot get beyond the poem because language is fallen; he is trapped on the inside. The opening of the second paragraph of 'The Burial of the Dead' may be read as a description of the poem, and of the reader's problem:

> What are the roots that clutch, what branches grow
> Out of this stony rubbish? Son of man,
> You cannot say, or guess, for you know only
> A heap of broken images . . .

The reader finds himself standing in the rubble of Babel.

There is one moment in *The Waste Land,* in the first section, which seems to escape the toils of language, by looking to a possibility beyond speech:

> I could not
> Speak, and my eyes failed, I was neither
> Living nor dead, and I knew nothing,
> Looking into the heart of light, the silence.

'Silence' at the end of its line rhymes semantically with negatives at the end of the three previous lines. And 'I knew nothing' is not the same as 'I did not know anything': like silence, 'nothing' is positive, as in Mallarmé (or Lewis Carroll). A silence beyond words and a nothing beyond matter are attained in an apparently ecstatic vision of 'the heart of light'.

This appears to register the reverse, joyful side of that similar experience a few pages later, in 'A Game of Chess'. There too, in what we suppose to be another encounter between a woman and a man, the man 'never speaks', can 'see nothing', 'knows nothing', and may be 'alive, or not'; but the 'nothing' that he has 'in his head' is clearly in this case a cause of terror.

Yet, as many have suggested, the feeling moving through the first passage is itself troubled, ambiguous; even before the next line, *'Oed' und leer das Meer'*, negates it.

It turns out to be implicated as much as any other in the fundamental ambiguity. And it is not the only self-contradictory moment in the poem, veering from one effect to its opposite.

Nothing in *The Waste Land* comes to the reader single. Allusions are overturned (Cleopatra/Dido becomes a woman whose nerves are bad); quotations are deviated (a passage of John Day brings Sweeney to Mrs Porter); lines are spoken by a plural subject (the girl who 'raised her knees' at Richmond is also a Rhine-maiden); scenes arouse opposite responses; juxtapositions yoke discrepancies; and so on. And the contradictions are not held, over all, within the firm, double angle of vision of mock-heroic, but remain unresolvable.

Various motives have been suggested: Eliot's conviction of the relativity of all points of view, his disbelief in the substantial unity of the soul, his desire for 'cubist' multiple perspectives.

However, we ought also to see the phenomenon in terms of the surface functioning of the poem's language – in terms of its being *about* language. We then remark that the poem is unstable, disjunct and at war with itself. A 'waste land' of writing.

The Notes to *The Waste Land*. We sense now that there is something funny going on. Seeking enlightenment, one learns that the 'dead sound' on the final stroke of nine at Saint Mary Woolnoth's is 'a phenomenon' which Mr Eliot has 'often noticed'. Urbanity and pedantry combine to inform us: 'The interior of St Magnus Martyr is to my mind one of the finest among Wren's interiors. See *The Proposed Demolition of Nineteen City Churches* (P. S. King & Son,

Ltd.)'. (Note that he has chosen a brochure about the *demolition* of buildings.) Above all, among passages in French, Italian and Provençal one is met by seven lines of German and no less than nineteen of Latin. One needs Notes to the Notes. They contain as many foreign languages as the poem.

Why this lack of 'seriousness'? Well, isn't the poem itself constantly subverted by its own humour? The tarot cards, which look as though they determine a narrative of judgement and purgation, are read by a charlatan, who 'has a bad cold'. References to Dante's hell lead to the church of Saint Mary Woolnoth, where that sound on the final stroke of nine is 'dead' for the city clerks because it tells them they are late for work. And so on through the poem. The Notes are more than a self-contained joke. They are a derision of the poem (and of the reader); or better, they are part of the poem's derision of itself.

With the notes as with the quotations in foreign languages, we move closer to the poem when we become concerned less with what they mean and how they fit than with why they are present and how they work. Whatever the circumstances of their composition, the Notes are now substantial to the poem, part of its armoury of aggression.

———————

As C. B. Cox points out,[1] self-contradiction in Eliot's work is at its most extraordinary in the contrast between 'Marina' and its epigraph — between Pericles' joyful reunion with his daughter, which is the ostensible subject of the poem, and Hercules' coming realisation of his killing of his children, which unobtrusively (and in Latin) trips the poem into hypothesis.

———————

     'My nerves are bad to-night.   Yes, bad.   Stay with me.
     'Speak to me.   Why do you never speak.   Speak.
       'What are you thinking of?   What thinking?   What?
     'I never know what you are thinking.   Think.'

We may take this non-realistic passage as the mimesis nevertheless of a psychological state and a conversational gambit. But we ought also to notice that it is a piece of language that fades. Each of the last three lines peters out in a diminished echo of itself.

As 'Wallala leialala' crumbles — after several lines, and after the word 'Nothing' – to 'la la'. The poem enacts a fall of language into broken words.

———————

Philomel's body is violated, but at least her voice as a nightingale is 'inviolable'. Nevertheless, that pure song (compare the song of the mermaids in 'Prufrock') turns out to be ' "Jug Jug" to dirty ears'. The ears are too corrupted to hear perfect language, and our language, attempting to reproduce that perfection, can only make 'Jug Jug'.

On Parsifal's approach to the Grail, children sing in the dome. Their innocent voices, however, produce a taunting, reproving nonsense:

> Twit twit twit
> Jug jug jug jug jug jug.

Something has reduced language to mere noises, to absurd monosyllables.

The whole of *The Waste Land,* indeed, reads like 'jug jug ... Tereu'. Except that, knowing the Elizabethan meaning of 'jug', we can translate the words as 'Tereus has forced sexual intercourse on me'. Whereas in the poem as a whole the translation is more problematical.

———————

Kenner begins his book on Eliot by surmising that every line of the poetry has been inspected, except perhaps the one containing the six jugs. And yet it is not unimportant. It relates the fall of language to illicit sex, via the song of Philomel and her rape.

The same link is made in another of the poem's references to Babel. Babel/Babylon is present by implication in the quotation from Psalm 137, though the word itself is replaced by 'Leman': 'By the waters of Leman I sat down and wept'. The substitution is pointedly significant. As well as being the lake near which much of the poem was written, Leman means paramour.

The earlier allusion to Philomel, moreover, associates a linguis-tic and sexual fall with the Fall itself. Philomel merges into the 'sylvan scene' of Milton's Paradise, where the particular 'lascivious' love-making of Adam and Eve seals their general 'guilt'.

The poem is concerned, in fact, with a Fall, very often in sexual

terms, and with the concomitant fall of language. The whole work
weeps by the waters of Leman and Babel.

_____

The end of *The Waste Land* alludes to Hieronymo's play 'in sundry
languages' in *The Spanish Tragedy* of Kyd. This enables Eliot, as we
know, to aim derisively at the reader, who is being 'fitted', like the
murderers of Hieronymo's son, by a show of his own vices; and
indirectly, to make a derisive though double-edged reference to
his own poem as a piece of 'fruitless poetry'.

More pointedly, however, Hieronymo's play is spoken in
languages – Latin, Greek, Italian and French – described as
'unknown', and enacts the fall of Babel. Hieronymo is quite
explicit:

> Now shall I see the fall of Babylon
> Wrought by the heavens in this confusion.

He discloses the crimes of his enemies while forcing them into a
confusion of tongues, and thereby involves the fall of man with
the fall of language. The murderers are even killed in the course
of his play – punished while babbling.

It is a luminous, startling idea, though Kyd makes little of it
dramatically. It may well have been Kyd who suggested to Eliot
the possibility of a polyglot *Waste Land,* with Babel as a constituent
myth.

_____

But we don't *feel* the cultural allusions, to the Grail legend for
instance: they are laid out as a mosaic in the poem and we can
only lay them out as a mosaic in the mind. The work is a refined,
decadent puzzle. Eliot even admitted that he was not too familiar
with the tarot pack, and had shifted it to his own purpose – a
purpose itself coolly erudite.

Yes: and that is the point. The work comes to us, and hints that
it comes to us, as 'a heap of broken images'. Times, places, cultural
marvels, lie about in the poem – as language lies about. (As
perceptions lay about in a 'heap' in Hume's mind.) The poem is a
devastation of history and consciousness, an appalled *musée
imaginaire.*

_____

The land lying waste is, partly, the land of language. So the poem looks beyond fallen, human speech to birdsong – of nightingale, hermit-thrush and cockerel – but that too is each time ambiguous. Then in the final section comes the non-human voice of the thunder. And what does the thunder bring? Another syllable: 'DA'.

If the poem offers salvation, it is (in part) a salvation through language. The last words are precisely that – words:

> Datta. Dayadhvam. Damyata.
> Shantih shantih shantih

In their utter foreignness, at once alienating and compelling, lies their significance. Salvation implies another language. The 'splendour' that the poem glimpses is 'inexplicable'.

And yet the words are not entirely foreign. As Kenner (again) has pointed out, Sanskrit is thought to be the oldest Indo-European language, and is therefore the root of all the languages in the poem. As DA is the root of the three commands. The languages scatter, to be gathered in the final words. The poem reaches back to a pre-lapsarian condition, before the dispersal of languages; and Sanskrit is its metaphor of a primitive, wise and single speech.

Is the end of *The Waste Land* joyful or madly sinister?

'Tomlinson: Of all the great of the older generation, we have not mentioned Eliot. Do you think that Eliot is still available to the American poet as a useful influence?
Creeley: No. '[2]

Though an allusive poem, about language 'The Hollow Men' is explicit. For the hollow men at least, language is fallen. Whatever has happened to them has 'dried' their voices, and made them 'meaningless'. They huddle in a hollow valley, the 'broken jaw' of their lost kingdoms, and 'avoid speech'. The language by which they construct the poem lapses into the repetitive menace of nursery rhyme (as the end of *The Waste Land),* and into fragments:

> For Thine is
> Life is
> For Thine is the

The 'Shadow' falls across the sentences, halting them and turning them into a 'whimper', at the 'end' of the world and of the poem.

Like Prufrock and Gerontion, an I-figure does perceive a living language, but elsewhere –'there', where

> . . . voices are
> In the wind's singing
> More distant and more solemn
> Than a fading star.

'There' language is song, and voices – with their verb transformed at the end of the line – 'are'.

What is a Christian poem? One that conforms to the genre of 'Christian poetry'? Or one that has Christian virtues?

In *Ash-Wednesday* Eliot is honest about what he wants. He recognises one desire that assorts uncomfortably with the genre, that is, the desire not to become a Christian. He allows it into the poem, in the passage almost at the end in which 'the lost heart stiffens and rejoices/In the lost lilac and the lost sea voices'. The lines recall the opening of 'Sailing to Byzantium', where Yeats too celebrates what he is renouncing at the moment of renunciation. Eliot's painful valediction, however, involves more honesty: he goes so far, in the making of a 'Christian poem', as to declare his unwillingness to be converted.

While discussing Blake in *The Sacred Wood,* Eliot writes: 'this honesty never exists without great technical accomplishment'.

A Christian poem should be Christian in itself. But there is another problem. The language of a Christian poem should also be Christian. (As the language of a tragedy should, arguably, be tragic.)

The subject is very complex, and has hardly begun to be

examined; its implications seem to me awesome. Eliot is the writer, I think, who made the essential move. A 'Christian' intuition about language before his conversion led to a poetry enacting the fall of language. *Ash-Wednesday* is an attempt to redeem language.

That is perhaps to overstate the matter. Think, however, of certain features of the work. In some sections especially, the language is loosened: discrete, sufficient lines are beamed to the reader, untrammelled by punctuation, each existing as a slow, beautiful space. The first three lines are (as it were) musical varia-tions, where they might have been a language breaking up:

> Because I do not hope to turn again
> Because I do not hope
> Because I do not hope to turn

In the fourth section, the 'music' airily mingles another voice, another language, and moves across spaces opened on the page:

Who moved among the others as they walked,
Who then made strong the fountains and made fresh the
springs

Made cool the dry rock and made firm the sand
In blue of larkspur, blue of Mary's colour,
Sovegna vos

Here are the years that walk between, bearing
Away the fiddles and the flutes, restoring
One who moves in the time between sleep and waking,
wearing
White light folded, sheathed about her, folded.

The repetitions throughout the poem of words and sounds give an effect of still music; as the cadencing, and placing, of the many long lines. The poetry achieves 'song'.

Or take the whole of the opening of that section, from 'Who walked between the violet and the violet', which gradually and exhilaratingly transforms a question into a statement, 'who' becoming a relative, depending on a main clause which the poem keeps silent. (Unless that clause is 'Sovegna vos' – the poem creating freedom for itself in syntactic variability.)

Or take the unlimited space at its end, following the words 'And

after this our exile', a space both filled and not filled by the rest of
the sentence, from a prayer to the Virgin Mary: 'and after this our
exile show unto us the blessed fruit of thy womb, Jesus'. The poem
has just alluded to 'the word unheard, unspoken'; now, in the
whiteness of the page, it presents that word in such a way that we
do not hear it, by not speaking it. 'Jesus' is quite literally the word
unheard and unspoken. The poem turns around silence, referring
to the silent word before the silence and after, as the world is
described, when the next section begins, as whirling about the
centre of the silent Word. The poem cannot speak for God; it
cannot be a divine language; but it can remove its own noise and
open itself to silence, as the intimation of the potent, creative
silence of Christ the Word.

Christ as *infans,* as a wordless baby, is the perfect image, for the
writer, for silence full of the possibility of new language. Symbolism and Christianity interpreting each other.

Some critics complain that the vivid detailing, the complex enactments of the earlier verse give way, after Eliot's conversion, to an
abstracting and generalising style, disembodied.

Eliot's concern, however, is for a world redeemed and remade.
The world of *Ash-Wednesday* hovers strangely on the edge of
experience, intense with nature yet beyond nature: 'three white
leopards sat under a juniper-tree', 'a slotted window bellied like
the fig's fruit', 'the voices shaken from the yew-tree drift away'.
The whole poem is a 'higher dream'.

The verse itself is not discarnate. Simply, the body of the poem,
in its 'musicality', has become lighter, aerial.

St Paul states, in a passage that I quoted in the first chapter, that
after resurrection the natural body becomes a 'spiritual body'.
(And not, incidentally, that the body is sloughed off by an
immaterial soul.) A Christian poet may want to intimate that new
condition, as he imagines, or 'dreams' it. In its presentation of
people and things, in the being of its verse, and also, necessarily, in
its humility, and honesty, *Ash-Wednesday* is – almost – a spiritual
body itself, the stirring, at least, of a nature towards resurrection.

The language of *Ash-Wednesday* is not, however, a redeemed tongue. It occurs, I take it, between 'the lost word' – Edenic speech now fallen – and the 'new verse' of a resurrected world, imagined as restoring that 'ancient rhyme'. It defines its status by reference to Cavalcanti's ballad, 'Perch'io non spero di tornar gia mai', written from exile to his 'Lady', to which it relates continually, at a significant distance, from the first line to the last (through the figure of the Lady and the Virgin, and through such phrases as 'Let these words answer', 'this our exile', 'Suffer me not to be separated', 'let my cry come unto Thee' . . .). Neither a merely fallen 'word' nor a 'new verse', the poem is a 'cry' from spiritual exile, a language in process of redemption.

And, because the poem's concern with language is comprehensive, it looks towards yet another 'word', the redeeming word of God:

> Lord, I am not worthy
>
> > but speak the word only.

Ash-Wednesday as a 'spiritual exercise' recalls the poetry of Mallarmé; particularly, in the way the sustained negativity of the first section leads later to the positive imagining of a world being remade.

But the ascetic denial of self (where 'oblivion' and 'forgetfulness' in the second section pick up Mallarmé's 'oubli') has in view an object beyond the self – 'Thus devoted' – and issues not in absence of self but in a dynamic of recovery:

> > strength beyond hope and despair
> Climbing the third stair.

(One might also notice the extraordinary humour that penetrates the gravity of that second section: a humour dealing with self.)

Because I cannot drink
There, where trees flower, and springs flow, for there is
nothing again.

Where is that emphatic yet tremulously ambiguous 'there'? It is no doubt a natural place, at which the speaker cannot drink because he knows that nature is fallen, so that flowering and flowing are eventually 'nothing'. But perhaps also a world glimpsed as re-created, where nature, buoyant in alliteration and Romantic (?) in its images of tree and fountain, really does flower and flow, yet only for those who are themselves redeemed; otherwise the vision fades to 'nothing again'.

————

Williams: 'Place is the only reality, the true core of the universal'. Eliot: 'place is always and only place'. The divide is dramatic, and readers of their work separate according to their own sense of place – most later poets, it seems, going with Williams.

I don't think any mediation is possible; we must simply be clear about why we react as we do. And also about what actually goes on in their writing. As far as Eliot is concerned, doesn't he ask a great deal of place, and not too little? A great deal of Burnt Norton, of Little Gidding? His poetry does not spurn place for an immaterial heaven: it has radical desires, and they are sited; it wants, and what it wants is a 'place of grace' *(Ash-Wednesday),* 'this grace dissolved in place' ('Marina').

This means, it is true, that he is unwilling to let place be; though there are moments where response comes in the act of percep-tion:

> Beside a public bar in Lower Thames Street,
> The pleasant whining of a mandoline
> And a clatter and a chatter from within
> Where fishmen lounge at noon: where the walls
> Of Magnus Martyr hold
> Inexplicable splendour of Ionian white and gold.

But what draws him is place remade. And at the extreme point, in *Ash-Wednesday,* the poem itself is a dream of place, an elsewhere, where re-creation imaginatively occurs.

————

Prufrock: 'It is impossible to say just what I mean!'
Sweeney: 'I've gotta use words when I talk to you.'

————

The inclusion, in the *Collected Poems* of such a writer, of 'Unfinished Poems'.

> Words strain,
> Crack and sometimes break, under the burden,
> Under the tension, slip, slide, perish,
> Decay with imprecision, will not stay in place,
> Will not stay still.

This is partly the familiar showing, in *Four Quartets,* of the practice of poetry as the index of a practice of life. Words fail to reach 'the stillness' because of the poet's own inability to 'sit still'. In the act of composition his words are assailed by demonic voices, and also, perhaps, by the voices of the fallen self that he wants to hear in the work, and that would pervert it from a still poem into one 'scolding, mocking, or merely chattering'.

The passage concludes in a line showing what can happen when the poet submits to temptation:

> The loud lament of the disconsolate chimera.

Plangent, clever melodrama.

The line, however, also 'falls' within itself, in the manner of the early poetry, its intricate sounds patterning in a void. (It is the only place in *Four Quartets,* that I can see, where a fall is enacted, the poem having another way of approaching the problem.) It thereby relates to the deeper significance of the passage as a whole, where words are described as failing not only through the fault of the poet but through their own inner fault. The passage registers dismay, once again, at the fall of language.

Eliot seems to conceive the act of making a poem as a struggle against fallen matter. Words, as well as selves, are in rebellion, and the theological overtones are clear: they 'slip, slide, perish', and they do so 'under the burden'. 'The intolerable wrestle/With words and meanings' is not merely an echo of the Flaubertian sense of the labour involved in giving form: it recalls the sweat of Adam tilling a cursed ground.

Indeed, why should language *not* be perfect, effortlessly? Why should we have to think of a literary work as an amazing order, achieved against heavy odds? Why did Pascal write the 18th 'Provincial Letter' thirteen times? Why did Yeats need any number of drafts for 'Sailing to Byzantium'? Why, to come down to our level, are there crossings-out on the manuscript of this page?

>   every attempt
> Is a wholly new start, and a different kind of failure
> Because one has only learnt to get the better of words
> For the thing one no longer has to say, or the way in which
> One is no longer disposed to say it.

Eliot's experience of the fall of language is partly involved in time. He discovers a continuous lapse of time between the poem he wants to write and the poem he can write.

It is another way of conceiving the fall of language. And the lines question the whole of *Four Quartets*: 'every attempt is . . . a different kind of failure'.

Eliot interrupted 'Prufrock', or had Prufrock interrupt it ('Shall I say . . .?'), to expose its lack of finality. At a notorious moment, he breaks into *Four Quartets* to indicate the faultiness of the writing:

> That was a way of putting it – not very satisfactory.

As it happens, the unsatisfactory passage, 'What is the late November doing . . . ', has just mocked itself. Eliot has indulged what looks like a writer's joke (though I am not sure that anyone has laughed at it yet): mightn't one murmur irreverently, after reading

> Scorpion fights against the Sun
> Until the Sun and Moon go down
> Comets weep and Leonids fly
> Hunt the heavens and the plains
> Whirled in a vortex that shall bring

– 'Sweeney to Mrs Porter in the spring'?
Whatever its manner, the interruption is searchingly serious.

Eliot stops his poem to question it. And the questioning does not
relate only to the preceding passage; nor only to the cognate
passages in the other quartets. It surely disturbs the whole poem.
One should read even the triumphant, definitive last lines:

> And all shall be well and
> All manner of thing shall be well
> When the tongues of flame are in-folded
> Into the crowned knot of fire
> And the fire and the rose are one

and then comment, 'That was a way of putting it – not very satisfactory.' Once that critical gaze has been trained on the poem
from within, it all shifts, and at every point the reader has to doubt
what he is reading.

The effect is unprecedented, and difficult to define. It is not
simply that certain passages are for good reasons badly written
(though some may display a 'conscious forcing of the tone'[3]), or
deliberately include inadequate wisdom so as to contrast with
others where the writing and the wisdom are offered unequivo-
cally. The whole poem is in question, and the whole poem is, from
one point of view, as it should be; yet, from another point of view,
it fails. Not only 'that' way of putting it but any way – even when it
produces the most accomplished and powerful poetry – is unsatisfactory.

The poem exists on a very fine edge, both celebrating and
subverting the possibilities of poetry. It derides itself, and warns
the reader away, from its compelling blandishments, asserting
that poetry is only poetry, and that 'the poetry does not matter'.
But it also believes intensely that poetry does matter, as Eliot
labours to show, by making it, and by giving it all that he has got.
As I imagine everyone acknowledges, at least some parts of the
poem are consummate; and if they are so, they are so. Yet for
Eliot, it is all written in a fallen language, by a fallen man; its vision
is limited, and possibly wrong, in any sense of the word. It is not a
speech 'tongued with fire', or only fitfully.

One of the paradoxes of the poem is itself. Language that is
fallen remains nevertheless an object of wonder. Contradictory
responses to it work against each other, in a fierce tension. The
paradox is Pascalian, and tragic: the poem, like language, like life,

is at one and the same time *grand* and *misérable,* great and
wretched.

The writer who believes that language (along with everything else)
is fallen, faces an intricate problem. He has to write poetry that, in
one way or another, fails, without simply being bad poetry.

Eliot faced the problem. Has anyone else?

Four Quartets is the most explicit investigation of the problem of
language. It is, of course, a poem that discusses its own poetics;
and no doubt the inquiry, especially at this level of paradox, is
best carried out in creative work. There is something not very
satisfactory about writing an essay on Eliot.

Readers who dislike *Four Quartets* point, among other things, to a
number of passages that seem awkwardly written and inappro-
priately engaged with the matter in hand. Passages like this:

> It seems, as one becomes older,
> That the past has another pattern, and ceases to be a mere
> sequence –
> Or even development: the latter a partial fallacy
> Encouraged by superficial notions of evolution,
> Which becomes, in the popular mind, a means of disowning the
> past.

I wonder, however, if such lines are not deliberately vulnerable.
The poem must not be perfect. It must also be humble, and I fancy
that Eliot lays himself open, that at certain moments he invites our
scorn.

He is certainly exposed, in a different manner, in the passage of
personal reflection which begins:

> So here I am, in the middle way, having had twenty years –
> Twenty years largely wasted, the years of *l'entre deux guerres* . . .

He comes forward simply, unadorned with quotations, indirections, compelling images, enticing rhythms, or interesting tricks of
syntax; without persona or dramatic mask. Compare this plain

confession of failure with the speech of Gerontion (which also begins 'Here I am').

Of course, it is a complex matter. The invitation of scorn is perhaps not humility. And truth-telling can be a means of rendering oneself unassailable.

It is said that the experiences of possible epiphany in *Four Quartets* are merely indicated, not described. Even listed:

> the moment in the rose-garden,
> The moment in the arbour where the rain beat,
> The moment in the draughty church at smokefall . . .

Isn't this intentional? Proust can afford to create – indeed, he must create – eloquent visions that delight the reader, since he has to show what it is that he means by transcending time. And, although he believes that the reader must find 'salvation' for himself, and not in the visions of *A la recherche du temps perdu,* he nevertheless assumes that salvation is involved with art. For Eliot, on the contrary, the reader must not be absorbed in any glimpses that the writing may vouchsafe, since they are only moments in a poem, and, in these terms, the poetry does not matter. He sends us away from the work, into our own life, following us with hints only.

It is also said that the epiphanies are not specifically Christian. No: but then it does not seem to be Eliot's purpose at these moments to report the experiences of his faith. He brings to the poem experiences that may be the reader's: intuitions at the edge of the natural, visitations of strange awareness, as 'the wild thyme unseen'.

I am supposing that the poem is admirably self-denying, concentrated in purpose. Still, one could wish for the imagination of a Christian poet to deliver something clearly and richly Christian (without being restricted, moreover, to epiphanies in nature). And to show Christ incarnate as more present in life.

Writing a poem radically disturbed as to the capacity of language, Eliot opens his work to the intimations of non-human sounds.

The passage at the end of 'East Coker', dismayed at the ageing which makes of each attempted poem a different kind of failure, leads to a wider meditation on age, concluding in the desire for a deeper communion through 'the wave cry, the wind cry, the vast waters'. 'The Dry Salvages', the next quartet, provides that scenario. It is through sea voices that the first section advances, both referring to them – the sea howl, the whine in the rigging, the tolling bell, and many others – and imitating them – 'The menace and caress of wave that breaks on water'.

The only quartet that contains no discussion of poetry, 'The Dry Salvages' turns towards another language, natural and yet strangely supernatural, hinting at 'the sea monster' and the Hound of Heaven, threatening and divine. Throughout the poem this language has many other sounds ('footfalls' . . .) and non-human voices ('go, go, go' . . .) to be listened to. A language beyond our own, gathered maybe at the end as 'the voice of this Calling'.

Convinced of the fall of language, *Four Quartets* looks to a language re-created:

> what the dead had no speech for, when living,
> They can tell you, being dead: the communication
> Of the dead is tongued with fire beyond the language of the
> living.

The surmise of heaven in the final lines includes the in-folding of the same 'tongues of flame'.

The problem, of course, is how to reach towards that new language, here and now. I am not sure that *Four Quartets* offers much help. Its perspective is largely moral. The same fire should 'purify' the earthly dialect of the tribe, while the poet too is being 'restored by that refining fire' so as to 'move in measure, like a dancer'. His words, evincing a moral rightness ('The word neither diffident nor ostentatious', etc.) will then form 'a complete consort dancing together', and thereby figure the cosmic dance alluded to elsewhere. If they can be persuaded to 'stay in place', they can also suggest 'the stillness' at 'the still point of the turning world'.

It is a vision of some beauty. Yet one may regret its lack of radical adventure; especially after *Ash-Wednesday,* which, with the same concern for the moral and spiritual quality of the poet and the poem, attempts actually to remake language.

The discourse of *Four Quartets* is itself, however, a kind of reconciliation. In *The Waste Land* allusions and quotations are subverted,
mocked, set at one another. They seethe in an exciting, deadly
ferment. *Four Quartets,* on the contrary, allows the voices outside to
speak for themselves, and binds them together in a single volume.
It recovers and reconciles them, as, beyond books and words, it
recovers and reconciles people, parties, attitudes, contraries in
natural and spiritual experience. It is a place where the tongues
are in-folded.

The project is very new, and very appealing. And the reversal of
the work of *The Waste Land* perhaps continues into language
proper. *The Waste Land* sets up Babel: languages scatter, and are
only perilously, uncertainly gathered in the Sanskrit of the ending.
Four Quartets is not concerned with the scattered languages
(though it is true that they may be hinted at in those 'tongues'
which are likewise gathered, and likewise at the close of the poem;
and that the text contains 'Erhebung', 'Figlia del tuo figlio', 'l'entre
deux guerres' and gallicisms like 'dawn points' or 'the unattended
moment', 'lotos' in its Greek spelling, and passages of overtly
Latinate vocabulary). It does, however, see language redeemed in
'pentecostal fire'; and Pentecost – which is present throughout the
last quartet, in the communication of the dead 'tongued with fire'
and in the final 'tongues of flame' – is arguably the biblical event
that promises salvation from Babel. But all that is, of course, image
and doctrine – image alluding to doctrine – rather than an actual
hint of Pentecost in the poetry.

A reversal of meaning for antithesis and paradox.

In *Four Quartets,* the desire for a language re-created is intimately involved, once again, with the desire for a re-created world. At
times its scene hovers beyond nature, beyond perception, through
'the door we never opened'. In the first section of 'Little Gidding',
however, an observable natural scene becomes the sign of a world
remade through the eliciting, as it were, of its rhetoric. Its
antitheses ('pole and tropic', 'frost and fire', 'melting and freezing')
tauten into paradox ('Midwinter spring', 'sun flames the ice', 'cold
that is . . . heat'), and, rather than figuring the division of a fallen
world, draw the natural beyond the natural. The imagination can
then refer to what it cannot imagine, the perfect world in re-
creation, 'the unimaginable/Zero summer'.

The verse is nevertheless curiously conservative after *Ash-Wednesday*. It shows, in an area of concern where one might have thought a more revolutionary language necessary, what great authority can be achieved in writing based on perception and the syntax of statement.

———————

The re-creation of matter and the re-creation of language are implicated in each other. In the midwinter spring passage of 'Little Gidding', a natural scene supernaturally suspended in time burns with a fire described as 'pentecostal'.

———————

All of Eliot's poetry is displaced with respect to a genre, without necessarily being parody. 'Prufrock' is a displacement of the love poem, 'Gerontion' of the dramatic monologue, *The Waste Land* of epic, *Ash-Wednesday* (a little) of Christian poetry, and *Four Quartets* of poetry itself.

This continuous undoing of kinds, forms, rhetorics: its end is partly, no doubt, to defeat ways of looking, so as to see afresh. But its chief end is to aggress literature in the act of creation, to both unmake and make, simultaneously – to exist always in paradox.

———————

(The Waste Land and epic: isn't the displacement here similar to that of *The Dunciad?* Both poems are at one and the same time mock-epics and epics. *The Dunciad* may magnify Dullness and employ the devices of mock-heroic, but its theme is highly heroic – the survival or destruction of civilisation. One notes, in fact, that both works have that theme, and that *The Dunciad* is already a kind of *Waste Land.* And also that for each of these outlandish creatures the other is the nearest point of comparison.)

———————

The sense of language in Eliot's poetry seems to have no corroboration from his criticism. Perhaps it is not in the poetry. Nevertheless, Eliot himself declares, in the Introduction to *The Use of Poetry and the Use of Criticism:* 'The critical mind operating *in* poetry, the critical effort which goes to the writing of it, may always be in advance of the critical mind operating *upon* poetry, whether it be one's own or someone else's.'

———————

There is, however, the well-known concern with the 'auditory imagination':

> What I call the 'auditory imagination' is the feeling for syllable and rhythm, penetrating far below the conscious levels of thought and feeling, invigorating every word; sinking to the most primitive and forgotten, returning to the origin and bring-ing something back, seeking the beginning and the end.

This seems to me a very enigmatic passage, and I am not sure that I understand it. It is introduced – dragged in, really – at the end of a discussion of Matthew Arnold also in *The Use of Poetry and the Use of Criticism,* and has a reverberating vagueness that Eliot does not usually allow into his prose. As if this were both an idea of great importance to him, and one that he did not fully grasp. (The writing also moves through an insistence of present participles – accompanied by no less than four other words in '-ing' – in a syntax one associates with the poetry, with the opening of *The Waste Land* and the fourth part of *Ash-Wednesday.*)

The auditory imagination appears, for Eliot, to go below consciousness, but also back through the life of the race, to 'the most primitive'. In a note to the final chapter of the same book, he refers, seemingly with approval, to a French article suggesting that 'the pre-logical mentality persists in civilised man, but becomes available only to or through the poet'. One can speculate (it is no more than speculation) that the 'origin' referred to in the first quotation is Adamic, and that the 'end' – in the expression 'the beginning and the end', whose importance we know from *Four Quartets* – may be the end of the world.

Certainly, the poet's sensibility goes below articulate language, to a pre-linguistic as well as pre-logical state, reaching downwards and back to wordless rhythm. Eliot writes on almost the last page of the book, with appropriate onomatopoeia: 'Poetry begins, I dare say, with a savage beating a drum in a jungle, and it retains that essential of percussion and rhythm.' (He continues: 'hyperboli-cally one might say that the poet is *older* than other human beings', to corroborate the earlier note.) The auditory imagination seems to be a means of overcoming a fallen language, in the rare moments of achieved poems, by penetrating below the conscious articulations of the mind, and of civilisation.

The result is a language remade – or, as Eliot says explicitly when discussing Shakespeare, 'the re-creation of word and image', 'reborn image or word'. It is unlikely that this vocabulary is not intended to have its theological meanings, in a book overtly aware of theology.

Of course, all that may or may not be the significance of a number of possibly diverse passages. They do not, in any case, constitute a finished thought, though they hum with suggestion; and they throw up any number of problems.

From the essay on Lancelot Andrewes: 'Andrewes may seem pedantic and verbal. It is only when we have saturated ourselves in his prose, followed the movement of his thought, that we find his examination of words terminating in the ecstasy of assent. Andrewes takes a word and derives the world from it; squeezing and squeezing the word until it yields a full juice of meaning which we should never have supposed any word to possess.'

From the essay on Marlowe: 'this intense and serious and indubitably great poetry, which, like some great painting and sculpture, attains its effects by something not unlike caricature'.

Eliot and Mallarmé.

It is not enough to say that Eliot's poems are 'about' language, as other Symbolist works: they are concerned with language as fallen and capable of re-creation; they aggress language, and attempt to remake it.

Eliot faced the problem of language and met it radically, in his own way. Leaving us with the problem. Which, in its depth, later writers seem to have ignored – or rather, later poets; or rather, English poets.

Eliot appears, in fact, to be almost outside English and American poetry, despite his almost unprecedented eminence, and 'influence'. He is not behind us, but way ahead of us.

'To understand anything is to understand from a point of view.'[4]

6   Writing and Re-creation

1

Having explored ways in which writing operated dialectically on language in the poetry of Eliot, I should now like to study that operation more generally and systematically, beginning with the relation of language to the self, or the human subject. We can imagine this relation in an Edenic condition, and it does in fact figure in the narrative of the Garden at the beginning of Genesis. I am thinking not of Adam's naming of the animals, though in that too, as in any language act, the relation between language and subject is in question, but of his communing with himself at the moment that he first sees the woman: 'This is now bone of my bones, and flesh of my flesh.' He does so by analogy with the self-communing of God, who talks with himself, so to speak, concerning both the creation of man: 'And God said, Let us make man in our image, after our likeness', and the creation of the woman: 'And the Lord God said, It is not good that the man should be alone; I will make him an helpmeet for him.' Presumably – but this can only be a way of putting it: not very satisfactory – in uttering his words Adam was at one with them, and experienced no hesitation or distance. To speak was to participate in a reality untroubled, and to conspire with it, by his psyche (as it were), by his body.

Such is no longer the case for us. It is not that we don't have immediate access to a perfect language by which to declare ourselves. The view that a clearly defined self, a firm identity, independent of language and existing prior to words, expresses itself in language, and that, possessing a meaning likewise independent and pre-existent, it uses language instrumentally so as to express that meaning, no longer seems tenable. (The fact that the view is common, in literary terms, to realism as to neoclassicism, and indeed to most approaches throughout the history of

writing, does nevertheless give pause, and its overthrow clearly
has consequences for reading.) This is owing partly to the destruction by psychoanalysis of the autonomy and penetrability of the
self; partly to the presently powerful theory that subject and
language are interdependent: that as the subject constructs a
language-world so it is itself being constructed by language. It may
well be that the subject is only discoverable in language, and that
it disappears behind – or rather, that it appears exclusively in – the
language that successively and variously names it. For all we know,
it is plural, discontinuous, different in each of its acts.

The view is usually presented in opposition to the 'essentialist'
psychology of Christianity. Yet the Bible itself, as against what
European thinking has made of it, necessitates no such psychology. It may imply that the subject, beyond our experience of it, is
a unity in the sight of God; yet its teaching is quite concordant
with the notion that, from where we are and in our fallen state,
the subject is indefinitely displaced, unknowable apart from the
signifiers in which we refer to it. In fact, it goes much further: the
subject is not only in a state of perpetual otherness: it is lost. The
vocabulary of Lacan in particular, in which the subject is
'decentred', or 'extraneous to itself', and experiences 'lack', 'gap',
'division', could be seen as the translation into a contemporary
psychoanalysis of the terms by which Christian writers have
named the self as involved in original sin – for instance, of Pascal's
'chaos' and 'abyss'; and while the Lacanian terminology dis-
comforts the subject away from a psychology of solid individuality,
it also comforts it away from the real anxieties of a theo-
psychology of transgression, loss, judgement. In a Christian
perspective, the indefinite displacement of the subject is not a
matter for report and for the reorientating of psychic energy, but,
in the first instance, a testimony to the Fall.

The language of the subject is also fallen. Like Adam, we are
not separate from language, however distant from it we may be;
we are inextricably involved with it, and are ourselves (to continue
the play of these ultimately falsifying metaphors), a text, a tissue of
words. In our case, however, since the constitution and also the
well-being, the possibilities, of the subject depend, in ways and to
an extent that we fail to understand, on the language in which it
states itself and its connections with what it takes to be not itself, if
language is fallen we fall with it. Language comes to us, from a
past, from a social experience, that are evil; we are named, not by

words that are ours, or that are unused, but by the words we inherit, and those words are entangled, obscure, tired. (By recalling it here, one discovers another meaning in Eliot's line about being impelled to 'purify the dialect of the tribe'.) Like Dante's Guido, as vain and corrupt selves we speak, with extreme difficulty, from the 'flame' of the vain and corrupt language into which we have been locked – from inside the tongue.

It is in this situation, however, that language – and specifically writing – operates re-creatively. The loss of the notion of an expressive self, and in particular of a fixed authorial identity, is all to the good, since it opens the subject to change. The operations of a renewing language, far from passively representing the writer, actively press in on him, presenting him with a new condition of himself which he only finds by creating it. If language is an act, which both articulates and modifies a subject, then writing is an especially complex act entailing an especially complex unmaking and remaking, where the subject acquires unprecedented and surprising qualities, of intricacy, design, cohesion. Nor is that subject immobile: as any literary work establishes not one meaning but a dense possibility of meaning, so the subject of the work is astir with potentiality.

The transformation of the writer, the achievement of a 'new man' from the concentrated resources of the old, is a sign, in a Christian perspective, of the transformation to come. And only, of course, a sign. I am not suggesting that the working of the subject necessarily has anything to do with grace, or is connected, otherwise than by analogy, with the writer's hypothetical salvation. I take writing, in any case, to be a deeply, radically, ambiguous act, as any act in a fallen world. It is as much a temptation, an incitement to play oneself, to illimit the subject in a ludic nowhere apparently free of constraint; to be merely fascinated by personal and verbal hypothesis.

That dialectical process of the subject can be seen in terms of the body, and in fact must be so seen, since it is in the body that language is located. The body, clearly, is not a merely instrumental relationship between ourselves and our words – the means, as it happens, for producing speech and writing. Language comes really from the body, and it remains bodily: the hands write and the eyes read, ink on paper, while speech involves the physiology of at least two people and the physics of air, and even gathers whole bodies into act, in poses and gestures. Speaking, including the silent speaking that we undertake when we read and write, reaches out into our general experience of the body, since, in terms of the bodily movements of which we are aware, all the 'organs of speech', from lungs through larynx and palate to nose, tongue, teeth and lips, also breathe, smell or taste – with the vocal cords themselves serving also to close off the lungs to make the rib-cage rigid for effortful action; while the unconscious activities along the neuromuscular speech-chain involve speech in the most hidden areas of the body's life.

That our language and our body are implicated one in the other is, from a Christian point of view, as it should be. It is shocking, of course, to the would-be Christian notion of the soul aspiring to freedom from the body, and to the 'Cartesian' vision of pure consciousness for which the body is an inconvenience: in their terms, an ideal language would be immaterial. The grounding of language in the body goes along, for the biblical Christian, with the fact that the body is present in each aspect of our most fundamental search – for ourselves, for each other, for the world, for God – and coincides with the teaching that a bodily man was made in the image of God (his first recorded words referring, moreover, to his 'flesh' and his 'bones'), that Christ the Word was made 'flesh', and that the body will be not destroyed but changed.

The whole of the body is solicited by writing and speaking, yet, because of the fall of the body and the fall of language, the bodily movements involved in the production of words commonly bear a troubled relation to them. We should like to believe – and the existence of works like Sir Richard Paget's *Human Speech* or Morris Swadesh's *The Origin and Diversification of Language* shows how much we should like it – that the meanings of our words correspond perfectly to the physical movements and the sounds that produce them. When Swadesh explains (pp. 193–4) the widespread use of nasal phonemes in the negative by the fact that negation is based on a grunt; or suggests that in speaking the mouth gestures meaningfully, the tip of the tongue serving as a pointer, for instance, or the lips closing on the object in a word such as 'capture'; or comments on the contrast in a large number of languages between words like 'mamma' or 'naná' for mother and 'papa' or 'tata' for father, that in 'each case the nasal of a given contact point . . . expresses the female parent, while the corresponding stop consonant designates the male parent', and that symbolically 'this can be understood as relaxed velum for the feeding parent, tensed velum for the loosely associated parent', he evokes, as do theories deriving all language from cries and onomatopoeia, a kind of golden agreement, a literal bodying-forth of meaning (though one which I fancy, in his description of it, is not to everybody's taste). Yet one realises that, even if such hypotheses were acceptable as to origins, we should soon exhaust the list of words in which we can now experience a bodily oneness with our meanings; and also that our desire is not for single appropriate words but for appropriate language.

Again, the re-creative process of language can, partly, answer that desire. Consider breath, by which we speak and continue to live. Writing emerges from deep down, being structured and paced, measured in time, by the binary movement of the lungs. And the writer does not merely exercise his breath: most clearly in poetry, where the working of the lungs is most present and the breathing most audible, but also in other forms, his breath is itself being remade. He never breathes so well as in his best writing, when his new breath becomes part of the signifying of his text. A poem especially is a place and time where surges, hesitations, pauses, long emissions of breath or gasping breathlessness, the self-delighting travails of the torso, mean, second by second, along the meaningful language they promote. A poem is where there is a reason for each move of breathing – where breathing and reason go together – from the 'high energy' generated by 'speech-force' as advocated in Olson's essay on 'Projective Verse' to the hardly breathing of Eliot's *Ash-Wednesday*, where the writer, in contemplation of a world remade, passes beyond normal breathing and, as the saying goes, holds his breath. The reader too is affected by the breathing of the best poetry, as almost the breathing of a regenerated body; as Mandelshtam saw when he wrote of Pasternak's poetry that it could cure tuberculosis.

Mouth movements also can become meaningful – they can join, that is, with the meaning of words – not often at the level of the word, unless the writer invents or distorts, and perhaps never over longer utterances, but at that of the letter and the phoneme. Here is an obvious instance, a line from Gray's 'Elegy written in a Country Churchyard':

> Some mute inglorious Milton here may rest . . .

Gray's theme is the enforced muteness of an obscure villager who may have had the makings of a poet, and he approaches muteness

himself in the act of speaking his verse. The lips of the poem's 'I'
continually close on to /m/, as if his words were emerging with
difficulty. Hence the appropriateness of Milton (whose choice as
representative great poet also has other origins), and of the
placing of the stanza's one main verb, '*may* rest', with the potential
poet rather than the potential Hampden or Cromwell to whom it
equally applies. (Remarkably, because their names also contain the
/m/ to which the context is giving a particular significance, they
too are seen as having been muted.) Hence above all the juxtaposing of two /m/'s in 'Some mute', which obliges the speaker, at the
very beginning of the line, to undertake a prolonged /m/ as if
trying to speak and failing.

In Sonnet 144, Shakespeare sets up a succession of *l*'s:

> Two loves I have of comfort and despair,
> Who like two spirits do suggest me still:
> The better angel is a man right fair,
> The worser spirit a woman colour'd ill.
> To win me soon to hell, my female evil
> Tempteth my better angel from my side,
> And would corrupt my saint to be a devil,
> Wooing his purity with her foul pride . . .

Every line of the poem except the eleventh contains at least one *l*;
the letter also occurs, unexpectedly, in three sets of rhyme-
endings, in the two quatrains quoted and in the third (*tell, hell*);
even its absence from the rhyme-words of the final couplet (*doubt,
out*) is compensated by its double appearance in both lines. As a
physical event prompting the mind, the recurrence of *l* emphasises the semantic bond between *ill, hell, evil, devil* and *foul*, and
relates them all to *female*, and also, in an even fiercer tension, to
angel. As a mouth movement, the repeated /l/'s suggest, in this
context, retching.[1] The suggestion is particularly strong at 'hell, my
female evil', where three /l/'s conglomerate, soon after the two of
'colour'd ill' and at the point where it is possible for two rhyme-
endings in /l/ to be juxtaposed. Once again, and more strikingly
than in Gray, the oral matter of the poem corresponds to its
semantics: the tongue movements simulate a retching related to a
fearful inner struggling and instability.

In the fifth of the *Astrophel and Stella* poems (the second of which
contains *l*'s similar to those of Sonnet 144), Sidney conveys the

difficulty of declaring the meaning as a difficulty of saying the words, or some of them. The speaker acknowledges, repeatedly but against his will, an objective, public, moral truth to which he has to give full credence, yet claims also, in the climactic last line, a subjective, private, psychological truth that exercises the greater sway over him. The poem ends:

> True, that on earth we are but pilgrims made,
> And should in soul up to our country move:
> True, and yet true that I must Stella love.

The anguish (apparent in the final undoing of metrical regularity by the stress on 'must'), has led in the third line to a startling sequence of vowels:

> It is most true that eyes are formed to serve
> The inward light, and that the heavenly part
> Ought to be king; from *whose rules who do* swerve,
> Rebels to nature, strive for their own smart.

The speaker's unwillingness to state the law which makes him a rebel issues in a laborious, inarticulate and ugly series of mouth movements and also sounds. (The passage is a superb example of voluntarily 'bad' writing, of the creative risk that a great poet takes by perpetrating something that a lesser poet would know how to avoid.) The repeated cry of pain, in this so sophisticated piece, is a kind of primitive ur-version of the whole poem.

Gray, Shakespeare and Sidney have devised in these passages what I should call oral onomatopoeia. If what we usually mean by onomatopoeia imitates by appropriate sound (in which the mouth participates without being focal), oral onomatopoeia mimes by appropriate mouth movements. Verbal sounds imitate, say, the rustling of soft silk; the mouth in forming words mimes not being able to talk, retching, or showing pain.

On the question of sound, take the opening of Shelley's 'Ode to the West Wind', where breath and mouth movements are also involved:

> O wild West Wind, thou breath of Autumn's being . . .

The burst of breath for the first four words carries an even more primitive cry in the vocalic sounds /au/, /ai/, /e/, /i/, which run together into an aural shape. The ambiguity of the cry – is it agonised or enthusiastic? – is the perfect ushering-in of a stanza where the west wind itself is to be described ambiguously as both destroyer and preserver. Between each vowel, moreover, is a *w*, to form which the mouth adopts the same position as for breathing out strongly. It imitates the wild wind, referred to in the same line as a breath; and the whole stanza, which is composed of a single extremely long sentence, mimes that breath by a human wind that comes not from the west but from the lungs. As well as another oral, the writing achieves a kind of respiratory onomatopoeia.

In all these ways, at rare moments, the writer's body attains a temporary oneness with his language. And although I have gone in, necessarily, for a kind of baroque focusing on isolated details, it is of course his whole body that enters this re-creative process, through rhythm. Rhythm is at once pre-existent in language, and therefore outside the writer, and also inside him, in the dense physiological activities that sustain him. By his writing he intensifies both rhythms, and so in saying – in bodying – his text he becomes himself a new rhythm. In that he surpasses himself and hints at a higher bodily state he is not unique: he joins the instrumentalist, the dancer, the tennis-player. He goes further than them, however, in that he attains this superior co-ordination, the new liveliness of the body, in language, that is, in the medium where we constitute ourselves and the world. The best writing offers a glimpse, in so far as we are capable of imagining it, of the resurrection of the body and of more than body.

2

As language is dialectical in relation to the subject, so it is dialectical in terms of communication between subjects. Again, we can imagine what an Edenic condition of this would be, though the Bible describes no actual communication between Adam and Eve. The humans would converse by analogy with God's conversing with them, and with his other creatures; and one realises that when addressing them in words ('God said unto them, Be fruitful, and multiply, and replenish the earth', etc.) he must have sounded them deeply, since it was by another act of language that he had created them. Founded by the word of God, they now resounded to God's words. Language was not merely an external means, an appropriate instrument, for establishing contact: it was internal to the relationship. When Adam and Eve conversed with each other, therefore, the language they exchanged derived from an immense language that had made and was sustaining them, as it had made and was sustaining their whole world.

Despite the Fall, we still share this common involvement in language and in each other. Language is not a congeries of idiolects but something we construct together, in society, the individual both inheriting it and actively collaborating with others to develop it. By the same process we construct our common reality in language, and in language we construct one another. If the individual is a text, we are jointly a collective text.

Because of the Fall, however, we are also disjoined, and the language that should be the place of our relating is equally the place of our dividing. Indeed, it is here that we experience the fall of language most pointedly, and it comes as no surprise that the fall in Genesis happens precisely in terms of communication. The serpent perverts language when persuading Eve, while the destruction of Babel scatters language into a multiplicity of tongues mutually foreign. (One even notes that evil inheres in all the early communicative acts of the Genesis story: the first instance of human communication is Eve's colloquy with the serpent; the first reference to inter-human communication concerns Cain's talking with Abel prior to killing him; and the first detailing of the actual words used in such an exchange occurs when Lamech says to his wives: 'hear my voice ... hearken unto my speech: For I have slain a man for wounding me'. RV.) The *misère* of language in this perspective is that it as much prevents as enables communication, or, as Sweeney has it, 'I gotta use words when I talk to you'; and that, given the social power of our language, we bear a terrible responsibility for what we make of each other.

Sweeney's complaint is, of course, Eliot's own; and the *misère* of communication is no less apparent in the most painstakingly wrought text than in the idlest talk. I take it that there is some shock involved in the fact that literary works, considered as acts of communication, are actually the focus of recurrent, acrimonious, bewildered debate as to what it is that they are communicating. Contradiction, ambiguity, discompose all texts, as they discompose any enactment of a fallen language, and relate a text to every other aspect of reality, as something demanding interpretation yet failing to provide it. Nor is the question answered by the theory, in Barthes and others, that the text, rather than offering itself for elucidation, withholds the signified indefinitely so as to set going a never-ending play of signifiers. By restating the communicability of a text as its capacity to incite the textual activity of the reader, who reads off one textual virtuality after another (as reality might be described as offering the *jouissance* of its infinite rewriting), it dissipates the problem only for someone who fails to feel the tragic disquiet in asking, 'What is meant here?'

Nevertheless, and contradictorily, it is also true that ambiguity or polysemy positively constitutes the writing that we call litera- ture, and that we welcome the fact: partly because this is one of the ways in which writing interests us in itself as well as in what it may be referring to; partly because we expect and delight in a measure of obscurity, of the unattainable, in everything that calls for a more than passing encounter; partly because we are thereby invited to participate, and to work at the contact. The reader *is* active, like the writer, in the meeting of a work which is some- thing other than a single fixed message from an immobilised authorial self to an immobilised reading self. As the writer as subject may be unmade and remade in the act of writing, so the reader as subject, in the act of reading, stirs with possibility.

Equally, what was said of the writer as body also applies to the reader. To read is to assimilate another body, the body of the work, and to experience the same bodily renewal, of breath, of the mouth, of the ear, while attaining a livelier body throughout by incorporating a new rhythm. Indeed, in the negotiation between writer and reader, communication is easiest in terms of the body, where the control of the former is extremely close moment by moment and where the latter knows what it is that he is experiencing. A literary work can be the hint, the sign, albeit fugitive and menaced, of what true interpersonal speech would be, if we could truly communicate, and of what it may be in the future, for true communication in a world remade.

Yet from the writer's point of view the communication, con- sidered as an act of relating, is deeply insufficient. The writer is, after all, alone, and he could be seen as figuring the fact in that tradition of poems where, according to a persistent commonplace, the male poet encourages a girl to 'gather rosebuds' while she may

– a tradition whose achievements include Catullus's 'Vivamus, mea Lesbia, atque amemus', Waller's 'Go, lovely Rose', Marvell's 'To His Coy Mistress'. One reading of such poems would be that a failure of communion in life, given the girl's refusal or the fear of death, is the source of a private literary work which transposes desire, by substituting writing for Eros, a lyric for the act of love. A consummate linguistic communication takes place, in the absence of a receiver. At times, as in Ronsard's 'Quand vous serez bien vieille, au soir à la chandelle', the communion is itself trans-posed and enacted within the poem, through the girl being placed there and so 'immortalised' in company with the poet. The most complex of such transformations occurs in another poem of Ronsard, the equally celebrated 'Ode to Cassandra', of which this is the first strophe:

> Mignonne, allons voir si la rose
> Qui ce matin avait déclose
> Sa robe de pourpre au soleil,
> A point perdu, cette vêprée,
> Les plis de sa robe pourprée,
> Et son teint au vôtre pareil.

(Sweet, observe with me if the rose, which this morning did disclose its crimson gown to the sun, has not, now the sun is down, lost the folds of its crimson gown, and its blush much like your own.)

To read this is to find oneself pronouncing an accumulation of p and b clusters, culminating in 'plis de sa robe pourprée'. Isn't Ronsard kissing Cassandra? Debarred from doing so in Talcy, he kisses her in the poem, artfully, and by a kind of oral pun. He even exploits the fact that he speaks or sings his poems to their addres-sees so that, even if he did not perform this one before the girl, it contains the idea of so doing; he mimes kissing her, as it were in her presence.

Mouth movements are harmonised with meaning here not for the writer only but in poetry where the writer–reader relation – or more strictly the relation of writer to recipient – is explicitly in question. Yet Ronsard's lips do not meet Cassandra's, and in any case the mouth movements are ambiguous. Don't they also suggest the sucking of the breast, as does, in this context, the very first word, 'Mignonne'? As if to confirm the suggestion, the next stanza, in which the rose is seen to have lost its petals, includes the lament, 'O vraiment marâtre Nature!', 'Oh truly Stepmother Nature!' The hidden and obsessive breast-sucking seems a response to a more general deprivation, to the loss, beyond Cassandra, of Mother Nature. This so simple poem, in other words, measures the depths of the convention it rehearses, in terms both of the life-experience involved and the poetic strategy to deal with it. A perfect, virtuoso miming, in the face of grievous absence or denial, the withdrawal of the whole world of desire, enacts at one and the same time the renewing power of writing and its inadequacy. As communication fails it is heightened in conclusive language, and as it heightens it fails.

3

That troubled relation to the world brings us to the third aspect of the dialectic of language. Here, the Edenic moment is of course Adam's naming of the animals, which I considered in the opening chapter:

> And out of the ground the Lord God formed every beast of the field, and every fowl of the air; and brought them unto Adam to see what he would call them: and whatsoever Adam called every living creature, that was the name thereof. And Adam gave names to all cattle, and to the fowl of the air, and to every beast of the field.

This is not, moreover, the only instance of his naming, since on two other occasions to which I have also referred, on either side of his act of disobedience but still within Eden, he also names the woman:

> And Adam said, This is now bone of my bones, and flesh of my flesh: she shall be called Woman, because she was taken out of Man.
> And Adam called his wife's name Eve; because she was the mother of all living.

Naming is clearly intrinsic to 'Adam' or the original man, who is presented, not exclusively yet nevertheless quite pointedly, as *homo nominans*, Man the Namer. His right and obligation to name presumably derived, as far as the creatures of the planet were concerned, from the 'dominion' that he had been given over them; while his power to name would follow from the fact that he had been made in the image of a God who was himself a name-giver, and who had named his creation as it issued from him: 'God called the light Day, and the darkness he called Night ... God called the firmament Heaven ... God called the dry land Earth; and the gathering together of the waters called he Seas.' Adam's nominative language would be at one with the world, because it corresponded, in a way incomprehensible to us, with the language through which the world had been called.

We are still of his race and are still moved to name, but we know that we can no longer do so with evidence and finality. We regard his naming across the divide of the Fall, from within a fallen world and a fallen language. Coming late, we encounter a world that has already been named, inadequately, time and again, by others like us, in thousands of languages many of which are dead. One inadequate way of naming that inadequacy is to say that the words we take over and the things among which we find ourselves fail to harmonise. Or: a hiatus opens between our experience of things through the words that designate them and our sense that, in so far as we do or might experience them outside words, they evade our language. As we say reality, it withdraws. 'A horse' is not quite a horse; the names for (a tree) fall from it like dead leaves. Yet there is no world clear for seeing and naming: names, to reverse the simile, cling to objects like graffiti, and graffiti is all, mostly, that we are capable of adding. The world, so to speak, is our misnomer.

The dismay that this should cause is not allayed by the argument that language is conventional rather than natural, and that its efficacy depends simply on the agreement of its speakers as to the relations it holds with a reality to which it remains otherwise unconnected. The absence of connection is precisely the problem, the lack of that perfect correspondence which would enable us not only to say the world but to meet it. The desire for a natural language expresses itself throughout history: the desire that a word should be inward to its object (though 'object' would then no longer be quite the term) – or even, in so-called primitive societies which maybe have more porous memories, that it should act upon its object magically – and that the relations among words should coincide with the relations among objects. Writers persist in wanting especially the sounds of words, as they emerge from human physiology, to chime not only with human meaning, as we discussed above, but with the very world; whereas we constantly hear a discrepancy, that confuses even the most ordinary of namings. Mallarmé, according to a well-known passage in 'Crisis in Verse', found the timbre of the word *jour* to be 'dark'. The wish is most acute in the making of a poem, where the demands of the ear are paramount; yet in Valéry's equally noted phrase in *Tel Quel*, a poem is a 'prolonged hesitation between sound and sense', and is the place therefore, one might add, where we are most aware of words and things as being at odds with each other.

At odds, yet not separate. Language and reality are confused, just as the individual, rather than being an autonomous 'I' confronting a 'world', is implicated in what he names. And the deeper problem is that, just as we desire to change the human subject and to change the relation with the other, so we desire not only to say and to meet the world but to change it. A language utterly adequate to a fallen world would show us where we are but would also leave us there. Moreover, to whatever extent Wittgenstein is right when he declares in the *Tractatus Logico-Philosophicus* that '*the limits of my language* mean the limits of my world' (5.6), to that extent a change in the world will involve a change of language. Hence the gravity of language, and the urgency of writing. For once again, dialectically, language does operate that change, and, in keeping with the paradoxical reversal which is central to this study, it is at precisely the locus of disquiet that possibility begins to occur. Sound does conflict with sense, as a word may equally scatter into a plurality of senses, or be distracted from its etymology; yet the contingent nature of a word is also a powerful source: contradictory sound produces further sense, and because of their 'unnecessary' relations words seethe with potential significance. The writer in deploying words disturbs innumerable 'echoes and recesses', and moves the mental air, as it were, with noises that arrive irrespective of semantics; he seems to be solicited by a *materia* of language and of experience ready for renewal. It is not that words are wells of meaning and that by sounding them we draw the truth, but that by virtue of their troubled relation to the world they may intimate another world, or the world become other. Unable to deliver reality, as a result of the Fall, they can remake reality, as a sign of the Resurrection.

Language and world together enter the re-creative process. One writer complexly aware of this, though from a position anything but Christian, was Mallarmé himself, who, after noting the obscurity of 'day' and also the clarity of 'night', suggests that without this anomaly 'there would be no verse' (or 'no line'), since verse 'recompenses the defect of languages'. It is not only that the writer can temper the unwanted sonorities by evoking appropriate ones elsewhere in the line: the line, as well as adjusting to the object, transforms it, and by the subtle relations, the 'reciprocal reflections', among its words, transforms language also:

Le vers qui de plusieurs vocables refait un mot total, neuf, étranger à la langue et comme incantatoire ... vous cause cette surprise de n'avoir ouï jamais tel fragment ordinaire d'élocution, en même temps que la réminiscence de l'objet nommé baigne dans une neuve atmosphère.

(The line which from several vocables remakes a total word, new, foreign to the language and as if incantatory ... causes you that surprise of never having heard the like ordinary fragment of elocution, at the same time that the reminiscence of the named object bathes in a new atmosphere.)

As the object changes in the 'new atmosphere' of the line, so language changes for the production of a 'new ... word' — remaking the object by remaking itself, going beyond its fall and imperfection into a condition of newness. And not only the line, surely, but the whole poem is a new naming in a new language.

For Mallarmé the change of the world in the word does not even occur, ultimately, through the design of the poet but through the nature of matter and of language. He has just discussed, and indeed enacted, that change in two previous sentences, if I may quote them after so many others:

A quoi bon la merveille de transposer un fait de nature en sa presque disparition vibratoire selon le jeu de la parole, cependant; si ce n'est pour qu'en émane, sans la gêne d'un proche ou concret rappel, la notion pure.

Je dis: une fleur! et, hors de l'oubli où ma voix relègue aucun contour, en tant que quelque chose d'autre que les calices sus, musicalement se lève, idée même et suave, l'absente de tous bouquets.

(What avails the marvel of transposing a fact of nature into its vibratory almost disappearance according to the play of the word, however; if it is not for there to emanate, without the constraint of a near or concrete recalling, its pure notion.

I say: a flower! and, out of the forgetting/the oblivion to which my voice consigns any outline, as something other than the known calyces musically there arises, idea itself and sweet, the absent from all bouquets.)

His perspective is Platonic, and supposes that, beyond mortal and imperfect actual flowers that one might gather into a bouquet, is the pure notion of flower, flower's timeless and perfect Idea; though the particular direction which he takes to attain idea, unlike the Platonic, is the mental destruction of the imperfect copies, while the way is language. And one notes that in this case he is not referring to the poem. It is not combinations of words here that transform an object by bathing it in unexpected sonorities, but the single word in isolation whose property, by designating an object, is to absent it, and to replace it by itself, and by the untrammelled concept which it suggests. Or more precisely, the mere, and perhaps non-poetic, saying of the word, provided it be attentive, achieves nothing less than the beginning of the re-creation of the world: by vibrating the object in the mouth, the air, the ear, it transposes it, not into an exclusively mental but into a 'sweetly' sonorous idea, still perceptible, since the object only 'almost' disappears, to sense. The *idée même et suave* in Mallarmé's terms corresponds, over some distance, to St Paul's 'spiritual body'.

The idea that in language we may discover the world in a new condition comes to us from a French poet; but Wordsworth, to whom we happily turn as a more real, more human, native voice to protect us from Gallic abstraction, held much the same belief. I refer you to the end of Book 5 of *The Prelude*:

> Visionary power
> Attends the motions of the viewless winds,
> Embodied in the mystery of words:
> There, darkness makes abode, and all the host
> Of shadowy things work endless changes, – there,
> As in a mansion like their proper home,
> Even forms and substances are circumfused
> By that transparent veil with light divine,

And, through the turnings intricate of verse,
Present themselves as objects recognized,
In flashes, and with glory not their own.

Wordsworth's concern is not with the intrinsic property of
language but with the power of language in poetry. Yet there is
the same sense of forms and substances finding their 'proper
home' in 'the mystery of words'; of objects being wrought by
'endless changes' in the 'turnings intricate of verse' so as to attain,
not their idea, but a 'glory not their own'. Although he doesn't
analyse the means by which language renews objects, or suggest
that language itself is renewed, Symboliste theory is evidently
stirring here.

It even seems that Wordsworth is presenting poetry, at this
point, as a resolution of his deepest disquiet, as the recovery of the
radical loss lamented in the ode 'Intimations of Immortality'. The
ode looks back to the 'Heaven' of childhood from the perspective
of the fallen adult. It remembers a time –

> when meadow, grove, and stream,
> The earth, and every common sight,
> To me did seem
> Apparelled in celestial light . . .

It acknowledges that, in the present,

> The Moon doth with delight
> Look round her when the heavens are bare,
> Waters on a starry night
> Are beautiful and fair;
> The sunshine is a glorious birth;
> But yet I know, where're I go,
> That there hath past away a glory from the earth.

It asks:

> Whither is fled the visionary gleam?
> Where is it now, the glory and the dream?

The lines from *The Prelude* respond to each of those familiar
passages. The reader discovers 'visionary' power in poetry, which
delivers objects anew with a 'glory' not their own; he 'recognises'

them, and sees them circumfused with 'light divine', their apparel now being the transparent 'veil' of imagination in verse. In the ode, the child quits the 'imperial palace' of a former heaven for a 'prison-house' on earth; in *The Prelude*, not the reader himself but the forms and substances of his world are gathered afresh into the 'mansion' of poetry. The perspective is strategically Platonic, well-nigh Mallarmean, and thoroughly dialectical: the move is from glory, to its loss, and to its recovery in verse.

I have been concentrating on poetry since it is there that one is most conscious of the re-creative work of writing, because of the closeness of a poem's linguistic moves and because a poem inevitably draws attention to its language more than a narrative or a play. But not only the poet is in question: it is true of any writer that, while he cannot clear the world of words, he can cause words to operate on the world. His text can be a place of endless change, where in the 'play' of language a particular 'marvel' can be achieved, a shift of the world or of our perception of it. The objects of a world expelled from its Edenic state can, in Wordsworth's startling terms, re-enter a mansion 'like' their proper home, since the poem resembles heaven (the Father's house, according to Jesus, where there are 'many mansions'), and the reader can see them in a kind of glory since the veil guarding the holy place has become transparent.

In one way or another the world is absented, so as to be re-presented and made anew, as the winds in Wordsworth become 'viewless' so that view can be replaced by vision. The process, one realises, is one of death and resurrection. And this linguistic remaking of the world is arguably not exclusive to writing which has that as its aim. All writing is re-creative − all writing, indifferent to any such ambition or even opposed to it, will involve the world in itself and will change it, in the transforming mystery of words. Writing, by its very nature, consumes and renews. Indeed, the constitution of language itself, even prior to writing, suggests a latent propensity for the contradicting and re-saying of fallen fact. Verbs, for example, reach out of the-world-as-given in tenses and moods such as the conditional, the subjunctive, the optative; a 'syntax of counter-factuality and contingency'[2] opens to a realm of possibility, of liberating hypothesis. And if the way we make language attests to an obscure, partly conscious desire to elaborate it as a strategy of renewal, it is already just such a strategy, as Mallarmé argues, in its simplest, least meditated form. The word 'fleur', when said, or when pronounced silently and heard in the mind's ear, is big with metaphysical activity. Language, however little we ask of it, is already a process of death and resurrection, and is thereby related to the process fundamental to everything.

What we are discussing is, of course, a theory of the relation of literature (or indeed of any art) to 'reality'. It seems that all think-ing about that relation resolves into one or other of two basic and apparently contradictory theories, the 'imitative' or 'mimetic' and what one might call the 're-creative', a version of which I am developing here. The former is loosely Aristotelian, the latter Neoplatonic. An eloquent champion of the re-creative view is Sidney, who maintains in *An Apology for Poetry* that the poet, rather than following nature, 'doth grow in effect another nature'. (Wordsworth also distinguishes, in the lines preceding those quoted above, between 'living Nature' and 'the great Nature' that exists in poems.) Poetry is a voyaging beyond the actual, and 'right poets ... borrow nothing of what is, hath been, or shall be; but range, only reined with learned discretion, into the divine consideration of what may be or should be'; they envision, accord-ing to some famous metaphors, a superior world: 'Nature never set forth the earth in so rich tapestry as divers poets have done ... Her world is brazen, the poets only deliver a golden.' He rein-forces the argument that the poet produces another world by tracing 'poet' to its root in Greek *poiein*, 'to make', and by referring to the other English designation of the poet as a 'maker'; the same reasoning from etymology gave rise in modernist criticism, one remembers, to the important though less decisive idea of the poet as maker of the poem.

To phrase it in dialectical terms, literature begins in the percep-tion of a conflict between *grandeur* and *misère*, and of a disparity between things as they are in a fallen world and things as they might be. It is the patterning of past, present and future, the attempt to deliver a new world out of the loss of an old. This imaginative ability to gainsay the present by conceiving a past and a future quite different from it, could even be taken as a sign, as Sidney claims, of 'that first accursed fall of Adam', not only because it implies an obscure sense of origin and end, the possession of a larger memory and anticipation, but also because 'our erected wit maketh us know what perfection is, and yet our infected will keepeth us from reaching unto it'. The power of human 'wit' derives, as again Sidney maintains, from the fact that

it has been set by God 'beyond and over all the works of ...
nature', or, in terms of a Romantic epistemology (specifically
Wordsworth's in Book 2 of *The Prelude*), from the 'auxiliar light' by
which the mind is able to bestow new splendour even on the sun,
the greatest of natural lights; and its function here, in a Christian
perspective, is to explore not a lost Eden or a past Golden Age,
nor a realm elsewhere of Ideas, but a re-creation for the future of
the here and now. Curiously, mimetic theories too are often
drawn by this intuition of possibility, of 'what may be', to suggest
that art imitates not a world merely observed by the artist but
'nature improved', 'la belle nature'. The French eighteenth-century
critic Charles Batteux even writes like Sidney: a poet imitates, he
asserts in *Les Beaux Arts*, not 'the true which is, but the true which
may be, the beautiful true, which is represented as if it really
existed, and with all the perfections of which it is capable'. Even
empirical theories may attest the same fundamental need, to re-
create the given.

   And yet, to move frankly into the area of personal judgement,
one realises the dangers to which writing and all art are inevitably
open. The adventuring into 'another nature' may lead away from
any reality that it is possible to inhabit day by day, and into a
nowhere, a merely nugatory absence. Writing *should* be concerned, after all, with 'what is, hath been, or shall be' – with plain
occurrence, with a common quiddity. On the other hand, to
convey an inert matter which had been perceived passively would
merely be to convey another kind of nothing. Writing is only
consonant with the orientation of language and of consciousness
when it operates change; to write, adapting a line from the
Immortality Ode, is to be 'moving about in worlds not realised', in
a reality unfinished, perpetually astir, on the point of becoming.
Again, if the language of the writer is intent only on transforming
the object, the object may well disappear. Language must also
adjust to the object; as it teaches it – virtualities of sound, for
example, or puissances of connotation – so it must learn from it,
deferring to what it gives, or to what is given. Or again, it is
possible for the working of the work to be self-enclosed, to be a
process of language so involved with itself that it seems to have
displaced all other worlds. Whatever our mistrust of 'reference'
and however cautious we are concerning the relations of a work
to a writer's experience, we need nevertheless to breathe a wider
air beyond the work, and to sense that the writer knows, in one

way or another, what he is talking about. Wordsworth claims that the reader only sees the new glory with which poetry invests the world if he is already intimate with such things as 'woods and fields'; and we assume that Wordsworth himself (who is, after all, more close) derived the 'great Nature' which is promoted by his poetry from a searching and constant familiarity with 'living Nature', and that he experienced a world vertiginously changing not only when he was moving among words at his table but when he was actually abroad in it. One recalls, say, the bird's-nesting episode from the first book of *The Prelude*, and its eerie ending:

> While on the perilous ridge I hung alone,
> With what strange utterance did the loud dry wind
> Blow through my ear! the sky seemed not a sky
> Of earth – and with what motion moved the clouds!

The situation is, of course, dialectical. On the one hand there is a need for language, a desire to be drawn into the world of the work, to pass the threshold of the first line of the poem or the first sentence of the story, to respond to the voice in the text. On the other hand is the need for what seems to be the thing in itself, as clean of intervention as possible. If Mallarmé is right about our reaction to the saying of a flower-word, so is Michel Butor, in *Travaux d'approche*: 'je dis une rose / et ces quatre lettres s'effeuillent devant elle', 'I say a rose, and those four letters lose their leaves in its presence'. On the one hand we need art: the reader will follow the writer in the constraints that he imposes on himself, willingly and indeed delightingly, so as to enter a difficult domain of order and otherness, since in the unnatural discipline of artifice lies a possibility of remaking the world, oneself, relation, language. On the other hand we need whatever is beyond our ordering, a world that escapes us, the obstinately alien; the animal which is not a 'horse', the plant which is not a 'tree'. The resolving need, there-fore, is to move dialectically, between things and words, while acknowledging equally and in tension, and without seeing them as merely opposed, the superiority of reality and the superiority of art. And a synthesis of desire, for this world and also for another, would be for this world remade. Not surprisingly, Eliot enacts that desire, in the section of 'Burnt Norton' beginning 'At the still point of the turning world'. In reaching towards *Erhebung* (a foreign experience named in a foreign language), he realises 'both a new world/And the old made explicit'; rather than the earth vanishing in the supersession of heaven, it is the body of the world that is touched by God, and one is surrounded by 'a grace of sense'.

A Christian view of this would indeed be that the dialectical swing is away towards another world free of the Fall and back towards the world in which we have nevertheless been placed and where alone we can be saved. It would suggest that both art and the dissatisfaction with art are gifts: that art is the hint of a new world, and dissatisfaction with art the realisation that it is no more than a hint. Writing really does re-create the world for us, but only a sign, an analogy, of Re-creation proper, which is in the power of God. Whenever it claims otherwise, whenever it proposes itself as a sufficient, autonomous realm to be inhabited, it is a form not of new life but of death, and we are once again in the presence of demonic parody.

To write is to be returned for the fourth moment of the dialectic. Even the constraints that we conceive and undergo, as well as entering us into a domain of necessity apparently beyond contingence, also remind us, from another angle, of the Fall, of the punishment of labour. They bring into the text our daily work, the quotidian limitations of which the sinless Adam was unaware; they let us know that we cannot create in liberty and sovereignty; they carry us into a new world, and carry this fallen world with us. To write is to succeed and fail, to remain in an unresolved dialectical process. And the paradoxical privilege specific to the writer is to know that his success and failure are directly related to the activity of God. He attempts to re-create the world through words, as God created the world and will re-create it through the Word; he fails to do so – his work being neither a scripture nor the text of the world to come – because of his alienation from that Word, because at the end of the day, at the end of the re-creative process, his text is still written in a fallen language. The writer, the best man with words, is also the one who best reveals our linguistic inadequacy. In his *Entretiens avec Georges Charbonnier* (p. 25), Raymond Queneau phrased it with accuracy and wit: 'with the writer', he said, 'you are sure that he will never succeed in using language in the most satisfying way possible'.

4

I have been considering language according to the three functions suggested by the German linguist Bühler, which coincide with the three persons of the verb and which one might call respectively, for want of more adequate terms, articulation, communication and nomination. There is also, as the Russian Mukarovsky saw, a fourth function, self-reflexion, which concerns the relation of language to itself. It is the function by which language is consti-tuted as a value, as something more than the dispensable purveyor of what it talks about. It too has its source in Eden, in the aural play of the words through which Adam on two occasions named his wife: 'she shall be called *Woman*, because she was taken out of *Man*', 'Adam called his wife's name *Eve*; because she was the mother of all *living*.' (One realises the care with which the opening of Genesis, among its other concerns, explores and analyses language, and specifically the language of 'the beginning'.) And once again there seems to be analogy, though of a less simple kind, with the divine language. Although the relation is too mysterious for our understanding, the words of God are reflexive, surely, in that they relate to the Word of God. Far from being only a means to an end, they are of absolute value, not only because they proceed from God but because they correspond somehow to his being. (One also notes the importance for the first Creation narrative of the idea of God as a speaker: it is almost as much the record of his words as of his deeds, and presents a divine Maker who speaks, continually and variously.)

In a fallen world, language draws attention to itself through its reflexive function as participating in the dialectical process that it relates, as being unmade and remade along with everything else. It answers to the reflexivity of the literary work as self-indicating artifice: to the fact that a story, say, or a sonnet, presents itself precisely as a story or a sonnet, as a literary world in a dialectical relationship to the everyday world that precedes and follows it. The four functions of language correspond therefore to the four participants in the literary act: writer (*I*), reader/hearer (*you*), reality (*it*) and work (*itself*).

I have discussed the reflexivity of language to a certain extent, and inevitably, when looking at the other functions; to focus on it directly I should like to examine the way in which writing, subverting a hallucinated order by opposing it, by casting words against things and language against the world, may recognise that language shares that hallucination and belongs to the reality on which it is operating. Subversion *by* language will then also involve subversion *of* language. (We glanced at this in connection with comedy.) Significantly, many of the devices of language and of literature are already subversive and auto-subversive, or are wide open to being made so. Consider in particular the figures of rhetoric, which have so often seemed to represent an especially fastidious order through being drilled into exhaustive and constantly renewed divisions and subdivisions. Take metaphasis, or the transposition of sounds between words. Isn't it a subversion of the 'natural' integrity of words, suggesting beyond a word's 'natural' combination of letters a chaotic contingence; and also a subversion of the 'natural' integrity of things? And doesn't it create, out of that primitive disruption, comic possibility? When our private life becomes filled with crooks and nannies, or we find in our hearts a half-warmed fish, there is the same production of a new world out of the old as when, by related processes, Mrs Gamp transforms half-a-dozen leeches into half a dudgeon, or Mrs Malaprop places a headstrong allegory on the banks of the Nile. In view of this confusion, in which language is shattered and made anew, one of the few apparently authentic metaphases or spoonerisms by Spooner himself, the spontaneous though unwilling expert in the figure, is deliciously appropriate: he is said to have declared that the Jewish story of the Flood was 'barrowed from Bobylon'.

Or take hyperbaton, which can mock the 'natural' order of words or phrases in the sentence and of things in the world through inverting them. Or zeugma, which by yoking together two or more different meanings subverts distinctions among meanings and among things, as in the classic examples in *The Rape of the Lock*:

> Here Britain's statesmen oft the fall foredoom
> Of foreign Tyrants, and of Nymphs at home;
> Here thou, great ANNA! whom three realms obey,
> Dost sometimes counsel take – and sometimes Tea.

Catachresis mocks the same distinctions by using words improperly, the word 'sea' displacing 'lake' and a lake becoming a sea. Antiphrasis, in which the stated meaning is the opposite of that

intended, mocks the 'proper' meaning of words even more
pointedly, and also the 'proper' fit between language and reality.
That latter fit is likewise subverted in pleonasm, which can also,
like most or perhaps all figures, be comic and re-creative. It may
contend with evil by stating and re-stating it, as when Touchstone
in *As You Like It* (V,1) plays with the slow wits of William but also
with death:

> . . . abandon the society of this female, or, clown, thou perishest;
> or, to thy better understanding, diest; or, to wit, I kill thee, make
> thee away, translate thy life into death. . .

Or it may suggest the exuberant redundance involved in the creative act, as does the different kind of superfluity of Mrs Gamp:

> 'Ah dear! When Gamp was summoned to his long home, and I
> see him a lying in Guys Hospital with a penny-piece on each
> eye, and his wooden leg under his *left* arm, I thought I should
> have fainted away . . .'
> 'Bite a person's thumbs, or turn their fingers the wrong
> way . . . and they comes to, wonderful, *Lord bless you!*'

Metaphor is another subversion of the 'natural' fit among words,
among things, and of words to things. It has also seemed, of
course, especially to Romantics, Symbolists and Surrealists, the
fundamental figure for the re-creation of reality, by the disclosing
or producing of affinities, analogies, correspondences. Its centrality in a certain kind of modern writing is indicative of the latter's
drive towards a world become other. The simile offers the same
possibilities, of subversion and re-creation. 'Like' is a mysterious
door to a universe in the process of being unmade, as when the
evening looks to a lover 'Like a patient etherised upon a table', or
remade, as when Cleopatra's barge appears, 'like a burnish'd
throne'. Hyperbole, which we considered in connection with the
greatness of the tragic hero, mocks the 'natural' limits of things. As
such, it is a figure characteristically oriented towards re-creation,
towards an overthrow of boundaries and, as its name implies, a
casting beyond. It is by hyperbole that, in Mandelshtam's words,
Pasternak's poetry could cure tuberculosis, and by hyperbole that,
for the wondering Miranda, Prospero's tale 'would cure deafness'.
Paradox, which figures, or so I have suggested, the involvement of

greatness with wretchedness and also that of wretchedness with possibility, and which is, therefore, a crucial, dialectical figure, subverts and transforms the 'natural' oppositions among words and among things. It can create a new world at odds with this one, as in the 'midwinter spring' passage of 'Little Gidding' or in the reversal and transfiguration of values in this 'Holy Sonnet' of Donne:

> . . . Take me to you, imprison me, for I
> Except you enthrall me, never shall be free,
> Nor ever chaste, except you ravish me.

If paradox is an apparent self-contradiction, oxymoron is a real one, with no articulating middle term. (Its relation to paradox is comparable to that of metaphor to simile.) It is an instantaneous change of sign, which, gainsaying a fallen world, glimpses another more intensely – one ungraspable in terms of this world and made present only through this world's undoing. It enables St Paul to speak of the resurrection of a 'spiritual body', and Vaughan to imagine, in 'The Night', 'a deep, but dazzling darkness'.

And take, finally, paronomasia, or the pun. Often involved in the other figures, its work is at once the most superficial and in a way the most radical, the most obvious and the most profound. It mocks everything that it lights on, particularly the distinctiveness of words and of things, and most particularly the apartness of sound and sense. It is a time-bomb lurking behind every syllable and every object, which at any moment can bring the whole elaborate structure of language and of the world tumbling about one's ears. It subverts all order, and dispels the hallucination. Beckett's quip: 'In the beginning was the Pun', is true as far as it goes, but it only goes back to the expulsion from Eden; a truer formula would be: 'Since the Fall is the pun' (or even: 'Adam was punished'. . .). Yet at the same time it is potently re-creative. As it descends to a depth of our linguistic disquiet, exhibiting the fault in our language, the gap between phonology and semantics, it also pretends, tongue in cheek, that the fault has disappeared, by demonstrating, for example, that it is perfectly correct to call a pony with a cough a little hoarse. Even the most trivial pun achieves, burlesquely, the semblance of a renewed naming, a comic pre-figuration of the nominative power of language in a world transformed. Also, by drawing attention to relations of sound between words that are otherwise unconnected it can suggest, as has often been pointed out, new relations of meaning. This is especially true of the alliteration, assonance and rhyme which, in their complex variations and repetitions, generate the text of a poem. It is paronomasia that links 'wild' and 'wind' in Shelley; that in Sidney links (and contrasts) *'up* to our country' and *'must* Stella love'; that in the recurring rhyme 'Oreste-funeste' in Racine's *Andromaque* causes 'baleful' to become the epithet of Orestes, or that in the inscription over the gates of hell in Dante's *Inferno* rhymes and associates, startlingly and with far-reaching intent, 'eterno dolore' with 'Amore'.

Rhyme is of special interest, since a rhyming poem (and so many poems do rhyme) derives in part from a complex of potential puns all of which are ready to be actualised. A subtle example of that actualisation – of a poem generated by a single, massive pun – where the pun is also explicitly re-creative, transforming one world, that of 'life', into another, that of 'the book', is another 'Sonnet for Helen' of Ronsard, which I shall need to quote entire:

> Afin qu'à tout jamais de siècle en siècle vive
> La parfaite amitié que Ronsard vous portait,
> Comme votre beauté la raison lui ôtait,
> Comme vous enchaînez sa liberté captive;
> Afin que d'âge en âge à nos neveux arrive
> Que toute dans mon sang votre figure était,
> Et que rien sinon vous mon coeur ne souhaitait,
> Je vous fais un présent de cette Sempervive.
> Elle vit longuement en sa jeune verdeur:
> Longtemps après la mort je vous ferai revivre,
> Tant peut le docte soin d'un gentil serviteur,
> Qui veut en vous servant toutes vertus ensuivre.
> Vous vivrez, croyez-moi, comme Laure en grandeur,
> Au moins tant que vivront les plumes et le livre.

The work of the poem is to transform 'vive' (live), exposed by being withheld until the end of the first line, into 'livre' (book), the last word of all. The transformation is forwarded by the unusual retention of the '-ive' rhyme of the quatrains, with a small modification, in the '-ivre' rhyme of the tercets. It is also advanced by the occurrence of v in every line (and of f in six), to keep the sound present; the change from v to vr is prepared by the closeness of r

after *v* on many occasions, by that entry of *vr* into the rhymes of the tercets, and by its appearance elsewhere in the last two lines in 'vivrez' and 'vivront'; *r* also enters the other rhyme of the tercets, while the introduction of *l* is made natural by the association with Laura – the beloved who entered a book – and by the rapid sequence in 'les plumes et le. . .' By this delicate word-play, in which vivre → revivre = livre (to live → to live after death = book), Ronsard conveys his more general meaning entirely through the power of the pun. (I fancy that there is even another, more concealed pun, by which he intimates to the reader no less than five times, in 'revivre', 'ensuivre', 'vivrez', 'vivront' and 'livre', that in contemplating Helen, in writing and in transforming experience into art, he is drunken – 'ivre'.) The poem reapplies the idea of the everlasting life of God – described in the Bible and in the Catholic Missal as '[vivens] in saecula saeculorum', an expression appropriated in the first line – and of the resurrection of the Christian, to the quasi-eternal life of art and the survival of the person in the poem; and it does so by literally changing 'life' into a 'book'.

Through this playing of word on word and object on object, paronomasia can indeed suggest, maybe beyond an abusive disfiguring, a ludic re-creation of language and of the world. It really is the lowest form of wit, the jester in the pack, the Fool. It reaches a kind of paroxysm in Joyce's *Finnegans Wake*, where all the linguistic matter is brought into a state of pun, and the whole is a kind of totalised pun, a new world/new language drawn by rhetoric out of this one. But the most amazing (or paronomasing) fact is that the connection between re-creation and the pun is actually established in the Bible. Both Jesus and the Holy Spirit are shown, at high, dialectically decisive moments, engaging in equivoque. In one of the most famous puns of all: 'you are Peter (*Petros*), and on this rock (*petra*) I shall build my church', Jesus founds the church on a pun and announces a new order in a calembour. One realises the appropriateness of the re-creative Word playing on words. At Pentecost, when the Spirit inspires the disciples to speak in other and miraculous 'tongues', he also sets 'tongues' like flames of fire over each of their heads. The descent of the Spirit is the beginning of the transformation of the world specifically by an act of language; the pun which he enacts is therefore appropriately self-reflexive, and concerns the very word for language and for the principal organ by which we produce it. In tune with the paradoxical reversal that governs the dialectic, therefore, from both these events we can apparently also say that in the new beginning was the pun.

To figures, considered not in terms of 'ornamentation' and 'persuasion' but as subverting and re-creating language and the world which it infers, correspond, among the larger devices of literature, those whose target, along with the world, is literature itself. A sizeable area of the literary enterprise is given over, in fact, to demolition – to the burlesque of genres and kinds, the parody or travesty of specific works, the caricature of styles. This can of course be a hygienic operation, attacking some disease in writing or in reality with a view to a greater health. But it can also set up a continuous impropriety and bring disparities clashing together, as in mock-heroic, which is a catachrestic and zeugmatic form. It can unstabilise literary monuments, as in the garbling of *Hamlet* by Mrs Malaprop or of the Gospel by Mrs Gamp. It can even raise a doubt about the whole literary undertaking, as in the notion, in Scarron's *Virgile travesti*, that Virgil (himself) could be spoofed. Not surprisingly, our own century has travelled this direction to what looks like an edge. Self-burlesque has been a characteristic mode, and a kind of maximised burlesque has emerged into full consciousness, in which writing itself is in question. Eliot is central to both, as both are central to Eliot – from 'Prufrock', which mocks far more than the love song, to *Four Quartets*, the most solemn, 'Virgilian', of his poems, which he (half-) dismisses as a not very satisfactory way of putting it. To see burlesque at its most powerful, however, unmaking and remaking with density and ease, one needs to return, once again, to Shakespeare, and to the moment in *A Midsummer Night's Dream* where Bottom, the Fool, wakes up:

I have had a most rare vision. I have had a dream, past the wit of man to say what dream it was: man is but an ass, if he go about to expound this dream. Methought I was – there is no man can tell what. Methought I was, – and methought I had, – but man is but a patched fool, if he will offer to say what methought I had. The eye of man hath not heard, the ear of man hath not seen, man's hand is not able to taste, his tongue to conceive, nor his heart to report, what my dream was. I will get Peter Quince to write a ballad of this dream: it shall be called Bottom's Dream, because it hath no bottom. . .

Isn't this one of the most searching as well as the most touching
moments in Shakespeare? Bottom has returned from another
world, whose entrance was the fiction of literature – the play of
Pyramus and Thisbe in which he had wanted to act all the parts
and which he was rehearsing at the instant of his 'translation'. To
penetrate that world he had had to be transformed, not heroically
but burlesquely. And by descending to the condition of an ass he
reached an ambiguous place from which, nevertheless, reconciliation proceeds, overcoming the confusion of nature, the quarrel of
Oberon and Titania, the frustrations of the young lovers. After
that descent, in the words of Oberon, 'all things shall be peace',
and in words of Puck that reappear at the end of *Four Quartets*, 'all
shall be well'.

Bottom has had a vision; but the only language capable of
alluding to vision in a fallen world is a 'foolish' one. So his speech
is hilariously amiss, making of a man and his faculties a zeugmatic
jumble. It even recalls the opening of the first letter of John –
'That which was from the beginning, which we have heard, which
we have seen with our eyes, which we have looked upon, and our
hands have handled, of the word of life . . .' (the sequence 'heard',
'seen', 'hands' is repeated) – so as to suggest that Bottom is unable
to report because, unlike the inspired apostle, he had not en-
countered the word. And it recalls more closely, while mangling it,
another New Testament verse, 1 Corinthians 2:9 in the Bishops'
Bible: 'The eye hath not seen, and the ear hath not heard, neither
have entered into the heart of man, the things which God hath
prepared for them that love him.' By travestying a passage that
refers specifically to a re-created world, that we are unable to
reach with our present 'heart' and senses, and by putting that
travesty into the mouth of his Fool, when the Fool is in the very act
of saying that only a fool would recount that other world, Shakespeare defines once and for all the inevitable, awesome foolishness of a re-creative language.

Bottom's speech is in fact the culmination of his usual talk,
which he shares with his fellows. The artisans disfigure words, like
Mrs Gamp, as when 'Ninus' becomes 'Ninny', and also becomes a
kind of pun since a ninny is speaking. They substitute words –
'obscenely' for 'obscurely', 'paramour' for 'paragon' – in the
manner of Mrs Malaprop, and also of course of Dogberry, the
linguistic 'ass' of *Much Ado About Nothing* who nevertheless catches
the rogues. And they disrupt language, by the unwitting use of

paradox, as when Wall describes his cranny as 'right and sinister', thereby also managing another pun; of oxymoron, as in 'odious savours sweet', where 'odious' is also a malapropism; and of the displaced punctuation that reverses the meaning of Peter Quince's Prologue: 'All for your delight,/We are not here. That you should here repent you,/The actors are at hand.' Even the abuse of alliteration in their play ('Whereat, with blade, with bloody blameful blade,/He bravely broach'd his boiling bloody breast') is more than Shakespeare's ridiculing of bad writing since it also belongs to their linguistic foolishness. A line that Bottom declaims as Pyramus epitomises the hilarity of this disordering:

Sweet moon, I thank thee for thy sunny beams.

Shortly after his soliloquy, Theseus and Hippolyta, serious charac-ters, debate the truth of the imagination. But it is Bottom who has been in that other realm, and has seen what may be shadows of even higher things – of the heavenly things that are not available, according to an expression of St Paul just prior to the passage that Bottom travesties, to 'the princes of this world'. The quoting of 1 Corinthians draws much of its context into the play: this is the letter where Paul declares that God has made the wisdom of the world 'foolish', and saves believers by the 'foolishness' of preach-ing; and where he urges any man who seeks wisdom to 'become a fool'.[3] So the 'rude mechanical' with the rude and comic name has the rare vision; and it is not the sophisticated poetry of the court that ushers him there but the burlesque patter of his mates. To meet Titania he has to become a pun: 'this is to make an ass of me'. Yet by being changed he does take one word – not 'love', or 'death', or 'glory', but 'ass' – and suit it by a foolish miracle to the thing. With the same aptness he is also called Nick, which meant in Shakespeare's time to 'hit off or fit with an appropriate name'.

His dream has no bottom, so Quince's ballad is to be called, by paradox out of antiphrasis, Bottom's Dream. Bottom will sing it at the end of a play; and remembering the play in which he is about to act, and which closes with the death of Thisbe, he thinks, 'peradventure . . . I shall sing it at her death', and adds: 'to make it the more gracious'. Is 'gracious' another pun? Does it allude to the grace by which, in the scripture that Bottom has just misquoted, God has prepared things to be enjoyed after death? Bottom, one realises, is truly Bottom the Weaver, who threads the way from artisan to visionary, from ass to grace. And as Bottom too he is appropriately named, since he is low comedy and lowly wit, the route, in this perspective, to the higher dream – another way down which is also the way up.

Our experience of language is dialectical, and corresponds to our experience of everything else. And that experience is most intense in writing, which works language as it works life, and which renders language particularly self-aware. From a writer's point of view the whole dialectic is travelled in two fundamental sequences: silence-speaking-silence, and blankness-writing-blankness. He may discover, in the silence that precedes speech and in the blankness of the page, the perfection that should be, unattainable and accusing, waiting for his move. It hints at a word, or a Word, before and above our words, essential to language yet missing from the elaborations of linguists: Saussure may distinguish between 'langue', or language as system, and 'parole', or the individual realisation of language, but has no place for a word surpassing language (a 'verbe'?), which language remembers and by which both language and our particular uses of it are judged. Writers sense it, however, and develop, for instance, theories of inspiration, to indicate that difficult perfection and our tenuous access to it. When Shelley writes in *A Defence of Poetry* of 'evanescent visitations of thought and feeling', and compares the mind in creation to a fading coal, he acknowledges the rarity and the mysterious perishability of the very sources of writing. The unmystical Valéry, claiming to receive 'given lines' or 'gratuitous lines' of verse, recognises something of the existence of a perfect word, mediated to us only by gift and grace.

Visitations like these are glimpses of an Edenic state. But since perfection is not the natural state of language nor inspiration the natural state of the writer, the latter has to follow Adam out of Eden and attain his text by hard labour, just as the fruits of the soil could only come to Adam through the 'sweat of his face'. A writer sweating to work the cursed ground of language, and inevitably failing and falling, can experience himself as the first man. He may reflect, if such is his ambition, that in a fallen world, writing that aims at anything as incongruous as the re-creation of the subject, of relation, of reality, of language, is 'naturally' monstrous. Among the norms that it may refuse are the norms of writing, so that it tends to the abnormal, the extravagant, the outlandish. Its means are parody, travesty, caricature; its form is malapropian, catachrestic, pleonastic, hyperbolic, paradoxical, oxymoronic, paronomastic, and like all those figures, a shade foolish. Yet the result of his labour may be a seemingly perfect work of art. Every detail may be right (or, as French has it, 'just'); there may be a satisfying marriage of all the elements of the language act; powerful changes may be operating endlessly. In that case, the dialectic will be momentarily fulfilled.

If the silence before suggests the absence of the word, the silence after – a renewed silence, a charged whiteness, that moves beyond the writer and his works – intimates a word and a world of strange possibility, and reveals the provisional nature of our perfections. Beyond palaver, it would erase the writer's preposterous noise, if he could reach a paroxysm in his own words and then turn them off. Or he may desire that word – the word of another, perhaps of the Other – to intrude in his writing, to quieten his fickle, sublunary language and to replace it by a firm and amazing new speech. It doesn't happen, but some works attest the desire by making it seem to. Suddenly in Bach's 2nd Partita for unaccompanied violin, the chaconne steps aside into the major and into what sounds (though it isn't) a quite different melody. The first note establishes the change, and opens a dimension between itself and the last note in the minor. As the new sounds in a new mode appear, everything is sovereignly transformed. The voice of a 'you' superseding the I.

7   Translating

If writing performs dialectically on language, translation performs
the same dialectic from one language to another. To turn to it is to
continue the concern with the reflexivity of language; and also to
move from a study where the linguistic *misère* to be contended
with was essentially serpentine to one where the *misère* is Babylonian.

We know the importance of translation as practice in general
literary and cultural terms. It can initiate or give direction to a
writer's work, as did Chaucer's version of the *Romaunt of the Rose*,
and it can operate extensively in a writer's 'own' productions, even
the very major ones, as it operates in the *Canterbury Tales*. If the
writer is of Chaucer's magnitude it can also determine a new
phase in a national literature. It can establish and advance a
language, as one gathers that Luther's Bible, Voss's Homer, the
Shakespeares of Wieland, Schlegel and Tieck made and remade
German. It can infuse and orient a whole civilisation, as St
Jerome's *Vulgate* in medieval Europe or the Authorised Version in
post-Reformation England. Not that we acknowledge this power
as spontaneously as we might: despite Pound's contentions, in
'How to Read', that in English literature after the Anglo-Saxon
period 'every new exuberance, every new heave is stimulated by
translation', and that 'some of the best books in English are translations', and his criticism that 'histories of English literature always
slide over translation', we still often fail to discuss translation as a
matter of course within our discussion of literature and to consider translators along with writers.

We also hesitate to allow that, as any theory of translation must
be part of a more general poetics, so, conversely, no poetics can
know itself thoroughly until it has absorbed a theory of translation. It would seem particularly necessary, for a poetics aimed at
the understanding of language and literature in terms of the
deepest routines of life, to explore in the same terms an activity

162

where the possibilities – even the possibility – of writing are pointedly in question, and where there is at work a fundamental process of change; and particularly useful, for a poetics concerned with the fall of language, to study an activity directly engaging with the consequence of Babel.

When a would-be translator sits down his situation is in part that of the would-be writer: he too is defined with reference to a blank sheet of paper from which he, the reader, the world and language are all absent. But he also has in front of him a text. His own writing activity will be governed by the existence of another writer who has already written and of a text that is already there and is apparently definitive. It is a strange position in which to find himself. And the fact that an act of writing has already occurred means not that his own undertaking will be parasitic, but that, with an extra linguistic demand to satisfy, in comparison with the writer of the first text he will be placed in language reflexively, moving not from no-language to language but from one realised language to another. He will pass through the same dialectic of language, with less risk and urgency (perhaps) but more acutely. Whereas the writer encounters the *grandeur* of language at large, as a wonder impelling him to write, the translator as reader encounters that *grandeur* locally, as a wonder actualised, and is then impelled, as writer, to translate. And whereas linguistic *misère* is general for the writer, for the translator it is specifically, though not exclusively, Babelic. When his work is finished he confronts two texts, a foreign original and his own version, and becomes aware of a third 'text', the silence between, the flaw. One notices, in fact, how commonplace this awareness is, the most persistent theoretical approach to translation turning on the definitive unattainability of a work in a foreign tongue, and thereby acknowledging *misère*; though it is also the case that, because of our changing attitudes to translation and our changing ambitions for it, we are in danger of forgetting that the commonplace, like so many of its fellows, is true. Dante is still right to have claimed that 'nothing harmonized by the bond of the Muses can be transmuted from its own to another way of speech, without disrupting all its sweetness and harmony', even though now we might want to point to the new 'sweetness and harmony' which can be created in the process. Cervantes is right to compare a translation to a Flemish tapestry looked at from the wrong side, even though we might argue that it is another tapestry which has been revealed, whose relation with the first is what interests us. Johnson is right, from one point of view, to declare that 'Poetry … cannot be translated', even if we are right, from another, to decide that it can. And it is not only 'poetry' that gets lost in translation: there is a whole world that we cannot translate or even reach, being foreigners, and being involved, as George Steiner says, in 'a special *miseria* of translation, a melancholy after Babel'.

Indeed, what translation also makes clear is that any text, even prior to the question of its being translated, is already Babelic. Its own language bears the marks of a catastrophe that occurred long before Auschwitz and Dachau, of a disruption much older than that of social classes. The plurality of tongues is not merely an inconvenience but a sign, that no one language is adequate – that separate languages, with their distinct modes of stating the subject, of addressing the other, of naming the world, move into areas from which others are excluded; and that the situation would be redeemed not by adding all the tongues together but by an equally impossible clearing away, since as Mallarmé wrote, again in the marvellously concentrated 'Crisis in Verse': 'languages imperfect for being several, the supreme one is wanting'. Relative to that absent language, each actual language is itself a translation, necessarily deficient and inevitably failing. So literature occurs *bon gré mal gré* in the aftermath of Babel, and is, furthermore, the only art that is not and cannot be universal. It is the art closest to us, since it derives from the common, everyday activity of speaking and writing, and the art that, by the problematic nature of its material, most closely questions our condition.

Any translation, directed by whatever theory or by none, will reveal the apartness of the two texts. One might desire a kind of translation, however, which, instead of doing its utmost to conceal the ultimate absence of the original, would voluntarily indicate it. At a Cambridge Poetry Festival the French poet Jean Daive read the whole of his book *Décimale blanche*, section by section, while alternately I read my translation of it. (I shall have to refer to myself on occasion in this chapter.) Preparing the translation, I realised that there was an unwitting deception in the offing. Given the circumstances, those members of the audience who were unable to grasp the French originals could well receive my versions as if the originals were somehow contained in them, and believe that they were listening to Jean Daive in a different guise – to Jean-Daive-in-English. So at one point, to scotch that, I re-read the French. The ploy, as well as being didactic, was an attempt, primitive enough, to be honest to Daive's poetry. Though something else also happened. The French poem, less when read than when it appeared typed among my English versions of the other poems, altered. It became more foreign, to English eyes, and it seemed also to have been rewritten, in the new context: it was not exactly the same poem as when it occurred in Daive's book. Even the question of authorship was raised. Here was a hint of the change, the possibility, to which translation always invites, and in which – to anticipate – the dialectic resolves itself.

One might even wish, on an appropriate occasion, to lead a text further into Babel. The contemporary Italian poet Mario Lunetta has a long poem called *Tredici Falchi*, or Thirteen Hawks, a section of which, concerning the founding of a political and cultural quarterly, is preoccupied with language. The writing frequently shifts into languages other than Italian, refers to the 'confusion of tongues' and the 'collision of the dialects', and mentions Breughel's painting *The Tower of Babel*. It even locates the latter in a Viennese museum, which it seizes the opportunity of designating in German. Since to translate is already to be involved in Babel, whatever the character of the poem being translated, when I came to translate Lunetta[1] it seemed that the only course consonant with both the nature of his poem and the nature of translation was to foreground and intensify the Babel. I increased the noise, by augmenting the number of languages present and also the frequency of their intrusion. And again something unforeseen occurred. The poem is Babelic and distances the Italian reader from a text which is in parts foreign; and it is already engaged in the translation process, in the sense that it obliges the reader to consider Italian renderings of the foreign phrases. To translate it, therefore, and to emphasise its polyglot character, was actually to develop it – to follow through the poet's original project. Far from being a matter of indifference to the poem, the translation was (however inadequately) the poem's genuine fulfilment.

Although these were rather special cases, it was only natural that the re-creative potential of translation should assert itself. For in the same place that the translator undergoes the *misère* of language he also works for its possibility. He is someone who steps out of his own language, to move in Babel, and to discover that Babel is also a strangely, powerfully gracious domain, where confusion is also exuberance and punishment is accompanied by gift. If Babel arouses dismay at the absence of language, the alienation of the word, it also convinces one that the multiplicity of tongues is to be welcomed, that each tongue, potent with some-thing of the profusion and variety of a universe, represents a unique system of experience and a unique manner of contending with its own contingence: Latin, for example, in its ability to amplify the sense of place by the complexity of its adverbs, has seemed to Yves Bonnefoy, in *L'Arrière-pays* (p. 109) an 'algebra of the word in exile'. Foreign languages offer abundant possibilities of being – of entering, through the spacious suggestiveness of words, other histories, physics, metaphysics, patterns of awareness and obligation. Multiplicity is, after all, no less than unity, a form of joy. As the translator encounters the most obvious yet also the most radical characteristic of the work to be translated, the fact that it is written in a foreign language, so his specific opportunity as a writer is, not to bask, but to negotiate with the foreign, the alien, that which is not himself – with the different-yet-similar from which all possibility springs; as he will likewise negotiate with the otherness of the other writer.

A large part of what a foreign work offers is precisely its articu-lation in a language different from ours. Yet this basic premise is implicitly denied in one of the most eminently reasonable atti-tudes to translation, as held by numerous writers including Dryden. A succinct expression of it occurs in the latter's preface to his translations from Virgil: 'I have endeavoured to make Virgil speak such English as he would himself have spoken, if he had been born in England, and in this present age'. That 'if', blandly accommodated in the sentence, or so it may seem, is decidedly vertiginous. Though it is true, of course, that such an approach is likely to be right for a certain kind of translating purpose, which is also the most general: that of making a foreign writer – or rather, something like him – readily available to one's contemporaries; and it is even true that, while ignoring essential difference and otherness, the approach may produce something genuinely new in the receiving language. The feigning of the 'if' may be just the fiction to engender novelty.

For in his own terms Dryden does assume that the translator enters the same linguistic and literary possibility as the writer, and that his task is not simply to attempt, with a greater or smaller degree of success, to transfer a work from one language to another. He would presumably agree that a translation, rather than figuring as a useful but basically inadequate accessory, is, or should be, a further act of writing, a new work; and perhaps even (as Henri Meschonnic phrases it in the second volume of his *Pour la poétique*) that it is not more or less 'faithful' and more or less 'transparent' but stands to an original as a kind of 'metaphor' (pp. 307–19). Instead of dissimulating the otherness of the original, a translation establishes a relationship, between two texts, two poetics, two languages, ultimately two cultures and perhaps two historical moments. In the light of which, one should add, a trans- lation likewise creates, and has its own originality.

A clear example of such a work would be another Augustan translation, apparently far behind the frontiers of contemporary research: Pope's Homer. It carries through the above 'programme' massively and comprehensively, marking the relation between Homeric Greece and eighteenth-century England (as Douglas Knight shows in Reuben A. Brower's *On Translation*) with delibera- tion at all levels. Pope takes Homer's distance for granted, and uses translation as a precise measure of that distance. He moves out towards what is in every way foreign, and causes it to correlate with the native. He can thereby examine Homer in the light of his own period and, more importantly, examine in the light of Homer the capacities of English epic, English prosody, the English language, English civilisation, and no doubt the capacities of his own talent. Pope's *Iliad* and *Odyssey* are decidedly poems, achieve- ments of English literature, to be received in the entirety of their project and not judged piecemeal in terms of the degree of their 'closeness' to Homer, of where they are 'successful' and where not. In a way, they are Greek–Augustan poems, the results of a collaboration between Homer and Pope.

Again, Pope does not rewrite Homer in a verse form which his own literature has to stretch towards but in one which it already possesses. Yet no illusion is involved: Pope and his readers know perfectly well that Greek unrhymed hexameters and English heroic couplets are not the same thing. The usefulness of the heroic couplet for Pope's translation is precisely the fact that it is so firmly of his country and of his age; it enables him to discover how Homer looks in Augustan verse and also how Augustan verse looks when negotiating with Homer. He proves that it can indeed be of great value to proceed as if a foreign writer were a com- patriot and a contemporary, especially if the translator and the reader are clear as to the meaning of the device, if making the foreign writer seem familiar is a means of indicating his strange-ness, and if the gap between how he is being made to write and how he did write is deliberately in question.

A more obviously creative relationship is established by another form of 'translation' associated with the Augustan as with the Restoration period, that is, the imitation. In Pope's imitations of Horace, say, or Johnson's of Juvenal – as also in Pound's 'Homage' to Propertius and some at least of Lowell's *Imitations* – the corres-ponding with another literary and cultural moment again enters the writing project. Titles or subtitles even direct away from the texts they introduce. The stress here, however, falls quite explicitly on the use of an existing work or body of work for the production of another. Augustan and Poundian imitations are overtly new acts of writing, works by their authors. As in Pope's Homer, it is once more the pretence that the foreign poet is writing now and in English that, instead of merely Anglicising him and rendering him powerless, becomes the means of extending English litera-ture by involving him in it. The same is true, one might add, of the ghost section of 'Little Gidding', which is another imitation, and Eliot's Homage to Dante Alighieri.

As a response to Dante's *terza rima*, however, Eliot did invent a new metre for English: tercets of basically iambic pentameters, with alternate masculine and feminine endings. Pound, of course, used Propertius no less than programmatically, to extend the executive possibilities of English poetry – a purpose for which he exploited a wide variety of remotely foreign works. Their practice suggests that, although translation may explore the new by embracing the foreign into what already exists in the prosody of the receiving literature, the deep bearing of re-creative translation – by which I mean translation that enters the universal, theologi-cal domain of re-creation – is outwards, to a meeting with the foreign on the latter's own terms.

The same applies on the level of language. Rather than acclima-tising a foreign work by totally absorbing it into a host language, the opportunity of translation is to stretch language, with more or less violence, towards the foreign. Yet the opportunity seems only to have been formulated quite recently, seemingly since the Romantics; and even now I suppose that a statement like the following by Rudolf Pannwitz (that Walter Benjamin quotes in 'The Task of the Translator') meets with some resistance: 'Our translations, even the best ones, proceed from a wrong premise. They want to turn Hindi, Greek, English into German instead of turning German into Hindi, Greek, English . . . The basic error of the translator is that he preserves the state in which his own language happens to be instead of allowing his language to be powerfully affected by the foreign tongue.'

And one must push further. The modification of language which that kind of translation intends is public and permanent: it is a modification offered for use. (Paradoxically, its success will be gradually to lose its strangeness as it merges into the language's evolution. Then, since Babel operates in time as well as in space, within as well as across languages, eventually it will recover its strangeness – but along with even the most conventional writing of its period – by virtue of that same evolution, which slowly and inexorably alienates us from our own works, written in the past of our own language.) Instead of wresting language, however, so as to serve it historically, translation may wrest it in such ways and to such an extent that it becomes itself half foreign. The language of the translation will be a sort of no man's land, where no reader can feel at home. Perhaps Hölderlin's Sophocles translations operate like this: they are sufficiently German for a German reader to know himself and the world in them, and sufficiently un-German for him to lose himself and to lose the world. In a way, a translation of this kind is more powerfully, more instructively foreign than a foreign text, since it withdraws the comfort of a native language. By removing the ground from under one's feet, it plunges one into the *misère* of language while at the same time hinting – in, it is true, a particularly off-beat manner – at a re-creation of language, of the self, and of the world.

Translation in this light becomes collaborative and even reciprocal: one translates a foreign work, but at the same time one translates, with its help, one's own literature and one's own language. The translator is a writer who changes language.

If translation encroaches on the literature and the language of the translator, so it can encroach on the work being translated. Instead of accounting the work untouchable, out of fidelity, or modesty, it may disturb it or even disrupt it. Once again the translator joins the writer, within a theory of language, and particularly of writing, as re-creative possibility. Just as language, rather than duplicating the world, operates upon it, so translation, rather than duplicating a work, may operate on the work and on the world of the work.

This is pre-eminently the moment where, in the dialectic of translation, the change of sign occurs. The translator cannot attain the original, and that is *misère*; but he can change it, and that is possibility.

There are many ways in which this may happen, only a few of which have been explored. My Lunetta translation interferes with the original poem by developing one of its features and rendering it more variously and densely multilingual. It changes the work, according to the terms that the work has already laid down. A translator may also use one poem as a stimulus to another, the first being the original in the sense not that it reduces the translation to a copy but that it originates the translation. Consider *Mono no aware* by the contemporary French poet Jacques Roubaud, which consists of a hundred and forty-three poems 'borrowed' from the Japanese. Each text, according to a preliminary note, has a Japanese poem as a 'point of departure', which serves as its 'subject' rather as the port of Concarneau would serve as the subject of a poem on 'The Port of Concarneau in the Rain'. The originals are worked on, in other words, until they become poems in French, as subjects are worked on until they achieve the status of poems; and the originals are chosen for the same kinds of reason that lead a poet to choose subjects. (At the same time, the originals intervene in French poetry, extending its possibilities by opening it to Japanese prosody and beyond.) And there is more. In the case of nearly all the texts, the Japanese original, a small, five-line *tanka*, is not set aside but is included with the French derivative, so that each poem comprises both Japanese and French. The Japanese, in a syllabic transcription, usually precedes the French or follows it; on four occasions the two mingle, as here:

> toshi no koi   le désir d'un an
> en une nuit   ko yoi tsuku shite
> asu yori wa   s'épuisera et de nouveau
> demain   tsume no gotoku ya   de l'un
> pour l'autre le désir   waga koi oramu   grandira

It is another way of inroading the original. The result is bilingual poetry/translation, a powerful inner rather than outer dialogue between two poems, two poets, two very alien poetics, languages and world-views. The compound texts represent a new type of translation, or perhaps simply a new type of poem.

The book also establishes a new kind of quotation literature, different from both the neoclassical and the modernist. It quotes poems whole, and plays them against French derivatives; it quotes, cumulatively, a poem-form, the tanka; and, also by accumulation, it quotes the Japanese language, and even Japan. Furthermore, it is a work that moves easily in Babel – rather than uneasily – inviting French readers to hear the Japanese 'with vowels as in Italian and consonants as in English'; and which contends with Babel by the new language that it contrives.

The bilingualism of *Mono no aware* is manoeuvred in written texts. It is possible to transfer that manoeuvre to the spoken word, and so achieve, between the original and the translation, a mutual trespass that is perfect, in the sense of being simultaneous. In the course of Jean Daive's Cambridge reading to which I referred earlier, we read some of the poems, at his suggestion, literally together, in a bilingual counterpoint which mingled his French poems vocally with my English versions. To the other relationships – of two poets, two languages, etc. – which any confrontation can enact, our reading added another, that of two Babelic voices.

A different way of obtaining new poems from old is represented by Celia and Louis Zukofsky's *Catullus*. Translation here is governed by interlingual punning, which saturates the whole of a Latin poem with corresponding English sounds and their attendant meanings. It is the pun that springs, miraculously and desperately, from:

> Amabo, mea dulcis Ipsithilla,
> meae deliciae, mei lepores

to:

> I'm a bow, my dual kiss, Ipsithilla,
> my daily key, eye, my eye's little leap-horse . . .

Catullus transfers to translation the totalised punning which produced *Finnegans Wake*. At the same time, although the Zukofskys do not include the originals, unlike Roubaud, they do involve them. The presence of the Latin is implied in the English, whose effect depends on that relationship. The English texts, though in themselves unilingual, move the reader at all points across to the Latin texts, printed on facing pages, and direct attention essentially to the passage from one to the other. The book as a whole is bilingual, and not merely a combination of Latin poems and English versions.

The newness of the English texts is attained here not by laying aside faithfulness to the original but by a form of extreme though restricted faithfulness, to the original's phonology. A tiny preface claims, moreover, a wider and unprecedented fidelity, a direct mimesis of rhythm and syntax as well as sound. Where the claim is founded, the translations both interfere with Catullus's poems, to engender any number of new semantic details in the English, and interfere with the English language, turning it, to adopt Pannwitz's phrasing, into Latin. Indeed, they make an English so strange, so disturbing and stimulating, that it operates somewhat like the German of Hölderlin's Sophocles.

Against all the odds, the poems even stay close, in the round, to Catullus's sense. Yet because of the ubiquitous, comic activity of the pun, the reader does not receive them simply as translations of Catullus. The pun both binds and separates: it marries Zukofsky to Catullus and English to Latin, while equally mocking what is also their *mis*marriage. It is right, surely, that we should marvel at the ingenuity which manages to gather up the semantics of the originals along with the phonology while at the same time being constantly aware of the jokes of schoolboy Latinists which that same ingenuity also recalls. The punning is deliberately exaggerated to accentuate the burlesque, and the strategy of the translation is not solemn but ludic. It ushers in, not 'a theory of immediate universal understanding' (Steiner), but hilarity. It mocks Babel, by abusing and renewing language with clownish virtuosity; it joins Bottom, Mrs Malaprop, Mrs Gamp and the Rev W. A. Spooner, and even produces an entirely new form of macaronic (none too digestible, I fear, in large quantities). Couldn't one also add that the book as a whole, by wrenching Catullus into English *nolens volens,* is also a kind of mockery of translation — indeed, a mock-translation, translation's *The Rape of the Lock?*

One can imagine other translation procedures to stimulate new texts via the pun. The writer may, for example, pun away from a work in a foreign language with no regard at all for its meanings, using it frankly as a means to his own end. There is also the case of the work whose structure is already paronomastic. Instead of translating the text, which in this case would be merely reductive, one might translate the system that produced it – in other words, generate a comparable text by using a comparable word-play in one's own language. I did this, in fact, when translating some of the poems in Raymond Queneau's *Pour un art poétique*.[2]

Since paronomasia is already an extreme and radical device for disturbing language and reality and for glimpsing the possible, the paronomastic disturbance of a text is particularly appropriate to re-creative translation. Yet there is another type of translation, the 'variation', which enters even more desirously into the processes of writing and of the world. We know the variation essentially, of course, in music. At times, when the source material is a piece by another composer, as in Brahms's opus 56 *Variations on a Theme by Haydn,* it resembles that literary strategy, for example Roubaud's, which treats a text in a foreign language as a subject. Its chief characteristic, however, is multiplicity, and multiplicity of a special kind; it is this that accounts for the appeal and the deep satisfaction of the master works, of Bach's *Goldberg* or Beethoven's *Diabelli*. Variations transform, not once but over and over again – perhaps thirty or thirty-three times. They persuade the listener that the transforming could continue for ever, and that there is no end to the possibility of the music. At the same time, each transformation is a version of the original material. Rather than replacing the music by something other, the variations keep it continuously present and change it further and further into itself. They develop, or unfold, the same substance, seemingly discovering layer on layer of what it already contained and allowing it to realise its own virtuality. They call thereby to a profound and complex desire: that the world should be transformed – that its possibility and our own should be endless; and nevertheless that the changed world should be, not a substitute for this world, but this very world itself.

The desire, as we have seen, is dialectical: it resolves two contradictory needs often experienced in isolation. We long for our world, because of its *grandeur*, and because it is the world we know and the only one in which we can imagine that we could be ourselves; we also long for a quite other world, 'no matter where, out of the world', because of the world's *misère*. Our world transfigured, however – this world in the achievement of its possibility – would reconcile those needs, and is our authentic vision of paradise. One returns to St Peter's reading of the promise, that after the destruction of the heavens and the earth there will appear, not something unimaginably different, but 'new heavens and a new earth', and to St Paul's prophecy of a future 'spiritual body', not utterly alien from our present 'natural body' but related to it as corn to corn-seed. Hence the significance of the last variation. It may leave us, as at the end of the *Diabelli*, in a distant domain which still wears the signs of home. Or, as in the *Goldberg*, where the initial Aria is repeated at the conclusion, it may bestow on us, as the final, startling gift, the Earth – the place from which we started, but a place nevertheless changed, immeasurably enriched by all that has intervened.

Given the power of this form in music it is strange that writers have hardly considered its adoption. Should he care to, a writer might proceed by any of several methods: he could use his own 'theme' or that of a writer in the same language, or he could compose variations on a work by a foreign writer. The latter course, the one that concerns us here, would remind us that change to something different but related is already of the essence of translation, so that the variation is its natural development. The variations might be based on a wide diversity of constraints, and could include any of the translation procedures discussed above. In their dealings with Babel, they would be continually exploring the foreign to reveal its successive possibilities, and continually celebrating translation, and its re-creative virtue.[3]

Translation, as Ortega y Gasset suggested, is a literary genre in its own right, distinct from the others. Its specific power is to transform, and that power can be realised by a practice based on a quite different theory from the one I have been pursuing, or indeed on no theory at all – by an intended effacement of the translator, a moralised attentiveness to the quiddity of the original, perhaps an attempt to relive the experience by which the original is supposed to have been produced. Translation changes, interestingly or uninterestingly, whatever end the translator may have proposed. It brings, or can bring, something unforeseeable into writing; while the work translated, instead of remaining passive and unmoved, co-operates with the translator and, as Goethe noted, continues its life by changing. But the context of that change is surely not, as for Goethe, evolutionary biology, and the metamorphosis that reigns in both organic and spiritual life.

The change wrought by translating draws its ultimate significance from the dialectic of Creation, Fall and Re-creation. In a fallen world, in which nothing bears its original intention whole, it speaks to a desire for a deeper change, in fact for the deepest change possible. It unmakes what is, and looks to a world remade, not in the labour of the translator, who both succeeds and fails, but in 'the twinkling of an eye'. Translation joins the other subversive and re-creative processes of writing, from tragedy to the pun; and although it is not the most important or significant form of change it is the most explicit, and in a way a clue to the others.

It is also the only kind of writing that engages with the fall of language explicitly. It opposes Babel, not only by doing what it can to remedy the confusion of tongues in contriving passages from one language to another, but also by looking to the end of confusion and the redemption of languages. All writing, I have suggested, is a search for that redemption, the search also giving rise to arts of poetry and arts of rhetoric, to the transmutation of speech into song, and to the fascination with other 'languages' such as music and mathematics. Of all writers, however, only the translator necessarily passes out of a single language and operates in the midst of the confusion. Hence Walter Benjamin's famous thesis, that translation works for 'the predestined, hitherto inaccessible realm of reconciliation and fulfilment of languages'. It does so by reaching beyond individual languages, imperfect in their isolation, towards the 'pure language' which is 'the totality of their intentions supplementing each other'. The translator causes two languages to meet and interact, and thereby releases the pure language in his own tongue. He is also necessary to the language from which he is translating, since upon it too he allows the pure language to shine more fully. His translation is the complement of the original work: by 'incorporating the original's mode of signification', he enables us to recognise both as 'fragments of a greater language'.

The vision is fired by the Romantic dream of universality, in which the reconciliation of languages accompanies the reconciliation of all phenomena in imagination and of all people in brotherhood. Its more distant source, however, as Steiner points out, is cabbalistic and gnostic. It depends on the notion that if a pure language somewhere exists it is 'the tensionless and even silent depository of the ultimate truth which all thought strives for'. The undoing of Babel is seen as the recovery of an absent language, the 'expressionless and creative Word' which underlies all the others. Is it a question of recovery, however, or of renewal? The biblical stress certainly falls on the latter – on the renewal of language and on the renewal of all things through the Word who is also *re*-creative. Benjamin's desire, though it looks to the future in seeing translation as 'ripening the seed' of pure language, is ultimately nostalgic, as is the desire in others for Eden and for a pre-lapsarian speech. The Bible suggests that there will be a new speech – or new speeches? – 'tongued with fire', for new creatures in a new creation. It implies that translation can enable us to catch, not echoes from the distant past but murmurs from the distant, imminent future, of a language deeply like our own but also profoundly different. In the light of which, the ironic interval I referred to between a text and its translation becomes the most eloquent of the three utterances, its absence a powerful presence, its blankness and silence a way towards Pentecost. Of course, translation cannot actually deliver that language; and the most extreme translations, in which desire is extremely acute, are also the most tormented.

Finally, if translation is a sign of the forms of change within literature and language, is it not equally a sign of the change by which literature, as indeed all art, comes into existence in the first place? When we refashion the world as art are we not already translating? There is a very large context, moreover, for this turning of one thing into another, since it happens in mimicry of the Creation, when, rather than making 'something out of nothing', it seems from the Bible that God translated what already was, drawing the visible from the invisible and making in Adam an 'image' of himself. This world would be the translation of another, and Adam the translation of Another. Furthermore, re-creation too could be seen as a translation, since heaven and earth are rendered into a new heaven and a new earth, and natural bodies are turned into spiritual. Translation, one might conclude, is a sign both of the initial Translation and of the Translation to come.

8 Renga

Translation contends dialectically with Babel, by producing a new work on the basis of an old. A writer can also operate the dialectic, from language to language, not in a text and its translation but within a single text. He may use a kind of interlingual harmonics in a work of his own, disposing sounds, etymologies, syntactic forms, in such a way as to set going, in the mind and ear of a reader capable of hearing them, overtones in one or more other languages; he may grapple a number of foreign tongues and actually draw them into his work, as Eliot in *The Waste Land* or Pound in the *Cantos*; he may combine an original with his translation of it in a new bilingual text, as Jacques Roubaud in *Mono no aware*. In *Renga* a group of writers – Octavio Paz, Jacques Roubaud, Edoardo Sanguineti and Charles Tomlinson – elaborated a multilingual work together, a long poem in which Spanish, French, Italian and English participate equally. Radically sugges-tive, it poses the question of translation in a new way.

It is based on, and named after, an ancient Japanese poem-form, which could itself be of great interest. Usually a collective work, it consisted of a series of small segments or 'links' of three lines, of respectively five, seven and five syllables, and two lines both of seven syllables. Each poet added the next link in turn, so as to further the whole poem but also in such a way that the new link would constitute a poem with the previous link. The completed text was therefore not one but many poems, and was susceptible of a plurality of readings. Moreover, as each link made a different poem with the links that preceded and followed it, it changed, and underwent that essential process of transformation of which trans-lation is a type.

Renga adapts the Japanese form to Western poetry. It is a sequence of twenty-eight sonnets – of which the last was left unwritten – without rhyme or syllable-count, grouped in four series. Each series employs a different type of sonnet, and also plays with the order of quatrain, tercet or couplet by alternately inverting it, so that the lines of the Shakespearian sonnet of the third series, for example, are disposed either in the pattern 4·4·4·2 or 2·4·4·4. Each poet contributed one section to each sonnet, in a pre-determined order, and then wrote in its entirety the final sonnet of the series which he had begun.

Renga translates the renga. It too is a plural work, each sonnet functioning as a simple poem while at the same time contributing to the one complex poem; and the latter offers two possible readings – the four series one after another, which is advancing page by page, or the first poem in each series followed by the second in each down to the seventh, which is the order in which the work was written. Moreover, although the sections of the sonnets don't of course form different poems with the sections that come before and after them, they do change, because of the vertiginous language-leap involved. The reader never quits a passage into the language that he enters it from, so that in the process of one's reading into and out of it, the passage alters. English-after-French, as just one instance, is not the same thing as English-before-Spanish.

In replacing the tanka, the basic five-line unit of the renga, by the sonnet, the European poets have renewed both the sonnet and the sonnet sequence. They have composed multilingual, collaborative sonnets and placed them in a multilingual, collaborative sequence; and they have given the sequence meaning by playing its structure against the structure of natural process. The twenty-eight sonnets rhyme with the twenty-eight days of the lunar month, and are divided into four series or weeks of seven sonnets or days. The twenty-four participatory sonnets rhyme with the twenty-four hours of the day; the four series also suggest the four seasons. Since the poems of the second series are curtal sonnets of eleven lines, the number of lines in the four first poems, the four second poems, and so on, is near enough 52; the total number of lines in the whole poem is close to 365. Once again, translation is involved: the Japanese renga also advances, or so one gathers from Octavio Paz's introduction, through various sequences or modes, based on the passage of the seasons or of the hours of the day.

Renga is far from being the first European collaborative work or the first multilingual work. There have been many of the latter produced by single writers, usually in societies where more than one language has been current, and there is also the special case of macaronic, occasioned by the continued deployment of Latin for specialised uses, and developed, I have suggested, as a device for overcoming Babel burlesquely by forcing Latin and a vernacular into a comic osmosis. Eliot and Pound transferred this polyglot writing into a new cultural situation with a different linguistic consciousness. Simultaneously, the Surrealists furthered collective works in a single language, as *Les champs magnétiques* of André Breton and Philippe Soupault, while Dada even produced examples of polyglot collective poems, like the German–French 'Balsam cartouche' by Hans Arp and Tristan Tzara. Nevertheless, *Renga* remains the first important poem to be multinational, multilingual and collaborative. It moves in the direction of Goethe's prophecy of a *Weltliteratur*, by sounding certain trends in twentieth-century writing and combining two of its major projects: the collective authorship of the Surrealists and the polyglot poetry of Pound and Eliot.

By 'translating' from Japanese into no single European tongue, Paz and the others have made, in the aftermath of Babel, a new language. No volapük, or esperanto, or Stefan George's synthetic *lingua romana* ('Las unas devorando las altras'), but a communal speech activating, and indeed intensifying, the diverse resources of each national speech. It is a kind of European, conveyed in the dominant European poem-form, the sonnet, and having Europe as its reference: the poets introduce their respective countries, with Paz's America entering as the splendid object of European desire. They also introduce their literary predecessors, through quotation and allusion, calling on Baudelaire, Donne, Dante, Quevedo and many others of the voices that have constituted the literary discourse of Europe to participate in their work. By bringing into the space of a single volume echoes from four of the national poetries within European poetry, they cause one area of the European tradition to operate in an entirely novel manner.

Renga also functions internally as a kind of serial translation. It is translation that governs the combining of the four dialects into a polyglot chorus – and 'translation' in a wide band of its meanings, from the strictest to the very free. Each successive poet continues the work by translating into his own lines the language of three foreigners. Often the translation is simple: Roubaud's 'livres de lierre' (books of ivy) become Paz's 'libros de yedra'. But far more is

involved. On one occasion, for instance, a word basic to our world
traverses a sonnet (the first of the second series) through each of
the languages, as 'terre', 'terra', 'tierra' and finally 'earth'. Whereas
translation usually separates, by replacing an original with its
version, here it combines, by placing all the texts together, in a
slow, numerous naming. Earth also gives rise to sphere and apple
(actually, by another and different process of translation), and
these too diversify as 'sfera-esfera-sphere' and 'poma-apple'.

Translation also proceeds by interlingual punning. In sonnet IV
2, the French 'poisse' of Roubaud ('makes sticky') is taken up by
Tomlinson as 'poises'. The change is in part polemical: Tomlinson
counters the verses that the Frenchman has passed him, on the
grounds that what he terms 'that syntax of deliquescence' is
refused by 'the hardness of what is real', and that, as against
Roubaud's troubled experience of 'air' and 'smoke' that 'make
sticky', poise is achievable by genuine 'relation'. It is a moment in a
running debate about the given which our 'Charles Pope (a Tory
anarchist)', as Sanguineti calls him, conducts with the others. It is
also, however, the point where, as in the *Catullus* of the Zukofskys
but within the same text, translation enters the process of burlesque. 'Poises' is a kind of instant travesty – you give me a word in
your language and I'll wrench it into one in mine – that unstabi-
lises the correspondences between two tongues and puts them
into a condition of creative play. (Had Roubaud cared to bounce
the word back into French he might have declared that Tomlinson's Augustanism was 'poison' to him . . .) *Makes sticky* is a 'natural'
transformation of *poisse; poises* is an unnatural one, that opens to
larger possibility.

A more customary kind of pun is at work in another line of
Tomlinson:

> . . . the shadow . . . spreads
> its inkstain into the wrinkles of weathered stone . . .
>
> (I l)

It is the pun as well as the sun's shadow that spreads 'ink' into
'wrinkles' and a 'stain' on 'stone'. (Duke Senior, one remembers,
with the same linguistic appropriateness found 'books' in the
running 'brooks'.) It partakes of that wider process of linking
words by identical or similar sounds, when sense is not necessarily

involved, that binds the poem as an aesthetic object, that binds the reader's experience of reading it, and that seems to bind the world to which the poem refers. The process is at times deliberately extravagant in *Renga*: perhaps it was the extra degree of linguistic self-consciousness, in that polyglot forcing-house, that led to lines like Sanguineti's 'Confusa ritorni, confusione diffusa, insetto incerto', or Paz's 'corales de coral en el caracol de tu oído'. In Tomlinson –

> Vague, vain
> implosion, a seepage, ghoststain
>
> (II 2)

– sense is in fact usually explicit in the play:

> The given is ground. You are bound by it
>
> (III 1)

and characteristically uses alliteration for different kinds of dual statement: 'calligraphy and confusion of boughs on air', 'speech of contingencies and quiddities – held/and heard', 'these lines that are life-lines,/these veins vines', 'syllables in search/of marriage, meaning'.

This word-play occurs on the inside of English, or Italian, or Spanish. *Renga*, however, offers the opportunity of doing something more. As each poet takes over, he changes the poem's language but is free to continue its sounds. If he elects to do so, he blends the sounds of his own language with those of someone else's, and thereby makes phonic connections not within a language but across languages. This is what they sound like:

> une parole préparée dans cette grotte
>
> Principi, tomba e teca . . .
>
> (I 1)

> . . .une ronde noire entrait dans l'eau
> et la nuit était une moitié de lac
>
> And love, a command no more, to each one
> the way lies clear . . .
>
> (II 3)

nidi per le mie vespe, giardini per i miei topi morti:

je déambule parmi tes lices de patelles

(III 2)

entre la maleza oscura, la espuma y sus profecías

Le même ensevelissement féroce nous sépare de la pierre.

(III 3)

Paz's 'corales de coral en el caracol' likewise takes the hint from Tomlinson's '. . . baptises/colours clean' (IV 2); and one conjunction of their writing contains considerable sound-play both inside each language and from one language to the other:

. . . a self
lost in a spiral of selves, a naming:

y la espiral se despliega y se niega y al desdedirce se dice.

(IV 6)

In all it makes a remarkable language to listen to, and one which can only exist in a multilingual text. It is yet another kind of translation that *Renga* has brought off, the sounding of a pentecostal language of phonological renewal.

And even when the move from language to language involves simple separation, it implies a delight in differences, a rejoicing in multiplicity. Already in the first sonnet, at the point where that punning of Tomlinson occurs, English and French eye each other, across what becomes a dizzy gap between a quatrain and a tercet:

. . . the shadow . . . spreads
its inkstain into the wrinkles of weathered stone:

Car la pierre peut-être est une vigne . . .

It is a thorough translation from English to French, which reveals how astonishingly they diverge in their ways of building sounds and of suggesting concretion and generality. The juxtaposition of the lines leads one, moreover, to rethink certain commonplaces about that divergence. At first glance, to Tomlinson's English, 'empirical', specificity of objects, carried in the closeness and detail of the consonants and in those persistent vowels, Roubaud replies with the Gallic 'abstraction' of 'la pierre . . . est une vigne'. It is true that 'weathered', which describes the look and feel of the stone while also placing it in time, in seasons and climates, proves intractable to translation: in their French and Spanish versions of *Renga*, Roubaud settles for 'vieillie' and Paz for 'gastada'. It is true also that the French definite article, as in 'la pierre', equally accompanies abstract nouns – 'la force', 'le calme' – and for the French may confer on stone the same intellectuality. However, 'la pierre', while it certainly designates the generality of stone, available to the mind, also designates this particular stone – where in the next line 'ants jet out their acid' – available to sight and touch; while 'stone' likewise hovers between the world as we sense it and the world as we conceive it. Moreover, if it lacks the article, so do 'force' and 'calm'. Wouldn't one say, in fact, that English, free from the weight of any deictic, names more directly than French? – and thereby recovers, strangely, the method of Latin. It moves not less but more easily towards the substance (say) of stone, or of wind, fire, water; of force, calm, majesty, desire.

Renga comes into being, springs into words, by a form of immediate translation. As a way of composing and as a finished text it blurs the line, therefore, between translation and creation. It continues the kind of blurring re-launched for modern poetry by Pound's 'Homage to Sextus Propertius' and modifies it (translates it) radically by making the process reciprocal – as if, Pound having worked on Propertius, Propertius were to work on Pound. The writing in *Renga* is fully collaborative, and involves a submission to other writers without the option to pull back. The poets belong, in Paz's expression, to a 'combinative system of producers of signs'. Each intervenes according to a mathematical sequence, surrendering his words and his sense of life to the otherness of his partners' literary and human habits and initiatives, the chance of a collective text and the remoteness of foreign tongues. He throws into the poem, almost as one might throw dice, an idea, a passion, a quotation, a rhetorical figure, a syntactical turn, a pattern of sounds, which moves beyond his power, to become the temporary property of each of the others, to do with as he will.

More deeply, each poet has to undergo, so as to further the emerging work, the spirit of the renga, of which Shinkei, apparently one of its greatest exponents, said: 'The art of renga is not the art of composing poems, or stanzas of a poem, but an exercise of the heart to penetrate the talent and the vision of another'. To participate in a renga is to venture on a special kind of literary criticism: to enter someone else's work (a work one has

helped to engender) so as to write not a study of it but a continuation. It involves writing in such a way that one is not the only one
writing.

The poets hear the voice of the other, submit to it, resist it,
modify it. It precedes their writing, to guide them in the presence
of several masters sitting in the same room. It follows them, once
they have relinquished separateness and ownership, to intrude in
their writing, perhaps to flare unpredictably all across it. And it
apparently continued to sound beyond the physical encounter.
Tomlinson, at least, states in his preface that even the making of
his own sonnet, after he had returned to England, was governed
by the group experience: 'One still found oneself speaking with a
communal voice.' The poem hints at a pentecostal speech uttered,
in a justness of spiritual discipline, by oneself and by more than
oneself.

Such collaborative and multipersonal writing has obvious
attractions, for the writer as well as the reader. It also throws light
on more conventional literature. Any writer, after all, can feel an
impersonal pleasure in viewing his own work, and can admire it
without vanity, as if it came from someone else. He may sense that
in a way it did – that the initial promptings arrived partly out of
the blue, and that the developing text was alive with surprises.
And isn't this even more obviously true of the translator? All
translating, we know, is or can be an 'exercise of the heart'. Isn't it
also, as I began to suggest in the previous chapter, co-operative
and bi-personal, the production of a dual text – not 'my' version of
'your' poem, but 'our' new poem in my language?

Renga is produced by the continuous translation of fellow-writers.
Someone considerably preoccupied by, and expert at, the making
of poems through the reworking of other poets' material was, of
course, Eliot; a section of *Four Quartets* which explores that theme
is illuminated by *Renga*, and illuminates *Renga* in return. I am
thinking of the passage in 'Little Gidding' where the narrator, in
the streets of London after an air-raid, meets a 'familiar compound ghost'. Here too we have an encounter, inside a poem, with
other poetic 'masters', albeit these are mainly, or perhaps exclusively, 'dead'. They are even more numerous than those of *Renga*.
The French connection is represented by Baudelaire, whose
'fusion between the sordidly realistic and the phantasmagoric'
helps Eliot in this walk 'Between three districts whence the smoke

arose'; by Laforgue, whose turning of the 'intractably unpoetic' into poetry is similarly in evidence; and by Mallarmé, in the line 'To purify the dialect of the tribe'.[1] Since Mallarmé's 'Donner un sens plus pur aux mots de la tribu' figures in his sonnet to Poe, maybe even Poe is included among the masters; the idea will appear less incongruous if one remembers that Eliot was prepared to acknowledge that he couldn't be sure his writing had 'not been influenced by Poe'.[2] Donne and the Metaphysicals are lightly insinuated ('valediction'); two of Eliot's contemporaries, Yeats and the undead Pound, seem to appear, as do various 'influences' like Virgil, Milton, Shelley (through his leaves blown by the west wind) and no doubt others; and in this section that sets out to be the equivalent of a canto of the Inferno or the Purgatorio the most massive presence is that of Dante, the poet whose hold on Eliot continually increased. His is the basic scenario, the meeting between a poet and a suffering spirit with the attendant style of dialogue, and his is the adapted prosody.

Another of the masters seems to be Eliot himself – that is, the Eliot of the early poetry. The passage on the 'gifts reserved for age', some of whose phrasing recalls Milton, draws also on Eliot's own account, back in the 1920 *Ara Vos Prec*, of the old age of Gerontion. It is natural, in this exploration of mastership and discipleship, that Eliot should include the availability of a writer's earlier self as a mentor to his later, in the altered context. The use of 'Gerontion' also provides a link with the Jacobean dramatists, who stand behind that poem as behind much of the early writing, and completes the array of Eliot's major benefactors.

That last point is worth stressing. Eliot does not simply introduce various masters as and when they are serviceable: he manoeuvres to include all his main sources, in this Quartet of gathering and reconciliation. And it is equally important to note that Eliot is not the only poet here in the presence of his mentors. Dante also appears with Brunetto Latini, whom he acknowledges as a teacher in *Inferno* 15, and with Virgil himself, 'lo mio maestro'. The *Commedia*, after all, is the archetypal work – and how strange it is – in which the poet is guided through his poem by another poet. Mallarmé is introduced actually describing the work of his master Poe; while the links Mallarmé–Baudelaire and Baudelaire–Poe are also there to be made. The passage places a concern for Eliot's relation with his mentors in a more impersonal theme of the poet–mentor relationship – that is, of the relationship by which a poet translates into his own work the work of another poet. And it is even broader than that, since it explores the transmission of poetry from poet to poet to poet, for example from Virgil to Dante and from Dante to Eliot; and even the further complication of such patterns represented, in this case, by the transmission from Virgil to Eliot direct.

What needs stressing even more, however, is that the narrator genuinely meets the ghost and relates to him dramatically; and that this relationship is not only one of recognition, self-awareness, repentance. Some of those masters, we know, are at work in the passage itself, guiding its composition – Baudelaire the matter-of-fact yet supernatural setting, for instance; Dante the prosody. So doesn't this section of 'Little Gidding' enact the strange and partly shifting relationship of a poet to his masters in the creative moment itself – in the very act of making the verse in which those masters are met with anew? That is why the ghost is both 'familiar' and 'strange', 'Both intimate and unidentifiable'. He has walked in Eliot's poetry before, but, in this quite new poetry which is shaping, his looks are changing and his presence is different. If Baudelaire is still the Baudelaire of *The Waste Land*, Dante for the first time offers his metre, and Milton, from being an adversary in so many matters, becomes someone able to help Eliot to articulate his sense of the terrors of ageing. And that is why Eliot, who is in the process of writing that new poetry, 'knows himself' yet also finds himself to be 'someone other'. Accommodating himself to a changed association with poets who influence him, he deliberately 'assumes a double part'; shifting into the fresh verse which that association engenders, he cries and 'hears another's voice cry'.

The passage occurs, in fact, 'In the uncertain hour before', and begins with two disturbed references to inspiration. The wind that blows the ghost and the metal leaves recalls the Holy Spirit as a breath; the 'dark dove with the flickering tongue', which is an enemy bomber, recalls the Holy Spirit descending on the disciples at Pentecost with 'tongues of fire', precisely so as to enable them to speak. The bomber has attacked and left. It is in this creative urgency and absence and distress that Eliot writes, and composes the 'passage' which 'presents no hindrance' to the ghost of his masters. The ghost's visit is prolonged; but as the passage completes itself in the final line, the ghost – Eliot's ghost-writer – naturally 'fades'.

That description of a flickering tongue, moreover, joins with two earlier references in 'Little Gidding': to another 'pentecostal fire' that 'stirs the *dumb* spirit' (my emphasis), and more particularly to the language of the dead:

> what the dead had no speech for, when living,
> They can tell you, being dead: the communication
> Of the dead is tongued with fire beyond the language of the
> living.

Those lines have a very wide significance. Yet, in the passage that we are considering, it *is* one kind of communication of the dead that Eliot receives, from the ghost who so appropriately enters the poem at this point. By communing with dead masters, and especially with Dante, Eliot is empowered to write, not exactly 'beyond the language of the living', but beyond what he had achieved before. Dante 'tongued with fire' leads him to an original and consummate verse, which one is not surprised to learn cost him 'far more time and trouble and vexation than any passage of the same length' that he had ever written.[3]

Furthermore, it is not only Eliot but the ghost too who 'finds words [he] never thought to speak'. Where he finds them, of course, is in the lines that Eliot gives him. Various dead poets stir the dumb Eliot, but, in this complex negotiation, Eliot also stirs their dumbness. Dante, Baudelaire, Milton, speak in this poetry, in ways recognisable but also new – familiar and strange. This verse-form is Dante's, but his verse-form was never quite like this. It is as if Eliot were speaking with a communal voice – or, as he phrases it himself, he and the ghost are 'compliant to the common wind'.

As in *Renga*, the making of that communal voice involves several processes of translation, at various distances from a strict meaning of the word. (Translation of the everyday kind occurs when Dante's 'lo cotto aspetto' becomes 'the . . . baked features', or Virgil's 'ulterior ripa' 'a distant shore'.) And there is one translation that draws attention to its deliberate mistake: for Mallarmé's 'mots de la tribu' Eliot substitutes the '*dialect* of the tribe'. 'Dialect' is, in fact, thoroughly consonant with Mallarmé's thought, for whom all languages were 'imperfect for being several' with the 'supreme' one lacking. By making the alteration Eliot points to the fact that, in this encounter with numerous, mainly foreign poets, he is writing in English, in one language among many, and that, although the ghost's communication may to a certain degree be tongued with fire, it still does not enable him to compose in a language beyond Babel. He pools the creativity of many writers to produce a new and 'purified' verse; but, in the very act of translating from one imperfect language to another, he acknowledges that the new verse remains dialectal.

This poem in 'Little Gidding' is an intricate creative moment, an act of writing in which other writers appear, merge and change. They surprise Eliot by showing a new face and stimulate him to an equally surprising poetry. Poet and ghost come to a new 'concord', in this artful transaction, this place of possibility, 'this intersecting time'.

So in the longest passage of *Four Quartets* Eliot has already organised a kind of renga. The poetry, in its own way, is collaborative and multipersonal, and implies Shinkei's 'exercise of the heart'. It enacts the meeting of the poet with other poets – on which Eliot's writing has, in fact, always been founded – not in a hotel basement but in the mind of the poet at the moment of composing. Like *Renga*, and like 'Homage to Sextus Propertius', it blends translation and creation. And it too prompts reflection on more 'conventional' writing. Doesn't Eliot make explicit here what is always true to a greater or less extent? – that to write is to meet with other writers, that writing is by nature collaborative, and that all writing is translation?

Renga exists through external translation, from the Japanese renga, and through internal translation, from one to another of its poets. It also raises, in a novel way, the question of its own translation. For one thing, a translation has already accompanied each of its successive publications, in France, Mexico, the United States and England; and these versions by Roubaud, Paz and Tomlinson differ in kind from any version that might be made by someone not involved in the original poem. They are implied in the poem, since in the process of composing *Renga* each writer was already translating for himself before continuing his partners' work, and they are not activities exterior to the poem but reworkings of it from the inside. In the absence of the others but in the presence of their texts, each poet in his translation prolongs the collaborative encounter. The others co-operate with him to produce a new work in his language; he gives them a new language in which they can speak together. Each of these versions is a new utterance, in a single tongue, of the communal voice.

Each poet, moreover, is not only translating the others: he is also translating himself. Here too *Renga* moves forward. The self-translator like Beckett or Nabokov who shifts his own text across two languages creates a different kind of space-between, or textual passage, from any other translator. Part of the interest of *Waiting for Godot* is that it is Beckett's translation of Beckett's *En attendant Godot*. Each poet translates *Renga*, however, less by turning it into another language than by restricting it to one of the languages which it already includes and in which his own lines are already written – through a process not so much of substitution as of saturation. He translates his own text by keeping it in the *same* language while placing it in a new linguistic milieu. So Tomlinson's English, for example, alters, when the reader, no longer modulating into and out of it via Spanish, French and Italian, receives it as part of a continuously English discourse.

Since the poet is translating the whole of *Renga*, he might also consider his own text as no more unchangeable than the others' and as being free to undergo modifications. In fact there are few examples of this, beyond some changes of punctuation and what is no doubt simply a second thought by Paz, when 'la playa' becomes 'una playa'. Roubaud does, however, occasionally vary the typographical disposition of his lines. The beginning of the first sonnet of section two:

> Aime criaient-ils aime gravité
> des très hautes branches tout bas pesait la
> Terre aime criaient-ils dans le haut

becomes:

> Aime   criaient-ils   aime   gravité
>   des très hautes branches   tout bas pesait la
>   terre   aime   criaient-ils   dans le haut

Perhaps he too is only revising his original, to match it to the typography of his verse in other poems of this section and in his final sonnet. (It is the new typography that Paz and Tomlinson translate in their versions.) One could actually imagine far greater changes in translating a work of this kind – occasioned either by the new pressures on one's own lines from lines which are no longer, having changed language, those to which one initially responded, or by the new stimulus of reliving the encounter.

Renga also disturbs the relationship of 'original' to 'translation'. There is still an original, authoritative (or quadri-authoritative) text: one would need to look elsewhere for the overthrow of that – to the sixteenth-century Dutch poet Jan van der Noot, imitating Ronsard in a poem in French which he then translated into Dutch, or to Eliot again, publishing 'Dans le Restaurant' in *Ara Vos Prec* and then translating a passage from it for the 'Death by Water' section of *The Waste Land*.[4] In each case the first text, rather than being the definitive original from which the secondary translation derives, is the means for the production of a text which is both definitive and translated. The effect of *Renga* is the reverse. The poem is so constituted that any translation becomes problematic. By placing four languages on the same level it disallows the relationship of a single original language to a potentially inexhaustible number of translations. A German version, say, would be inappropriate through being unilingual. By placing four writers on the same level, it disallows the relationship of a single original writer to a potentially inexhaustible number of translators. A German translator would be inappropriate through being alone. The only apt translation that one could conceive would be bizarre, and perhaps comic. Since the poem, quadrilingual and collaborative, ought to be translated on its own terms, presumably it should be approached by four translators of different nationalities to produce a quadrilingual and collaborative translation – maybe passing their translated passages each to each, in a kind of translators' renga. At which point the obvious thought occurs, that they would be better employed composing a new renga of their own.

It also troubles the notion of 'foreign'. If we read the line, '– Et, ô ces voix d'enfants chantant dans la coupole!' in Verlaine's 'Parsifal', we are aware that it is French and perhaps that its foreignness places us in Babel. If we read the same line in *The Waste Land* its foreignness is foregrounded by the fact that it occurs in a basically English poem – Verlaine's French changes in this new context – and the awareness of Babel is far more pointed. The Frenchness of Roubaud's French is similarly underlined in *Renga* by occurring among three other languages; it changes from what it would have been in a poem by Roubaud. Here, however, there is no home language from which to consider it – from which to deem it foreign – and in which to feel secure. The English of *Renga* no longer has the status it had in *The Waste Land*: all four languages being equal, English becomes one language among many (as it does, it is true, at the end of Eliot's poem), and is no less foreign than French. While intimating Pentecost *Renga* is also sharply Babelic, since it leads us, linguistically, into exile.

And so it also poses in a new way the question of the reader. It fails to do what we take for granted from a literary work – to posit the reader's nationality – and thereby makes any reader a foreigner. But it equally makes *all* readers foreigners, together. An English reader has to acknowledge that English in the space of the poem is one language among others, and that his ability to read the poem is limited at those points where, say, an Italian reader is better equipped. In the same way, therefore, that *Renga* links the poets in their separateness, each having surrendered the primacy of his language and of his writing activity, so it links readers in their separateness, each having surrendered the primacy of his language and of his reading activity.

Renga is a new kind of literary work – multinational, multilingual, collaborative poetry – written in a new language. Like all languages, it needs to be learned. One has to discover how to read a composite volume that is more than the sum of its parts; to respond to a text that has no author, but not because the author is unknown; to find the ground in a poem which deploys places, times and other poetries as never before, by establishing literary and personal links across the presents and into the pasts of four cultures.

Appropriately, language is one of its themes. It talks about its own existence as a special tongue, and about the meeting of the four poets within itself. The self-reference enters in the fourth line: 'Dream ceases: languages begin', and persists in the last: 'from east to west to north to south above below flow forth the languages'.[5] The languages flow, in fact, into a final silence, since Sanguineti's sonnet which should have closed the poem remains unwritten. According to Tomlinson's preface to the Penguin edition, Sanguineti decided that his sequence was already complete: 'his silence was his sonnet'. Whatever the reason for it, the silence is deeply right. At the end of a work engaged, in a quite novel way, with Babel, it is the necessary muteness, a sign that the confusion has been used, ordered and beautified but not removed. At the same time, dialectically, it gathers into itself all those many pro-cesses of linguistic re-creation that the whole poem has brought to bear. It is not empty, but full with those possibilities.

9   Sublunary Music

Although we are still far from having completed a move towards a Christian poetics, I should like in these next two chapters to suggest, by glancing at music and painting, how such a poetics might be developed to comprehend other forms of art. Considering music will also further the exploration of sound, of breath and of body. I have chosen to write about it in a sequence of tentative theses.

1.   In a fallen world, everything is fallen. Music is our response to the fall of sound and to the fall of hearing.

2.   Sound exists. How mysterious! A natural thought is that it has no meaning in itself and only accedes to meaning in human and also animal language, and in music; a small area of the sonorous world is genuinely sound while the rest is noise. Yet Michel Butor is surely right to presume, in 'Music, a Realistic Art' (*Inventory*), that all sound is sign. The problem is to hear that signifying.

A theology of sound (if I may move straight to that) might begin by placing us dialectically, as hearers, between the sound of Eden and the sound of Paradise. They of course are inaudible, though the mind can listen to the sounds of 'the beginning' that Genesis records, after the event, and sends echoing: the sounds of God 'saying' the creation and 'calling' it and speaking to the humans, the sounds of Adam 'calling' the animals and the birds; and can note that the beginning of the new creation equally issues from sound – from the sound of the Spirit at Pentecost: 'And suddenly there came a sound from heaven as of a rushing mighty wind, and it filled all the house where they were sitting' (Acts 2:2), and from sound on sound at the Second Coming: 'For the Lord himself shall descend from heaven with a shout [or, at the word of command – *NEB*], with the voice of the archangel, and with the trump of God' (1 Thessalonians 4:16).

At the Fall, as one would expect, the world of sound is vitiated. Adam disobeys because he 'hearkens' to the voice of Eve (Genesis 3:17) who has herself listened to the serpent, with the result that hearing becomes fearful. Adam hides among the trees and when God challenges him, replies: 'I heard thy voice in the garden [or perhaps, as according to the New English Bible, I heard the sound as you were walking in the garden], and I was afraid' (3:10). After the expulsion, the sounds of the world, even figuratively, speak of the Fall, as when the blood of the murdered Abel 'cries' to God (4:10). They also continue, however, to speak of Eden: for the sounds that we hear, with the ears and with more than ears, are, like everything else, antithetical, the rumours of *grandeur* as well as *misère*. A created world still rejoices sonorously in its Creator:

> The pastures are clothed with flocks;   the valleys also are covered over with corn; they shout for joy, they also sing.
> (Psalm 65:13)

> Let the sea roar, and the fulness thereof: let the fields rejoice, and all that is therein.
>   Then shall the trees of the wood sing out at the presence of the Lord, because he cometh to judge the earth.
> (1 Chronicles 16:32–3)

Moreover, according to that vast figure of St Paul's that I referred to in connection with story, even the sounds of a fallen world, the cries of its *misère*, are not closed and desperate but look towards the resolution of the dialectic. They signify as the 'groanings' of 'the whole created universe', 'in all its parts', for the bringing to birth of a new world (Romans 8:22, *NEB*). What we hear in the world is the yearning for another, and the cries, the birth pangs, that tell of its coming.

3.   Music, even more clearly and decisively than writing, is an art for the ordering of sound, for exploring and renewing fallen sound, for 'dressing' and re-dressing the sounds of a marred garden. It is the imagining of what the world would sound like if . . .

4.   I presume that notes too 'slip, slide' and 'perish', that a composer also labours in a fallen world 'in the sweat of his face'.

The result of his labour is a work that intimates, even more than story, the hope of a world where everything is in relation and all relations are right.

5. Although each of the four functions operates in music considered linguistically, the self-reflexive function is uppermost. Music is a plainly self-reflexive language, as, indeed, it is the most plainly self-reflexive of all the arts. It can, like language proper, directly mimic the sounds of the world: its onomatopes are Messiaen's imitation of bird song, for instance, or Russian constructivist imitation of an iron foundry; but otherwise its language is its own. It can elaborate massive designs from small items of thematic material, using itself to fabricate itself; it can unfold inexhaustibly from variation to variation. The threshold into the transforming world of music, which hints at the sounds of another world, is therefore the most sudden, mysterious and amazing.

6. Music deploys sound, and also silence, as does language. And, as musical sound differs from verbal sound, so musical silence differs from verbal silence.

7. Everyday silence is part of the world of the senses, and not other than, or prior to, that world. It changes when used in a piece of music or a piece of writing, especially a poem. As an element of the work's measuring of time, it is no longer the undifferentiated silence outside, which remains not timeless but merely untimed. Within the work it has duration, a characteristic that it shares with sound. And doesn't it also, in music, have pitch, intensity, timbre and form, and in poetry form, place, and the pitch, intensity and timbre of feeling?

The mind can also hear silence as a virtual perfection that precedes sounds and discloses their imperfection. I suggested in the chapter on 'Writing' that the writer can discover in silence, as in blankness, the unattainable Word which accuses his words. Although he may hear that silence, however, as threatening specifically the phonic aspect of his work (as he may see the blankness of the page as threatening the graphic), presumably the composer knows this silence more directly and more literally, as the judge of sound.

There is also another silence. The Japanese composer Toru Takemitsu claims to take inspiration from 'the sound that exists between things and the silence that accompanies sound'; he listens to both the sounds and the silences that are, as it were, not there, and that are inaudible to common sense. It seems an oriental plotting of space, which can also be discerned in a number of Western poets and in the music of Webern, where notes may be points of intensity in a largely empty pitch–time continuum. By such writing we have learned to hear silence, in the work and in the world, a silence that exists beyond existence, fulfilling sound by emptying it.

Even the musical work furthest from such concerns can be heard as the middle term of the dialectic silence–sound–silence. The silence of before is revealed in the opening note, the silence of after in the silence that follows the end.

8.   In John Cage's *4'33"*, the pianist remains silent, leaving the members of the audience to hear the sounds of the concert hall, their own sounds, and the sounds that the piano does not make. They are led to distinguish between actual sounds, of a fallen world, and virtual sounds, beyond it.

9.   Many artists of the last century or so have turned to silence as to a desirable absolute. It has been a beckoning angel, or perhaps a siren call. It has offered an absence beyond the clatter of music forms and verse forms whose validity was no longer evident, and beyond the clutter of European civilisation, experienced as a jumble of objects in a museum or second-hand shop. Its espousal, however, can be merely negative, a denial of the real. The medium of sound is air and breath: should we set them aside in the name of purity, of transcendence? Physical, supposing we understood them spiritually. There are suggestions from many climates of the spiritual dimension of air. In the Christian story of history, we were made alive by the breath of God and are re-created by breath: the first Adam became, through breath, an animate being, while Christ the last Adam is a breath or spirit who gives new life (1 Corinthians 15:45). All things, in fact, were created by breath (as well as by the resounding Word), by the Spirit of God moving on the face of the waters. Air, the place of music, is the source of our life and, by analogy, of our rebirth.

10.   Silence is a mystery, but sound is far more mysterious.
Silence is mystical; sound is spiritual.
After sound there is silence. Beyond silence there is sound.

11.   Music also renews fallen hearing. Composer and listener never hear so well as when an approaching or an achieved music is soliciting and tuning their ears.

12.   We place hearing high in our hierarchy of the senses, which we establish partly on the importance of the information they provide and partly on a metaphysically charged reading of mind and body: the closer to the mind, the more elevated the sense. Situated just in front of the brain, the eyes are as it were the means by which the mind sees. If we are sighted, moreover, we imagine ourselves not vaguely diffused through the body but gathered as a consciousness just rearward of the eyes. We are the 'I' behind the eye. Hence, arbitrarily or perhaps correctly, our metaphors for describing certain qualities of a person – which may include, it is true, 'touch', 'taste' and 'flair' but which culminate here in 'insight' or 'vision'.

Hearing is secondary to sight, and not only because we should feel more deprived by blindness than by deafness. Although the ears are equally close to the brain, they are set not in front (we walk 'forward' into the future, leaving the past 'behind' us) but to the side.

We don't seem to place the 'lower' senses in any order. For touch we need contact with the object, whereas sight and hearing, and also smell, enable us to probe far beyond ourselves. On the other hand, we refer touch mainly to the delicacy of our finger-tips, and apart from our brains themselves our hands are the only parts of our bodies where we score over the animals, as animals. Smell we know to be capable of great refinement, yet we rarely use it. We also associate it with animals and animal need, and with humans engaged in 'animal' activities like hunting. Taste occurs near to the mind – as, of course, do smell and a region of touch: all five senses crowd around consciousness. It belongs, however, to the process of eating, and therefore to the lowly stomach. It serves Messer Gaster not Monsieur Teste.

If we had a classification of the arts in terms of the sense or senses to which they correspond, it would reach down to the minor arts of perfumery and gastronomy. At which point we could remember Proust's choice of the experience of drinking a spoonful of tea containing crumbs of a madeleine cake as Marcel's initial and decisive encounter with involuntary memory, mother of the Muses.

13.   Music, like writing, operates in fact on more than hearing, and, although not necessarily involved with any other sense, like writing it is grounded in the body and also in matter. Song and speech, including the speech of writing, emerge from way down in the body's gestures and rhythms: their organisation depends on the beating of the heart, the breathing of the lungs, the walking of the feet, on the pulse of our fundamental binary system. Among literary forms, poetry most evidently welcomes and enacts this dependence: a poem is a piece for body-instruments – being scored for strings (or vocal cords), wind instrument (a baroque contraption stretching from lungs to nose and mouth), and various percussion (including palate, tongue, teeth ridge, teeth and lips) – which causes even our ideas to flick along the tongue or launch at the ankles; and this is even more powerfully true of song. All music, indeed, involves its executants in their body (a violinist, like a speaker, plies his arms; like actors, trombone players sweat) and enables them to surpass themselves bodily; even more effectively than a literary work, all music surges through the whole body of its receiver.

Yet Charles Ives complained: 'Why can't music go out in the same way it comes into a man, without having to crawl over a fence of sounds, thoraxes, catguts, wire, wood and brass?. . . Is it the composer's fault that man has only ten fingers?' His desire to have music flow untrammelled, avoiding the passage through the contingencies and physicalities of the world, is the persistent longing to live in a world without a Fall and to bypass the labour of Adam. Indirectly it acknowledges the Fall, but it ignores the re-creative work that music performs by its labour, by its tram-melling in body – as indeed in mind, since I presume that no music 'comes' fully shaped. One of music's achievements, in fact, is to renew, via the 'intellectual' sense of hearing, body and mind together.

14.   Ives's desire would evade the human body and also the body of the world, the wire, wood and brass of a reality all too material. Yet again, music – which derives its sound waves from human matter, like writing, but also, unlike writing, from mineral, vegetable and animal matter – by incorporating the body of the world into itself transforms it. As the fall of hearing is an aspect of the fall of the body and of the body of the world, so its renewal is part of the renewal of body. Music anticipates transformed hear-

ing in a transformed world. When music moves, everything stirs.

15.   Music also proceeds from time and from the rhythms that measure time, which we carry in our bodies and perceive in the world. All its rhythms centre on the primary one of binary pairing, as we know it in the day-night of the sun or the systole-diastole of the heart. It also takes control of time, during the fragile moment of performance. It teaches time new and intricate paces, leading it into a harmony of other relations which points backward to Eden and forward to Paradise.

16.   Music, like literature, is not another world, or an anti-world, but this world in a particular condition. It is penetrated by the sounds, intelligences and bodies of the real. Its space-time is the world at a distance and in a state of change. The change is for the better, and one would say that the patient's health is considerably improved. If he continues, he will become a new man.

17.   Art is a way to the future.

18.   Victoria said something to the effect that 'music is the being of God'. Rilke's more famous statement: 'song is being', might be a secular version of the same vaulting surmise. Being is not a notion that I could handle; the word that springs to replace it is 'body'. Isn't music a special kind of body, a strange bodily evolution that is at once both material and non-material? Thoraxes and catguts are there but are also transformed and lifted. Music is perhaps pre-eminently the way, to return once more to St Paul's oxymoron, in which we conceive, beyond the natural, a spiritual body.

19.   (That extravagant formula of Victoria's: does it nevertheless pluck at the truth? Music on rare occasions does seem to invite beyond even the re-creation of the subject and of the world, to something like the contemplation of God. Tallis's forty-part motet *Spem in alium* sounds miraculously open to God, and to his hosts.)

20.   Music also renews speech. A radical then common view of last century was that literature, along with the other arts, aspired to the condition of music. Does it aspire, more specifically, to song? To speak is to make our vocal cords and the air vibrate in unison but with only a beginning of order, in that the order involved is in the meaningful language that the vibrations configure and not in the vibrations themselves. It is true, as Michel

Butor suggests, that speaking already implies a certain musical competence, and that pitch, rhythm, continuity, timbre, are necessary to even the simplest utterance. It would be possible, having recorded the reading of a poem, to develop notes from its pitches and to observe its musical make-up – perhaps as the basis for an electronic transformation. The material untouched, however, would almost certainly be of little interest musically. To sing, on the other hand, is to cause our vocal cords and the air to vibrate according to the severities of a mathematic. To sing words is to bring language into those ordered relations. Sung, language achieves the music that it implies, and intimates a possible speech in a world new-made.

21.   As well as renewing the sound, song also, like writing, renews the breath of speech.

Although song and speech imply and use the pauses of breathing in, we sing and speak basically on exhaling, as we purify our blood of carbon dioxide, not on inhaling, as we oxygenate our blood. Not when receiving (as Adam having life breathed into his nostrils) but in an act of self-purging. Set going by the tongue, moreover, a 'world of iniquity' also procedes from us. We all suffer from bad breath. By transforming speech, song and writing are a sign, though only a sign, of the perfect renewal of breath – of breath becoming spirit.

22.   Speech and song belong to the breath. They occur at a point of fundamental need.

23.   One might consider instruments in terms of their closeness to the breath. The flute would presumably be the closest, after the voice itself, as it not only works by breath but also makes the breath particularly audible: even more than other woodwind it carries the breathing person into its sounds. At the same time, because music, produced by the human body but also by bodies in the world outside, is, more than writing, a move beyond ourselves, it suggests that its other ambition is away from breath, voice, language, towards instrumental or electronic sounds that remove, as far as is possible, the malady of the human. It looks to renewal via voices that are other. The writer may experience the same desire, as when Eliot moves, in a text unable to use non-human sounds but able to refer to them and imitate them, to the many sea voices of 'The Dry Salvages'.

On the other hand, the power of writing is precisely that it is freighted, not only with reference, however problematic, to the whole gamut of our experience, but also, and uniquely, with the daily patter of our conversations with others and with ourselves.

24. Music, like literature, is a dialectical process whereby a fallen world, in this case of sound, of hearing and sometimes of speech, is transformed, and suggests the possibility of a greater and future Transforming. It functions like any art, between nature and re-creation.

At the same time, as we are approaching the end of this study this may be the moment to extend its theological context by noting yet another passage of St Paul's, which places both litera-ture and music less flatteringly. For anyone who accepts the theology of 1 Corinthians 14, there are, in the world as it is, truly spiritual and non-artistic activities that reach beyond literary speech and musical song. In what he calls 'speaking with tongues' and 'singing with the Spirit' a new order is actually announced and is even partially present.

10   Painting and the Art of Change

A space traveller arriving on the earth and discovering so many millions of paintings might be surprised at our valuing our world so highly that we should be endlessly reproducing it, and might also wonder what it is that we find wrong with our world, that in our paintings we should be endlessly changing it.

To see, we know, is a most complex act, and the *grandeur* of the visible, and of our seeing it, is evident and inexhaustible. As I look through the window in front of the desk where I am writing, the sunlight reflects off the wall opposite, but not just at that angle and not so as to present the wall to my sight. It spreads into the whole of the room, flowing generously, superfluously, to the eyeless chairs and carpet, to the bookcase invisible behind me. By being here and looking from here I enjoy one of the continuous and infinite possibles of the visibility of the world. Should I move, even slightly, I can enjoy any number of other possibles, all of which are both there and not there before I realise them. My body, in fact, is unceasingly moving (and unceasingly varying for anyone who observes it); where it moves is itself a world perpetually moving with respect to the sky, light, space, and perpetually, as a single body, varying relative to itself. Seeing is creative, as by the positioning of my body I procure a visible world, in those particular configurations; and yet seeing is also given, as the world shines on itself and offers itself to the eyes.

For in a way the sun *is* making that angle available for me, along with the other angles that I choose. I am given to see the Victorian bricks, chipped, pitted, and masters of so many colours, the green paint flaking around the irregular windows, the lead-clad wooden stub of a hoist beam projecting from the wall with its now idle ring. The light does reveal all that, and liberally provides surprises

of seeing – like the face of a carving through another window
suddenly there, for the first time as far as I am concerned, as the
sun has touched it. All things await me, and all things come to me,
by what the Reformers would have called a common grace.

We also refer to sight the perceptions of the mind, as when I
'see' what you mean or understand your 'point of view'. And isn't
seeing continually giving rise to 'seeing'? I see the weathered
bricks of the former Assembly Rooms outside, and I 'see' their age;
I 'see' the skies and seasons that have collaborated with them to
produce that variously interesting façade, that wall in time. More
than that: I 'see' that the mahogany of my desk is also weathered,
in another way; that although it has been protected from climates,
its patina tells likewise of days and years, of a surface rubbed and
worked. And so I 'see' the relation, between harsh, exposed brick
and shining, domestic wood. Active rather than passive, but not
wilful or fanciful, the 'seeing' comes, from looking hard and long
enough to see what is there.

The means by which we see is also mysterious. Our eyes meet
the light (all our senses are of touch), which is as close to us as it is
possible to be and strikes our most sensitive surfaces; yet through
its medium our eyes act at distances from us which are unimagin-
able. Moreover, the light is not what we see : indissociable from
sight, light is itself invisible. One would say that it is rather the
light which sees us, and which after tracking through aeons of
space offers us the images of its origin. Yet in another sense it is
not originated but originating. It is the ground of visibility, the
condition for there being a visible world. It precedes the world
and, itself unseen, reveals it, rather as in the first creation story in
Genesis the initial command is 'Let there be light'. The primacy of
seeing also is discoverable in that account. God's seeing is
repeatedly stressed, as (unlike ourselves) he sees the light that he
has made and then sees the rest of the creation as it successively
appears: 'God saw the light . . . God saw that it was good . . . God
saw . . .' To experience light and to see by its intervention is to be
placed, however imperfectly, in contact with that primal visibility,
that first 'day'.

The theology of light (if you care to follow me into it) even
suggests a further reach of mystery. We are used to thinking that
there exists a real light which then serves conveniently and
powerfully, in the intellectual, moral and spiritual domains, for the
naming of various metaphorical lights, such as a luminous idea or

a shining example. Light, however, may itself be a metaphor. When St John states famously and with some boldness that 'God is light' (1 John 1:5), is he applying the physical properties of light figuratively to God – taking advantage of a handy comparison by which to express his meaning – or is the implication, on the contrary, that the real light is God himself, and physical light its metaphor? If the light by which we see in this world is merely a translation of the 'glory' that surrounds God and that God is, one perceives another reason for the description of Jesus, in John's Gospel, not simply as the light but as the 'true light' (1:9); as if the wave band of electromagnetic radiation that affords us the most impressive aspect of our world were only a marvellous derivative, a version of the truth.

The *grandeur* of the visible is that, as far as we can see, the light is still 'good' as it was for God in the beginning, and that it con- tinues to present, as in Eden, things 'pleasant to the sight'. Even in a fallen world all things have their 'glory', according to this item from the expansive, constantly surprising poetry of St Paul: 'There are...celestial bodies, and bodies terrestrial: but the glory of the celestial is one, and the glory of the terrestrial is another. There is one glory of the sun, and another glory of the moon, and another glory of the stars: for one star differeth from another star in glory . . .' (1 Corinthians 15:40–1). In a strictly Christian perspective, the whole earth is also full of the 'glory of God' (Isaiah 6;3). Here, of course, for seeing to become 'seeing' we need more, should the premise be accepted, than the natural power of sight. Only by faith can we see *that* glory, as only by faith we can see the visible revealing the invisible, and the universe radiant with a careless diffusion of *figura*. There is a point beyond which seeing the world involves, if one may put it this way, knowing its Creator. The recesses of the very visibility of the world need to be revealed, and believing is seeing.

Which means, I take it, that not only the body, the mind, but the subject himself is in question in the act of looking, and even trivial observations have their consequence. There is no purely objective seeing, for we see according to what we are, and are therefore judgeable by what we see. As I change, my world changes, for better or for worse; *credo*, to adapt Anselm, *ut videam*.

The *misère* of the visible is most obviously that, the world with all its glories having lost its origin, we see the tokens of that loss in suffering, destruction, death. In more properly visual terms we also see ugliness: the *uggligr*, the fearful and dangerous, which by its clownish, dark disfigurement draws us into contemplation of the Fall. Of course, paradoxically, the sights of a fallen world may also be, as sights, inexhaustible, astonishing, elative – beautiful. (Constable claimed, according to Leslie's *Memoirs*, never to have seen an ugly thing in his life.) When Aristotle in the fourth chapter of the *Poetics* remarked of imitation that 'though ... objects ... may be painful to see, we delight to view the most realistic representations of them in art', he could have added that a careful eye may delight in the objects themselves; for while art can turn the unpleasant into the pleasant by transforming it into itself, the pleasant, in one perspective, is already there, this *misère* has its *grandeur*, and a common grace continues to illuminate fallen form.

And isn't the sharpest evidence of the fall of the visible actually in the reversal of that paradox – in the *misère* of *grandeur*, in the fact that, not the ugliness, but the beauty of the world, fails? This is what really pains: that the extreme perfection of the visible, instead of satisfying, dissatisfies, and leaves one stupid and puzzling. The dissatisfaction has often been noted, differently by different writers. It may be that the visible appeals to consciousness yet rejects it; or advances a need for meaning while at the same time refusing any; or indicates a God who hides himself. It may be that the wholeness of the visible seems nevertheless a shattering, a scattering of unity. It may be that its plenitude appears a lack, its presence finally an absence, as the visible is fulfilled to a point beyond which we are at a loss to imagine anything more and yet constitutes a 'there' as in *Ash-Wednesday*, where 'trees flower, and springs flow' but where also, rather than a constant exuberance of being, 'there is nothing again'. A sight, a site, withdraws as we contemplate it, and if we see 'glory' we also see, in Wordsworth's biblical phrase, that 'there hath past away a glory from the earth'. We may come to think that this passing has not occurred only because we have become adult.

Equally, our own seeing is flawed. As collaborative makers of a visible world rather than inert receivers of impressions, and responsible for our sight, we in part inherit our seeing, as our language, from others. We see as we are led to see, in a measure through others' eyes. The history of our race, and of its depositing film after film on the visible, tells in our simplest glance; it is a fallen Adam who now looks on the world. We need as much to 'purify the vision of the tribe' as its dialect, to wash our eyes of accumulations of faulty sight.

The surprises of seeing, however, are also on occasion glimpses
of the renewal of the visible world. If the visible witholds itself,
doesn't it also, at times, at the moment of drawing back, offer itself
again as something strangely different? A fragment of a scene,
that small, defined area on which we are able to focus while the
rest of the image shades away from it in progressive indistinctness,
appears as if suddenly changed. It is not that the natural has
become supernatural, or that one could point to any element that
is anything more than a tree, a road surface, a patch of sky; everything remains what it is, yet the whole has somehow caught hold
of itself, and formed, hardening the place to a kind of picture. The
view seems to have become a vision, and the see-er an unsuspect-
ing seer. Foreign, all but paradisal, the site contains within itself its
own beyond, as if a limit of perfection were in reality a threshold.

Light itself can appear lighter, as though, in the light where we
see, we 'saw' the inkling of another light, a coruscation almost of
glory. At the estuary the sea and its boats, the high clouds and
even the air seem to burn with an afternoon light so intense that it
quivers through them like a single flame, but not so as to destroy:
rather, it purifies and reveals them. The metaphorical trembles on
the edge of the real, and the biblical sense of light can be very
close. The Bible, indeed, looks to the end of created light and its
superseding by the true light of which it is the figure: the heavenly
city, in John's vision of it, has 'no need of the sun, neither of the
moon, to shine in it: for the glory of God [does] lighten it, and the
Lamb is the light thereof' (Revelation 21:23). Even body, the body
by which one contemplates the seascape, will become a kind of
transfigured light, according to a variation that Paul plays on his
own distinction between the fallen or 'natural' body and the
resurrected or 'spiritual' one. His phrasing in the letter to the
Philippians (3:21) is that Christ will refashion 'our body of humilia-
tion' so as to conform it to 'his body of glory' (my version). One
realises too that at one moment during Jesus' life on earth that
'resplendent body', as the New English Bible translates the last
expression, was actually visible. At the Transfiguration, his face
'shone as the sun' (Matthew 17:2), even his clothes were 'exceeding
white', with a whiteness such as 'no fuller on earth can white
them' (Mark 9:3), and the disciples who were present saw his
'glory', and Moses and Elijah beside him 'in glory' (Luke 9:30–2).
Even now, in the protracted 'last days', we may see in flashes, it

seems, the world illuminated by that other light.

For it is near us, around us, that the intimations of a renewing of the visible occur; possibility is local, native to where one is. The windows in the wall at first-floor level opposite me give on to what was once a sail loft and is now part of an antique shop. (That wall issues from a building of some complexity.) The wall faces south, and the shadows of birds often roam across its surface. Also, from time to time, a bird, usually a gull, will be suddenly reflected in one of the windows, should I be fortunate enough to be looking. By spying these shadows and reflections I too see the south; but *where* do I see the birds? The gulls in particular I catch against the bright-ness of a blue sky, yet bird, sky and white clouds are seemingly behind the window, in the depth of the shop. They share its inner space with objects and pieces of furniture which, in their turn, inhabit the heights of the sky. A new space has been created, and the visible transformed, not by an arbitrary *diktat* of the imagina-tion but by the fact that transparent glass is made mirror-like by relative darkness behind it and by the fact of my happening to glance up.

Mirrors, indeed, are especially fascinating – vertical waters through which we look into a world that is identical to our own yet utterly different. Why is this mirror world so inviting? It is not only the sky on a pane of glass that appeals: so does my study as reflected in a glazed bookcase. Why should I desire to enter that other room, to cross that carpet, walk out through that door and step into that beginning of a passage? The house, which seems to swell back through the wall into a side road and blend with the wheeling of martins, is simply a rearrangement of my own house, its unfamiliarity only a part of its attraction. The reason, surely, is that in a mirror the visible is no longer contingent but, as it were, necessary. Though recognisable, it is another place and another time, discrete, weightless, quite coherent and calmly self-sufficient. I can modify it, by moving this lamp, for instance, but I can only do so by interfering with the world on this side of the mirror: the other is invulnerable. It is also unattainable, and secretive. There is a limit to the number of angles from which I can observe it, so that most of its recesses and obverses are forever hidden from me. It is a different world, resembling this one; like a picture.

Hence the not inconsiderable interest of a Hall of Mirrors at a fairground. The mirrors' first office is to deform the visible; they participate in the ongoing process of the burlesquing of a fallen world. Specifically, they deform the already spoilt human body, the debased 'image'. Popular, comic, laughably ugly, lawless, among mirrors they are the clowns, and being abusive clowns they also have a touch of the demonic. By the same act, however, they also burlesque that other world which ordinary mirrors procure. If they guy reality they also guy art (as an art-form they are rather pointedly self-reflexive . . .); as they mock the visible they also mock one of the signs of the renewing of the visible.

It is from this dialectical situation that the visual arts derive. We paint (or draw, engrave, sculpt) a world 'glorious' and 'pleasant to the eyes', where, in Christian terms, the visible reveals the invisible, every sight is a sign, and a man is even the image of God. (Painting is no trifling matter.) Yet we also paint a fallen world, as, in a fallen world, we compose music and we write. The original 'day' has been lost, and the visible Eden has taken on 'corruption' and 'vanity'. In Eden one can imagine no need for painting, and one glimpses its painterless, visually sufficient world in the blank canvas, just as the writer and the musician can intuit their own Eden in the unwritten page and the silence before sound. But that canvas is also a glimpse forward, to a desired paradise, to a fulfil-ment of vision. Dialectically, it suggests a painting so exact that it would be the world itself, either in its first perfection or perfectly renewed. Actual paintings, between the two, contend with a fallen world and look beyond it.

They act, as do all works of art, by unmaking and remaking the real. A flower undergoes in painting the same process as in speak-ing, and one might appropriate Mallarmé's assertion with hardly a change: 'I paint: a flower! and, out of the forgetting/the oblivion to which my brush consigns any outline, as something other than the known calyces pictorially there arises, idea itself and sweet, the absent from all bouquets.' From one point of view, the world *must* be reworked: only in its dialectical absenting and re-presenting is the dynamic of its recovery enacted. Interestingly enough, this function of the art work is acknowledged implicitly by people who give no thought to the matter, judging from certain conventional exclamations that one catches from time to time. When Auntie declares that her niece is 'as pretty as a picture', or the gentleman at the flower show finds the roses 'so perfect they could be artifi-cial', aren't they inferring, in silent recognition of the Fall, that the visible perfection of objects is not expected to be found in themselves, and that the role of the visual arts is to remedy this in a perfection beyond nature? From another point of view, the world is reworked in any case. Painting deals with the most familiar reality, perceived by the most familiar sense; it is, or can be, the art most like the world, which it delivers with a greater show of simili-tude than either writing or music. Equally, however, painting is least like the world. The nicely calligraphed *boutade* that Magritte inscribed under his painting of a pipe: 'Ceci n'est pas une pipe', really is fundamental: in a painting a pipe is not a pipe, a tree is not a tree is not a tree, but pigments, washes or inks on canvas, paper, wood. Whether the artist, with his eyes and with his hand, sees well or badly, by painting he inevitably changes; the most faithful transcription will be a transformation, however weak, and to imitate is, facilely or exigently, to re-create. If music is the most amazing threshold, because of the irruption of its sudden other-ness, painting amazes as it were quietly, by insinuating its seeming familiarity. It is another world that may look 'just like' this one.

That world is achieved by a system of exclusions. For a start, painting removes sound; and when one thinks of it, how strange that is. The seen has become mute. The Houses of Parliament on Turner's canvas burn with an entirely silent crepitation. The painter may use this necessary absence, by leading the observer in one way or another to take cognisance of it. The scream in Munch's painting of that title has all of a real scream's anguish but none of its release in noise; the expectant and terrified silence in Goya's *The Execution of the Rebels on 3rd May, 1808* is forever poised before the moment of its shattering by the levelled guns. The effect is more pervasive, however, when the silence itself is silenced, when the painting keeps quiet about its being quiet. The effect can accumulate overwhelmingly in a gallery, where picture after picture offers, with no reference to the fact, its bordered soundlessness, its hollow within noise. As one advances along corridors and into airy rooms, one penetrates further into a kind of lucid dumb show; as if the Muse of this museum had taken a vow of silence. Deprived of sound, the visible appears different; it re-appears, inviting one to look at it newly, and perhaps, in the words of Claudel's *Introduction à la peinture hollandaise*, where he is thinking specifically of the silence of Dutch painting, to 'hear . . . that conversation beyond logic which things hold with each other simply by virtue of their coexistence and their compenetration'. For we do 'hear' paintings. In dumbfounding the noises of a fallen world they procure a novel silence, beyond what we can obtain merely by blocking our ears, and give it location; but the curious, unworldly world from which that silence emanates is also potent with the possibility of renewed sound. The form of silence that painting achieves is one that seems on the point of being broken, by a not quite imaginable rumour, a sound absent from all noises.

Painting also removes movement. As the visible enters the painting touch by touch, it is doubly changed, becoming both silent and still. Again, many works avail themselves of the fact, on the one hand suggesting movement nevertheless, or, as in Duchamp, developing the static image as a means to analyse it; on the other, perpetuating a moment, as in Rembrandt's *The Supper at Emmaus*, or concentrating their enforced immobility, as in Piero della Francesca, into the semblance of a motionless eternity. Yet it is once more the mere fact of immobility which is most significant. By stilling the movement of a fallen world, painting frees the visible to discover new ways of moving. Those figures of the seen have been arrested in the clumsiness or indeed the extreme elegance of their motions in this world, but their immobility is provisional, a pause to which they consent while we observe them, and the movements on which they seem about to embark would be those of a world remade. Painting localises an immobility, and draws from that negation a potency of renewed moving.

And it removes language. One might be tempted to think that painting, which refers to things independently of speech, enables us to see without words, presenting the visible naked of its linguistic disguise; yet to see a painting, as representation, involves as much naming, as much discourse, as seeing the apples before they become a still life or the person before he becomes a portrait. What is the case, surely, is that the *painter* has seen wordlessly – or rather, that he seems to have done so: he has excluded the incessant verbal blur in his head from the world of the painting in the act of painting it. He thereby admits us the observers of his craft to a totally visible world where, within the frame of its own self-reference, fallen language has indeed been quelled. A 'tree' inside a painting both demands our language in so far as it designates a tree outside and is beyond our language in so far as it is something other than a tree. The process, moreover, is again fully dialectical: along with all the other un-named objects, the 'tree' looks as if it needs to be re-named, in a renewed language capable of the task.

Noiseless, motionless and wordless, yet calling for new sound,

new movement and a new language, painting is a special concentration of the possible. Mere visibility has enchanted the world.
Furthermore, in making everything come to sight, painting also
engages with what Merleau-Ponty calls, in his exemplary essay
'Eye and Mind', the 'obscurity of the *there is*'. It suspends intention :
those fruit are not for eating, those hills for walking in; that line,
those colours, cannot be drawn out for our use. Even a nude, even
a historical or a genre piece claiming our emotions or some kind
of political commitment, continue to exist in front of us, independently of those intentions and those responses, and, like all
paintings, solicit our gaze. As the painting is a sight, so the
observer becomes someone who looks, and looks again, at the
visible there-ness of a world.

So as to achieve that perception of the *there is*, painting changes
it, however little, and is therefore of particular interest in a
Christian perspective. It is true that the Christian tradition has
often asserted that the world is a mere appearance – not an
illusion as in Asiatic religions but certainly no more than a veil
concealing a quite different reality situated elsewhere. Yet the
biblical presentation of the bearing of this world to any other, if I
may return to it yet again, would seem to be that the world of 'the
beginning' still inheres in this fallen world, as its *grandeur*, and that
the world of 'the end' will be this world re-created. The world has,
not to fade and disappear, but to alter. What the visible tree
reveals is the tree itself, rendered glorious, and it is by looking not
through it but at it that we may come to 'see' it, in its virtuality;
even if the interior distances are too great for our imagination;
even if the oak is merely the acorn of the future plant. No
painting, of course, can attain that futurity, but by closing with the
visible in a gaze that modifies it, a painting shows us the way. It
affords a glimpse of the even more obscure *there will be*.

Painting has peculiar force, therefore, in terms of the dialectic
of our desire, for this world and for another. Poised, like writing
and like music, between two worlds, the fallen and the possible, it
is a hint of what the world would look like if . . ., while at the same
time being steadily engaged with what the world looks like
already. This dialectic seems to have been felt by Cézanne. In one
of the 'imaginary conversations' that Joaquim Gasquet compounded, in his biography, from the painter's talk and from his
letters, Cézanne exclaims in front of Veronese's *The Marriage at
Cana*: 'Isn't it beautiful? Isn't it alive? . . . And at the same time,

how transfigured, triumphant, miraculous, in a world other and yet utterly real.' He says, actually, all that I want to say, and I am glad that a painter said it; especially as he continues: 'The miracle is there, water changed into wine, the world changed into paint-ing.' One tends to think of Cézanne, who described his 'code', his 'method', as 'realism' and 'the hatred of the imaginative', return-ing time and again to the intractable Mont Sainte-Victoire, or becoming all outward attention before the posed but still objective apples. Yet he equally saw painting, by that attention, as changing and indeed transfiguring its object, and producing a world that was other; and he responded to *The Marriage at Cana* with the thought that the miracle depicted on the canvas is also enacted in the painting. All one can add as a Christian is that a miracle through which Jesus, in the world as it is, announced by a local instance the future re-creation of the world into something related but far more excellent, is a deeply appropriate subject for an art which, like all art, endeavours within its own means to do likewise.

Painting transforms the body of the visible, and it transforms our seeing. For this too there is a Christian context, in the theo-logy of sight, where once again the pattern is dialectical. The original creation, 'good' to the divine vision and 'pleasant' to the human, is countered by the temptation of the serpent which is equally directed to the eyes. The serpent shows Eve the forbidden tree, also 'pleasant' to look at, and promises her that if she and Adam eat its fruit they will acquire the knowledge of good and evil through their 'eyes' being 'opened'. (His words, to reinforce the analysis of them in the first chapter, are ambiguous: they are true in so far as the humans do acquire that knowledge, but false in implying that it will bring them happiness.) In acquiescing, there-fore, Eve falls not only by hearing, as discussed in connection with music, but by both sight and 'sight': she is misled by seeing the fruit and by desiring to 'see' good and evil. Appropriately, her punishment and Adam's is to undergo the fall of sight, and the next words of Genesis are heavy with tragic irony: 'she took of the fruit . . . and did eat . . . and he did eat. And the eyes of them both were opened, and they knew that they were naked.' As hearing brought fear so seeing brings shame, the first thing they learn, when their eyes open on to a fallen world, being that they are exposed. That vitiation of sight, however, is itself dialectically reversed, in its redemption by the Messiah. For the mission of Jesus, among so many other things, is precisely to 'open the eyes'

(Acts 26:18) of Adam's descendants. One might say, in fact, that Jesus makes and fulfils the true promise of which the serpent's version was a kind of demonic parody in advance.

Again, painting is not the power of God, but it is a sign of that opening of the eyes. It relates to the ultimate renewal of seeing as writing relates to the ultimate of speaking with tongues and music to the ultimate of singing with the Spirit. Here, the painting with a particular internal aptness is Rembrandt's *The Supper at Emmaus*. Referentially, it concerns the moment during a meal when, in Luke's narrative, disciples who had failed to recognise the risen Christ realised whom they were with when he broke the bread and (I quote) 'their eyes were opened'. The seeing was a 'seeing', and was, indeed, the focal and the most fundamental 'seeing' of all, since what they perceived was Light itself. In painting the moment of that endlessly repeatable experience, Rembrandt re-enacts it, in the terms of art, by his own work of seeing and by the work of seeing with him that he makes possible for us. As in Veronese's *The Marriage at Cana*, the action of the painting signifies in function of its subject, the painter having homed to one of the subjects by which, precisely, the action of painting is defined. In Veronese a painting is a miraculous conversion; in Rembrandt, an opening of the eyes.

With regard to painting both as changing the visible and as changing sight, one kind of work, the self-portrait, is of special interest. In making such a portrait, the painter places his own visibility in the real yet distinctive world of the picture. He transforms even himself into a painting, and enters an otherness, a locus of prodigy, not by the force of grace but by the force of art. Similarly, what his eyes open on to is himself. By bringing his act of seeing into the picture – if his portrait appears to be looking at us we assume that he has taken himself, as a looker, in the very moment of looking – he also stresses that every painting is an act of seeing; and by that reflexivity of gaze, through which the painting sees the eyes that see it, both those of the painter and those of the viewer, he emphasises that seeing is always in part the subject of a painting.

The self-portrait is a kind of mirror, where a painter is painted and a look is looked at. Actual mirrors in painting are even more telling. They too draw attention to seeing, by placing another eye within the picture. In a room, the eye of a mirror sees only as and when we see, its possibilities of sight depending on our gaze, as if in our absence that ever-open eye were blind; but it does not see what we see. In a picture, where observer and painter collaborate in seeing, that hint of a seeing that is both ours and not ours is reinforced. At the same time, the other world framed by the mirror is placed within the other world of the painting. The painted mirror is reflexive: it refers the painting to itself, and figures the 'necessity' of its visible world; but it also suggests a further dimension of otherness, not beyond that world but within it. Rather than there being, in Merleau-Ponty's words when discussing self-portraits, 'a total or absolute vision, outside of which there is nothing and which closes itself over ... the painter', a mirror in a painting offers an extra glimpse inside a glimpse, and portends an unending otherness of visibility.

It also produces that otherness in part by simultaneously reflecting the scene in front of itself and projecting it 'behind'. A mirror, even in a common room, is a kind of oxymoron, where one sees both backwards and forwards; in the re-creative world of the painting, this fundamental re-creative figure comes into its own.

A painter who explores mirrors with a particular subtlety, on the few occasions he employs them, is Vermeer. In his *A Lady and Gentleman at the Virginals*, the warmly cool, light-modelled space of the painting, so 'real' in the heavy falling of the carpet, the detailing of design on the instrument, and yet so more-than-real in the stillness and consonance of the room, issues into a more distant space, a further change, in the mirror hanging on the far wall. The enclosed interior is also in the presence of another world outside, whose being there is merely intimated by the many windows on the left. Although the street, or the garden, remains invisible, however, one does sense it, as always in Vermeer, from the fact that the windows do not consist of plain glass. Its visibility is stated, at one remove, in the patterning of the leaded lights. The suggestion of something else is also augmented by the presence and absence of music. The virginals, whose keys the woman is presumably touching, send into the otherness of the room the silence of their other music, while another silent sounding is hinted at by the viol lying on the floor. Inscribed on the lid of the virginals is the Latin motto, 'Musica Letitiae Comes Medicina Doloris', 'Music' – not painting – 'the companion of joy, the balm of sorrow'.

Music is, of course, a defining theme in Vermeer. Many instruments are being played in his paintings, or have just been played, and several stand idle; while in *A Lady with a Lute* – sometimes known, surely perversely, as *A Lady playing a Lute* – the woman seems to be tuning one of the strings. She listens intently to the changing note while gazing into the radiance from the window.

The effect of the mirror is to lead the woman at the virginals, who has already been transformed into a portrait, even deeper into the world of the painting by portraying her over again, by creating an image of her doubly pictorial. The otherness of that image is further enhanced by the leaning forward of the mirror, which causes the portion of her that we see, along with a fragment of her room, to slope at an uncustomary angle. An even more delicate indication of this change within change occurs in *A Girl reading a Letter near a Window*. There are only five open windows in Vermeer, and in the two cases where an open window and a human figure relate – here and in *A Woman with a Water Jug* – something very special happens. The girl is facing the light with the window drawn inwards and past her, such that her head and neck reappear tessellated in its panes. The reflection is arresting, uncanny. Softer than the mirror-image, it is even less locatable within space, and seems to exist in a space, and in a manner, of its own. Its execution, moreover, not only ignores naturalism (it does not reconstruct the girl's head correctly according to the laws of optics), but actually alters the model. The girl in the reflection has ringlets, for example, which are tighter and straighter. One is tempted to think that Vermeer, having wrought a first transforma-tion on the girl by painting her, worked a second transformation when painting, so to speak, her painting.

The extreme of this research, and presumably the impassable limit, comes in *A Young Lady with a Necklace*. The mirror here is situated on the left-hand wall, as also are nearly all of Vermeer's lights, and attention is drawn to it by the fact that the single figure in the painting is gazing into it. Although we are induced to think of the reflection, however, and although we know it to be, as it were, there, because of the angle of the mirror we are unable to see it. That further glimpse is referred to but not vouchsafed, and so becomes even more fascinating. And another effect of our seeing the mirror sideways-on, with only a sliver of suggested glass, is that we are excluded. It is not simply that the girl's look, returning to her from the glass, creates a powerful barrier, since Vermeer usually does debar us from his figures' preoccupations. What is specific here is that we are pointedly not shown what we are led to look for.

Which brings one back to *A Lady and Gentleman at the Virginals*, and to its even more peremptory exclusion. In this one instance Vermeer has placed the mirror directly in front of the observer, in the middle of the opposite wall, and thereby invites him into it; yet at the same time he has tilted the mirror downwards and made it impossible for the observer's reflection to appear. The fact that we do not see ourselves in the painting is present in the painting, and our invisibility is almost explicit. Our everyday selves are not capable of entering the transfigured world of the art-work, and so we are drawn in and then rejected, obliquely dis-graced, sent back into our own world with a heightened sense of its fallen condition and of its possibility.

Finally, painting transforms light. The 'light divine' which circumfuses forms and substances in poetry, according to the visual terms of Book 5 of Wordsworth's *Prelude*, along with the 'glory not their own' which it lends them, are clearly figurative. The light in painting however, though only hyperbolically divine, exists literally for the eyes. And yet it is not, of course, literally light. The painter has prepared a surface such that the light catches it in a particular way; but the light of the room where the picture is hung, the light that plays upon the picture, is not the 'light' that shines within it. That light is the sign of another light, of an otherness of light, towards which the world is turning and the painting turns.

Cézanne is once again a powerful witness, at least in the words that Gasquet attributes to him:

The hazard of light rays, the advance, the infiltration, the incarnation of the sun through the world: who will ever paint that? . . . All of us more or less, beings and things, we are only a little solar heat, accumulated, organized, a memory of the sun . . . My wish would be to release that essence. The scattered morality of the world is the effort it perhaps makes to become once again the sun . . . Everywhere a ray of light knocks at a dark door. A line everywhere encircles, holds a tone prisoner. I want to free them.

His is a Mediterranean and pagan vision of the world straining towards the light and of the painter as the artist who figures and perhaps even assists that movement. The sun, become almost a Mithras or a Helios, enters the world by 'incarnation' (in mimicry of the real Son, who in his own way 'lightens every man' and was made flesh), and draws the world towards itself, with the artist as its acolyte. The painter is even involved, in Cézanne's terms, with the world's *misère*, since he contends, quite pointedly, with darkness, and with a darkness that imprisons. Of course, Cézanne's 'vague religiosity' (as he himself calls it) would be far from the concerns of other painters. Yet all painting, whatever the artist's interest, whatever his desires for the world and for his art, engages with the light, and creates, on a flat surface deep with the distances of another reality, a metaphor of that metaphor.

Cézanne also told Gasquet of wanting to seize 'this smoke of being above the universal blaze', which he saw not in relation to an apocalyptic, final fire but as 'a minute of the world which passes', and which it was his task to 'paint in its reality'. He also spoke of 'a great being of light and of love, the vacillating universe, the hesitation of things', and interpreted colours as 'the dazzling flesh of ideas and of God'. One becomes aware once again of the visionary quality of his realism (he was a reader of Lucretius); and one also recalls, with that last phrase, Victoria's definition of music as 'the being of God'. Is it simply that artists in their enthusiasm pitch the value of their art as high as they dare? Or may it be that each of the arts, relating as it does the deepest process of the world, through life, death and resurrection, strains even further and looks ultimately to God himself, to his recovery, and to the reconciliation of the universe in him? Painting reaches towards the Light, as writing towards the Word.

11 Word, Breath

1

I have been concerned in this study to explore a Christian poetics, in the light of a biblical interpretation of the world's process. My reading of writing has been based in particular on a dialectic of language, the focus being naturally our own language – human, fallen, tragic, comic – with the divine language only entering by way of occasional reference. I should now like to advance further, and to place the study in a larger context, by taking that language of God into consideration.

The Bible's exposition of the matter is again dialectical; it also contains two quite extraordinary notions. The first is that God not only has a language but that he is language, or at least that one way of describing him, or an aspect of him, is to call him 'the Word'. Indeed, to use the conventional formula, it is not only the second Person of the Trinity but the third who has this linguistic reference, for God is also the Spirit, or the Breath, and although *pneuma* has an absorbing variety of meaning, as has *logos*, it does suggest the breath that is the basis of speech. One even notices in the creation story that opens the Bible that the account of the Spirit or Breath of God 'moving on the face of the waters' is followed immediately by his speaking: 'And God said, Let there be light', as if his breath were moving partly for the purpose of voicing those words.

The second notion is that language does not follow the world but precedes it. From what came to be the outset of its discourse, the Bible is at pains to establish that in 'the beginning' itself 'the heaven and the earth' resulted from a series of divine speech acts. The suggestion continues through the Old Testament, and refers, moreover, to both word and breath – in Psalm 33, for instance: 'By the word of the Lord were the heavens made; and all the host of

217

them by the breath of his mouth' − to culminate in the most
familiar and scandalous statement of the doctrine, at the opening
of John's Gospel: 'In the beginning was the Word . . . All things
were made through him.' That originary speech was not, furthermore, a single and final utterance, for the world, having
proceeded from word, is now preserved by it. Peter in his second
Letter designates the 'word. . .of God' as 'keeping in store . . . the
heavens and the earth' (3:7), while the Letter to the Hebrews
describes the Son as 'upholding all things by the word of his
power' (1:3). And if 'all things' are maintained by the Word, having
had their source in him, so they will be reabsorbed into the Word,
or at least into Christ, according to Paul's contention that God will
finally 'gather together in one all things in Christ, both which are
in heaven, and which are on earth' (Ephesians 1:10).

A divine language produces reality, supports it, and awaits it. It
also produces, supports and awaits ourselves. For us too, beginning and end, memory and desire, have the face of language. Our
furthest origin is in God's word: 'And God said, Let us make man
in our image' (Genesis 1:26), and in his breath: 'And the Lord God
. . . breathed into his nostrils the breath of life; and man became a
living soul' (2:7), so that our very existence depends on an act of
language. Not that this dependence, of course, is to everyone's
liking: Raymond Williams considers, in *Marxism and Literature*, that
'there is an obvious danger . . . of making language "primary" and
"original", not in the acceptable sense that it is a necessary part of
the very act of human self-creation, but in the. . .sense of language
as *the* founding element in humanity' (p. 29). One understands in
the light of that defence of human self-creation why such a
position should be 'dangerous' and 'unacceptable'. The commence-
ment of our re-creation is, if anything, even more suggestively
linguistic. Not only may a man be 'quickened' by the Word and by
the Spirit, but the language that changes him dialectically will
consist of literal words. Peter tells the recipients of his first letter
that they were 'born again . . . by the word of God, which liveth
and abideth for ever', and adds that this 'word' is the gospel that
was preached to them (1:23−5). As the 'word of God' − that is, the
truth that he establishes, his utterances in the world, and also the
scriptures − is related to the 'Word of God' his Son, so contact with
the language of the gospel can lead vertiginously to the Ground of
language.

In the meantime, our relation to the divine language, as well as

to the human, is problematic, because of the nature, once again, of
the serpent's ploy. The serpent in Genesis 3, when tempting Eve,
aggresses specifically the language of God, by questioning it: 'Yea,
hath God said, Ye shall not eat of every tree of the garden?', and,
as we have already noted, by contradicting it: 'Ye shall not surely
die'. There seem to be two profound intentions in that economical
attack. It calls into question the whole universe, since it was by
words of God that the universe had been created; and it calls God
himself into question, since, at least according to John's New
Testament exegesis, the Word *is* God. What is presumably meant
here is that the serpent assaulted, verbally yet comprehensively,
not only belief, or obedience, or truth, but 'the heaven and the
earth' and the Word through whom they had been made.

From the moment, therefore, that the humans listen to the
wrong words – to the words that are wrong – untroubled relation
is lost, with God-as-Word, and with the divine word in the universe
and in men. Yet the language of God remains literally vital, a
nourisher of life as Jesus describes it in the Gospels: 'It is written,
Man shall not live by bread alone, but by every word that pro-
ceedeth out of the mouth of God' (Matthew 4:4). (This occurs,
significantly, during Jesus' temptation, when he re-enacts and
reverses the temptation of Eve by resisting the verbal assaults of
the Devil, and having, like Eve, quoted the words of God, by
assenting to them.) And our own language becomes correspondingly urgent, a matter of deliverance or damnation. Once
again, the biblical statements, although they have become
commonplaces, are capable of arresting. On the one hand, there is
Paul declaring that as the faith which leads to righteousness is in
the heart (a notion for which we are prepared), so the 'confession'
that leads to salvation is in 'the mouth' (Romans 10:10). On the
other, there is James inveighing against the tongue: 'the tongue is
a fire: the world of iniquity among our members is the tongue,
which defileth the whole body, and setteth on fire the wheel of
nature, and is set on fire by hell' (3:6, *RV*). Jesus himself warns that
'every idle word that men shall speak, they shall give account
thereof in the day of judgement', and continues: 'For by thy words
thou shalt be justified, and by thy words thou shalt be condemned'
(Matthew 12:36-7). Whether or not one fully understands this, one
sees the appropriateness of a God who is the Word making
heaven or hell depend on words, and the particular appropriateness of the Word himself proclaiming it.

Language, if one accepts this teaching, is neither additional to the rest of our experience nor merely of extreme importance. It is within us and we are within it, rather as if language, like air, were the medium through which we move and which moves through us. It is our way, to ourselves, to this world, to another, and to God. And it is disturbed, a divine word challenged by lapsed human words.

Hence, among other things, the problem of the sign, that we might approach by considering what I take to be two opposing errors. It could be assumed, on the one hand, that, because our reality and our transactions within it are upheld by a God who is the Word, a tranquil *logos* guarantees the sign; or it could be argued that, if there is no God, the notion of *logos*, in all its inter-connected meanings, must be renounced along with him, at the risk of leaving the sign unresolvably mute. The latter claim has been made, influentially, by Jacques Derrida, and it will be convenient to examine his work, in particular *Of Grammatology*, with a view not to 'refuting' Derrida but to situating him and, by so doing, understanding him, and above all understanding the situation.

Derrida's project asks to be read as an onslaught on logos, in its recessions of meaning from the (spoken) word to the founding Logos of Hebrew and Greek thought, seen as the 'infinite under-standing of God', and as reactivated in Spinoza's 'understanding' or Hegel's 'absolute concept'. It aims, by deconstructing Western metaphysics, both within the tradition, from Plato to Hegel, and apparently outside, from the pre-Socratics to Heidegger, to expose logos as subtending it, whether acknowledged or not, and as being the condition of our most tenacious but uncritical assumptions: of self-consciousness, or the presence of the self to the self, and of world, or the presence of 'the infinite signified', of a vast intelligibi-lity secure beyond word and thought. For Derrida, the notion of presence is no longer tenable. In 'metaphysics' it is the voice – speaking, hearing oneself speak – that gives access to presence, to being, to meaning, as it also produces the idea of world and of world-origin. Reality is experienced or constituted within a 'parole pleine', a full word or plenary speech, and 'logocentrism' is a 'phonocentrism' or a 'phonologism'. For the word to be full, however, the signifier, in Saussurian terms, must lead to an inexpugnable signified, whereas according to Derrida the signified functions itself like a signifier. As the signifier depends on the signified – the sound-image 'tree' depending on the concept 'tree' – so the signified depends on the signifier, being unthinkable without it. If there were God the signified would not be dependent, since it would refer to a thing, 'to an entity created or at any rate first thought and said, thinkable and sayable, in the eternal present within the divine logos'; and even when thought in the mind of a finite being through the intermediary of a signifier, it would still have *'immediate* relation with the divine logos which thought it within presence'.[1] To remove God, the guardian of the 'transcendental signified' which guarantees that the difference between signified and signifier is 'somewhere absolute and irreducible', is to cast the signified back towards the signifier, within a process of signifying from which there is no exit. The signifier remains locked within a play of differences, that is, within the system of distinctive oppositions, between signifier and signified and between one signifier and another, which according to Saussure constitutes language; and instead of delivering a signified it defers it indefinitely. Meaning, being, truth, no longer exist outside of the sign, before language and independently of it, 'within the full presence of an intuitive consciousness', but are inseparable from the 'movement of signification'.

Many reactions to Derrida's 'terrorism' and 'nihilism' have been fierce, and I dare say that a Christian response would be expected to come sharper than others. Derrida seems, after all, to be removing all the requirements for a Christian thematic: the knowability of the self, the accessibility of the world, the autonomy of truth, the permeation of being and the existence of a Supreme Being. Although his position is self-evidently atheist, however, what I suggest is threatened here is not Christianity but a pseudo-Christian philosophy unaware of itself. Much of his deconstructing is, to change the metaphor, a genuine hygiene.

To deconstruct logocentrism is to discover the fallacy not of Logos but of what our worldly metaphysics has made of it, by proceeding as if there were no Fall. However firm God's knowledge of the self may be, if the self is fallen and its language is fallen then, as I suggested in the chapter on 'Writing', there can be no true inward and immediate experience of presence in the act of speaking oneself. A biblical critique of Descartes' *Cogito* – the classic instance, which one might assume to be highly compatible with Christianity – where the self regards itself within a perfect limpidity, would note how blithely sinless it is. One should add that presence is also dislocated because of our separation from the Word who 'said' and the Spirit who 'breathed' us. In the same way, however clear the thought of the world may be to God, for us there can be no simple presence of a world, since, as again already suggested, creation has fallen into 'vanity' and 'corruption', and we deploy a contradictory and ambiguous language in our efforts to name it. One should add that the world fails of presence above all owing to its lapse from the Logos through which it was made. If we suppose that the existence of God provides, of itself, easy access to person and to reality, we slide into a basically unbiblical metaphysic, and remain exclusively and self-deceivingly within *grandeur*. We ignore the distance opened between ourselves and the Word in that most celebrated of all the texts that refer to him. Having declared, 'In the beginning was the Word', John continues by describing the Word as 'light' and then swings vertiginously, only a few sentences later, to saying that 'the light shineth in dark-ness; and the darkness comprehended it not [or, has never mastered it – *NEB*]'. At the very moment that the Bible asserts the priority, creativity and divinity of the Word it also pronounces our own uncomprehending or hostile remoteness.

To follow the implications of grammatology, on the other hand, would be to remain exclusively within *misère*, within a reality powerless to move dialectically backwards or forwards. Undone by Derrida, language would become a lexis without logos, a dis-position of marks or syllables where words and things, 'I', 'you' and fragments of what is not a 'world', creep by in a snarled and merely self-reflexive signifying. A man, 'in endless Error hurl'd', would be surrounded, not by an absence but by a superfluity of signs, with a dearth of posts – of signs leading to signs in a desperate infinity of transfer, in which everything only manages to mean everything else. He would be undergoing a con-temporary version of hell, in a world un-named and incapable of being re-named. So with a text, which, rather than establishing meaning, would locate an unending potential of meaning, as a narrative would proliferate fictions. Its language would yaw between aphasia, silencing or throttling speech in a silent and breathless world, and logorrhoea, streaming from a plethoric self abroad in a plethoric universe, 'wordloosed over seven seas' (*Finnegans Wake*). There would be, not the subversion, the mockery, of an hallucinated order, an overthrow of the Fall, but a demonic parody, a revelling in disruption.

A reading of the Bible would suggest that the crisis of the sign, which we are aware of passing through now, is in fact inevitable and permanent, and only a Christian, dialectical theory would seem capable of fully comprehending it – of grasping both *grandeur* and *misère* and also the possibility that opens beyond them. In Chapter 6 I considered a dialectical response to the flaw between signifier and signified, and between the sign that they constitute and the thing to which they refer. I have also alluded from time to time to the dialectics of the next stage in the sequence of signification: the relation, that is, of the thing, itself become a sign, to what it signifies. This – the world's dialectical meaning-making – could clearly be the object of another book; an entirely preliminary and brief sketch might go something like the following.

The *grandeur* of signification, in these rather grandiose terms, is, I take it, in a Christian perspective, that the cosmos reveals God, the 'invisible things of him' being seen in 'the things that are made' (Romans 1:20), and that man is even his 'image' and 'likeness' (Genesis 1:26, etc.). The act of man's creation is also evidenced, analogically, by a process within the world. When a man engenders another, he post-figures, so to speak, God's creating of Adam, for shortly after the reference to the divine decision to make man, Adam's fathering of Seth is described in exactly the same terms: 'Adam . . . begat a son in his own likeness, after his image' (5:3). The 'visible' having been drawn, moreover, from the 'invisible' (according to one understanding of Hebrews 11:3), it seems that what we call the real is the figure of that other, invisible real: that the earth is heaven's metaphor. I considered apropos of painting the relation of light to the Light which God is, and specifically to Jesus as the 'true light'; the startling polysemy of Hebrew *ruach* in the Old Testament and of Greek *pneuma* in the New, each denoting both 'wind' or 'breath' and also 'spirit', suggests the same relation of wind and breath to the Holy Spirit. When Jesus in John 3:8 says to Nicodemus: 'The wind [*to pneuma*] bloweth where it listeth, and thou hearest the sound thereof, but canst not tell whence it cometh, and whither it goeth: so is every one that is born of the Spirit [or – in the NEB – from spirit, *ek tou pneumatos*]', he not only compares wind and Spirit in their operation, according to the method of the parables, but indicates, via the bearing of the first word to the last, a stranger bearing, of the earthly breath to the heavenly. The Spirit, one might say, is the 'true wind', and the third as well as the second Person of the Godhead is witnessed·to in one of the fundamentals of our world, in an occurrence of everyday.

The *misère* of signification is that the creation as a sign has become 'vain' and 'corrupt', and that the image of God in man is damaged. (The fall of man, his spiritual 'dying', seems to be evidenced by analogy in his physical death.) 'Seeing', moreover, the discerning of the invisible in the visible, is no longer simple, according to that haunting phrase in Paul's first letter to the Christians at Corinth (13:12): 'For now we see through a glass, darkly'. Paul is contrasting, towards the end of the celebrated passage on love, what we can see 'now' with what we shall be able to see 'then', when the resurrection will have taken place. No doubt a simple reason for the choice of figure is that a looking glass gives only an awkward and partial view of a large vista. Isn't he also suggesting, however, that as we try, from the earth, to look at the reality of heaven, we see only a mirror·image? That this world reveals another not straightforwardly but (since the Fall) by an economy of inversion? And we ourselves, of course, are among those puzzling reflections – in fact, at the centre of them. In attempting to see ourselves as we shall be, we peer at a self obscurely reflected, in an obscurely reflected world.

Paul returns to the figure in the second Corinthian epistle, when making a quite different contrast between Christians and the Jews whose minds are 'veiled'. He says, according to one reading of the text (3:18), that 'we all, with open face reflecting as in a glass the glory of the Lord, are changed into the same image from glory to glory'. Rather than seeing God directly, we see him indirectly on someone else's face. According to the other reading, we 'behold' the glory of the Lord as in a mirror; in which case the image of God is quite explicitly a mirror·image. As in real mirrors we see an apparently 'necessary' world, to recall the discussion in the previous chapter, so in this figurative mirror we see the truly necessary world, culminating in the glory of God, but, as it were, reversed.

Signification in the third movement of its dialectic is creation revealing the possibility of re·creation, through its 'groaning' and 'travailling' for a new birth (Romans 8:22); and a man revealing God in a new way, by bearing two 'images' and progressing from one to the other. It is again Paul who claims (1 Corinthians 15:49) that, having borne the image of the 'earthly man', or Adam, we shall one day bear the image of the 'heavenly man', or Christ – the new man of the new creation and the perfect image of God – and who asserts (2 Corinthians 3:18) that our being 'changed' into that image is already underway. The remaking of man is also evidenced by the analogy of another of the world's common processes. To return once more to the first Pauline figure referred to in this study, when a 'bare grain' having descended into the earth rises as corn, it prefigures the 'natural body' of a man being consigned to earth at his death and rising as an even more astonishingly same-yet-different 'spiritual body'. When the process is complete, moreover, there will also be an un-reversing of the mirror-image. The passage that presents us seeing in a glass, darkly and indirectly, continues by declaring that in heaven the geometry of sight will alter, and we shall see 'face to face', our face looking directly at the face of reality. Paul even mimes that reciprocity of regard linguistically, in the interaction of the nouns in 'face to face' and of the verbs in the clause that follows: 'then shall I know even as also I am known'; while in the Greek, the word for 'to' continues the first syllable of 'face', with a change of accent: *'prósōpon pròs prósōpon'*, as if to perfect, in this ultimate of seeing, the consummate movement between.

One notes how bodily that signification is, despite Derrida's claim that logocentrism depreciates the body, and despite the fact that, even within a logocentrism quite explicitly Christian, this has often been the case. Biblical teaching disallows, certainly, the detraction of what is not body, in materialist arguments in favour of body as the only, or as the founding, reality; but it also disallows the detraction of body, in various confused cele-brations of the metaphysical. The latter derive from a number of traditional but biblically unwarranted assimilations, of 'soul' to 'spirit' and of both to 'mind', within a mind-body duality and hier-archy; and from the location of fallen nature in body, as the gross matter in which the immortal soul is obliged temporarily to languish. Whereas, according to Paul's first letter to Timothy, God alone possesses immortality (6:16), and, according to the letter to the Romans, immortality is something we have to 'seek' (2:7). In that fifteenth chapter of 1 Corinthians from which I have so often quoted, where Paul is considering the resurrection of the dead, he asserts, not that the body dies so as to free the soul, but that '[what] is sown in corruption ... is raised in incorruption' (v.42), and that this corruption must 'put on' incorruptibility and this mortal 'put on' immortality (vv. 53–4). The body, moreover, is evidently included in that process, and is even emphasised, by the fact that Paul is answering the question, 'How are the dead raised up? and with what body do they come?' (v.35), and that the 'sowing' refers specifically to laying the body in the earth.

(Isn't the suggestion of the assured immortality of the soul actually serpentine, since it represents a particularly subtle glossing of God's words to Adam and Eve? It says that, yes, in a way you will surely die, but in a higher sense you will not: your soul will merely shuffle off your body.)

Two biblical passages popularly associated with a theology hostile to body also turn out to be teaching something quite different. To read Paul's statement: 'if ye through the Spirit do mortify the deeds of the body, ye shall live' (Romans 8:13) as if he were making 'spirit' the hero and 'body' the villain of the piece, rather than urging his readers to strive in their entirety towards spirit – specifically, the Holy Spirit – and towards the spiritualising even of the body, is to overlook a statement that precedes this one: 'he that raised up Christ from the dead shall also quicken your mortal bodies by his Spirit that dwelleth in you' (v.11), and another that follows it: 'we ourselves groan within ourselves, waiting for the adoption, . . . the redemption of our body' (v.23). To read Jesus' warning to the disciples: 'fear not them which kill the body, but are not able to kill the soul', as if he were going to continue: 'but fear the Devil, who can kill your souls but is not interested in your bodies [any more than I am]', is to forget how he actually continues: 'but rather fear him which is able to destroy both soul and body in hell' (Matthew 10:28). And the body is given vast and, indeed, awesome dignity in the Pauline teaching that the Church is the 'body' of Christ (Ephesians 1:22–3, etc.), and that our own bodies individually are 'members of Christ' and the 'temple' of the Holy Spirit (1 Corinthians 6:15, 19).

To distinguish between the immortality of the soul and resurrection – which implies a dialectical process where life is continuously mined by death yet is capable of passing through and beyond it – is important not only for theology but for literature. Immortality reduces the human body and also the body of the world (the 'flesh' which the Word became), along with the writing that operates in the world, into a kind of shadow-play, in a reality destined merely for destruction. Whereas resurrection considers the human body and the world's body, not as solely 'great' nor as already inhabiting their possibility, but, to return to my constant theme, as able to change into a further version of themselves, into 'spiritual body' and into 'new heavens and a new earth'. It impels the writer, not to idealise, nor yet to materialise, but to re-create.

I wonder if we should not even reconsider the 'metaphor' of the body of God. We are used to supposing that references to God's 'arm', 'hand', 'feet', 'mouth', are anthropomorphic figures enabling us, by analogy with what we experience closely, to describe with an acceptable approximation what we can only imagine at a great distance. We assume, for example, that God did not 'really' lay the foundation of the world with his hand and spread out the heavens with his right hand (Isaiah 48:13), but that the implied comparison with a human builder is 'a way of putting it', more or less satisfactory. We assume that his words do not really issue, as ours do, from his mouth and lips. Yet while it is true that many such descriptions are certainly figurative in another sense – God's arm, for instance, is often a metonymy for his power – it is also true that they would already be figurative when applied to humans, who *do* have arms. And although one can happily see figuration when the psalmist calls the heavens 'the work of [God's] fingers' (Psalm 8:3), there is a stubborn literalness in the statement that Moses was given tablets of stone 'written with the finger of God' (Exodus 31:18, Deuteronomy 9:10). What, moreover, of the notion that Adam was made in the 'image' of God? Given the physicality, the visibility, of the word, only a particular cultural emphasis would limit Adam's likeness to God to, say, his 'power of choice', his 'rationality', his 'possession of a soul', while excluding his body. Similarly, it is the Christ who was made flesh who is called, with the same physical suggestion, the image of God (2 Corinthians 4:4) and even 'the stamp of God's very being' (Hebrews 1:3, *N.E.B.*), and of whom it is said, with a pointed emphasis on the body, that the glory of God shines on his 'face' (2 Corinthians 4:6). One might conclude, to be sure, especially in the light of Paul's describing Christ as 'the image of the invisible God' (Colossians 1:15), that Adam and Christ are the 'carved image' or the 'icon' of God simply in the sense that they are a (partly) physical representation of a non-physical Deity, in the way that a sculpture might represent an abstraction such as 'power' or 'anguish'. Nevertheless, just as the Church would seem to continue for ever as the body of Christ, rather than losing that definition with the loss of its members' physical bodies, so the existence of Jesus as a man survives the ending of the incarnation at his death. Paul looks forward to the Church finally attaining 'mature manhood', which he describes as being measured by 'the full stature of Christ' (Ephesians 4:13, *NEB*).

Perhaps we should be right to suppose that 'Adam', or man, bears God's image in part because he looks like him, because he is a translation, in terms of manhood and in a created world, of the bodiness of God. (It is true that the Bible contains no reference to the 'body' of God as such.) The translation would be supremely accurate and yet also, for us, dizzily free, and it is only through Paul's idea of a 'spiritual body' that we could begin to imagine what kind of body God might have – like ours yet immensely different, far further removed from man's even than growing corn from seed. In which case, allusions to God's 'arm' or 'mouth' would not be metaphoric: they would be the correct way of representing, in our language and in our world, the reality of God. It is our arms, our mouths, that would be metaphoric – metaphors or translations within the total Adamic image of the real arms and mouth of God. Figuration, as I began to suggest in the previous chapter, would function in the opposite direction.

At which point one might question all the biblical descriptions of God and of heaven that we take to be metaphoric. When John in Revelation sees books being opened, for example, is this a metaphor drawn from our experience of opening books literally, or is it the exact way of describing an event which, in heaven's terms, is the real opening of real books? When we open a book, do we do so by metaphor, sustained in our figurative action by the literal opening of books in heaven? Is everything fundamental in this world sustained by its derivation? – as light by the Light, wind by the Spirit, words by the Word. Rather than our vision of God and of heaven being anthropomorphic, isn't it a man who is theomorphic, and the world which is, so to speak, ouranomorphic? We and our world are God's creation, his language, his tropes.

Derrida's claim that logocentrism depreciates the body is linked to a claim that it also depreciates writing. 'Writing', he says, 'the letter, the sensible inscription, have always been considered in the

Western tradition as body and matter external to spirit, breath, speech, logos', and have consequently suffered in the traditional subordination of the outside to the inside and of body to soul (p.35). (In fact he sees the problem of 'body' and 'soul' not as giving rise to that of writing and speaking but as deriving from it.) He cites an array of witnesses – all of them, of course, writers – from Plato and Aristotle through Rousseau and Hegel to Saussure, Jakobson and Halle, to the belief that our experience or our meaning is represented naturally by spoken words, whereas written words, which are mediate, secondary and parasitic, merely represent those spoken words over again, as signs of signs; and that writing is actually a danger to speech, which it 'enervates', and even to the interiority, the living presence to itself, of the soul.

It may well be that Western metaphysics places speech above writing from the conviction that voice is a direct act of being, an immediate raising of the objects of consciousness, the place and time of logos as both word and thought. It may well be, as Derrida also argues, that Western linguistics is inevitably based on phonology. One might note, however, that speaking is quite as physical as writing: the interiority of breath is of a bodily kind, since it rises from a pair of complex bellows, and vocal sounds are produced by activity in any number of the body's components. Speaking is decidedly part, if you will, of a material practice. And one might also note that a speech-based metaphysics is given no warrant in the Bible, which presents God himself as both speaking and writing. The creation is said to proceed – or rather, is written as proceeding – from the divine Word and Breath, but there may also be a suggestion, in the psalm quoted above, of God's fingers having written it. There is similarly a wide variety of reference to God 'writing' the heavenly 'book of life' (Philippians 4:3, etc.), to his 'writing' his laws on the hearts of his people on earth (Jeremiah 31:33, etc.), to Christ promising to 'write' the divine name on his followers (Revelation 3:12). It is true that writing here is figurative, of the kind which, according to Derrida, the metaphysical tradition has placed alongside speech and over against physical writing. He quotes Rousseau asserting that the law of God is to be sought 'in the heart of man where his hand deigned to write it' and not in the Bible, that is, 'on a few sparse pages' (p.17). Yet the Bible's own view is that the scriptures – 'the writings', *hai graphai* – are as much the word of God as are his figurative writings and his speaking; as is, moreover, the rather pointedly physical inscription of the commandments on tablets of stone. The formulaic preface, 'It is written', *gegraptai*, by which the scriptures are quoted within themselves, presupposes the authority of what follows. Similarly, at the end of Revelation John is concerned for the integrity of his writing, and warns against taking away 'from the words of the book of this prophecy' (22:19); while in the composing of the scriptures, the relation between speaking and writing is close and untroubled: Moses, like other prophets, speaks and then writes: 'Moses . . . told the people all the words of the Lord . . . And Moses wrote all the words of the Lord' (Exodus 24:3–4).

Whatever may be the case in the so-called logocentric tradition, the Bible itself fails to assert the superiority of speech over writing, just as it remains silent as to the historical priority of the one over the other. And in terms of strictly human language, if it is true, as Derrida claims to be the case within logocentrism, that writing is fallen, so, according to the Bible, is speech. It is the tongue that 'setteth on fire the wheel of nature', and 'every idle word' spoken that will have to be accounted for.

Both speech and writing are also involved in the whole of the dialectical process as I have been expounding it. We considered speech, in connection with Mallarmé's meditation on the words 'une fleur', as absenting the world so as to transpose and re-present it. Writing, which logocentrism, according to Derrida, sees as 'laborious, finite and artificial' by way of denigrating it (p.15), does have those qualities, but as aspects of its possibility. (Speech has them as well.) It is laborious since it is part of Adam's labour, finite because it occurs outside Eden, and artificial in that it opposes to fallen nature the artifice by which we conceive the world re-created.

It also has 'aphoristic energy', which Derrida contrasts with the metaphysical idea of the 'book'. He argues that logocentrism implies a book, that is, 'a totality . . . of the signifier' pre-existed by a 'constituted totality of the signified', which 'supervises its inscription and its signs' while remaining 'independent of it in its ideality' (p.18); or in more familiar terms, that a book having beginning and end and comprising a whole is for logocentrism the expression of a consciousness and of an idea, which exist before it and can exist without it. Once again, however, for a Christian logocentrism acknowledging the Fall, including the fall of the person, of the world and of the language to name them, the book *is* problematic; and aphoristic energy, the activity of bounding, limiting-off along an unbegun and unended 'text', is indeed the appropriate writing to 'disrupt' a world at odds with itself.

(One remembers Pascal, and the fact that his early death prevented the composition, in the period of Descartes, of a discursive Apology of the Christian Religion, and left behind only bundles of 'pensées' – fragmentary, sometimes incomplete, and definitively unordered.)

One might even conclude, in a Christian perspective, that writing is actually more oriented than speech towards re-creation. A difference between them is the way they are involved in time. We labour when we speak, but only when we write do we labour over and over again, during days and months. We undergo time as the enemy that destroys us until we die, which is the context of our labour as writers and which threatens that labour with being left unfinished; but we also co-operate with time, as that which advances us towards resurrection, and which enables us to advance our writing, and the modifications that it produces, towards its achievement. Not only inscription, moreover, but even crossing out – the negative form of the act of writing, equally fundamental and just as mysterious – participates in this process. As I suggested when discussing Eliot, crossing out is a sign of the fall of language; it arises from the fact that the serpent, to return from yet another perspective to Genesis 3, metaphorically crossed out the language of God, by substituting 'You shall not die' for 'You shall die'. It is also, however, a sign of the possibility of language. Punctual and continual crossings-out effect a change of language, as language effects punctual, continual and, for Wordsworth, 'endless', changes on the world.

2

If God is Logos, and if his Logos, sustaining everything, makes possible language and the sign, his disappearance over the cultural horizon will shake the most fundamental assumptions. Derrida is far from being the first to explore the implications of the 'death of God', and to expose those elements of our sense of things which, though dependent on a theistic or a deistic model of the universe, have survived the demise of that model. The usefulness of his critique, however, is that by its central and radical attack it enables one to realise in a new way that the deistic model, in so far as it is constructed from a 'religious' metaphysic ignorant or else negligent of the Fall, is fallacious and hallucinated. He may well be right in reasserting that we are at the closing of an epoch, where the future, in terms of the present 'constituted normality', can only be 'absolute danger' and 'monstrosity' (p.5) – though a Christian might believe that it is an idol, 'the God of the West', who is waning (I am aware that there will be a measure of idolatry, perhaps a large one, in my own articulation of a would-be Christian dialectic), and that the God of revelation will be discoverable within the danger and via the monster.

I suggested, however, that a Derridean complacency in signlessness, in an inferno of endless signifying where nothing is signified, would amount to a demonic parody of what, for the Christian, is the true *misère* of the sign. The same is true of a nexus of literary theories that see literature as the contestation of the same hallucinated order, from perspectives not Christian but 'Romantic' or Marxist. (Not that either Romanticism or Marxism is in any way exhausted by those perspectives, which many Romantics and Marxists would reject.) We know that since, say, Sade and Blake, a major project of writing has been the exploration of the *enfer* of scientific deism or Enlightened humanism, towards the marriage of heaven and hell, the cultivation of flowers of evil, the taking of life, via the diseased and the deadly, 'à rebours', the worship of Satan. Reviewing that project in *Literature and Evil*, Georges Bataille claims for it a superior truth, on the grounds that the very 'meaning of literature' is to be 'the expression ... of Evil' (Preface), a transgression, an entry, through violence, unreason, eroticism, into the anguish of death, of the forbidden, the sacred, so as to find, beyond the law of the Good, 'the *impossible* and the *reverse* of life' (p.98). Philippe Sollers is concerned similarly, in *Logiques*, with the notion that the culture into which one is born presents itself not as a creation and an interpretation but as a reality, a cause exterior to oneself and functioning as 'judge, measure, guarantee, supreme identity, paternity, law, truth, Being – in a word, God in all his forms' (p.80), and that the exit from the 'collective neurosis' which this engenders is Perversion, that is, what Neurosis decries as mysticism, eroticism (again), obscenity, madness, the unconscious. Specifically, he suggests a literary 'theory of exceptions' that recovers certain 'censored' texts, which have been placed beyond the pale or rendered innocuous by misreading but whose role is permanently to undermine that fake normality.

A biblical critique of such theories, while concurring with their sense of literature, or writing, as rejection and quest, would claim that they ignore the Fall no less than does worldly Christianity, and that they merely parody the Bible's contesting of the natural and the normal. They function like black masses, which Bataille rightly and conventionally sees as the 'inversion' of a Christian theme, but which are also the paroxysm of a world already inverted, a demonic celebration of its wretchedness. The 'reverse' as conceived by Sade is not the other side of a now fallen life – that is, God – but the other side of life as originally given, that is, the Devil, who only seems other because we neglect to recognise that he is, for the time being, 'prince of this world'. 'Le Mal' does not oppose the way of the world: it *is* the way of the world, and Sade's *The Hundred and Twenty Days of Sodom* can be described as 'the book that . . . dominates all books' by expressing 'the true fury which man holds within him and which he has to control and conceal' (Bataille, *Literature and Evil* p.88) only because it takes us further than we dare to go in the disclosing of *misère* and of our complicity in it; just as the great sinner's power to terrify comes from the fact that he makes our own case clear.

Moreover, if dialectical materialism argues that certain texts are censored by a succession of ideologies, what one might call dialectical spiritualism would argue that all texts are always liable to censorship in one form or another (and incidentally that this censorship is rather well practised by the ideology known as Marxism). For what renders a text or parts of a text unacceptable or unreadable is not only the culture that surrounds us but the sin that guards us jealously. And the texts that are most persistently and heavily censored are surely those of the Bible – despite their appearance of having founded in part the culture of the West. If Sollers is justified in claiming the following:

> Whatever the society in whose grip we find ourselves, it only needs Sade's text to be in existence somewhere for a hidden contamination to work its way to the surface, for a silent mockery to unmask, without respite, the foundations of our knowledge, for the stay of the *natural*, of the *norm*, to be once and for always shaken and undermined (pp. 79–80),

one would be even more justified in substituting, for 'Sade's text', 'the biblical texts', and for 'a silent mockery' (which is demonic) something like 'the love and the wrath of God'.

On the other hand, just as a belief in Logos ought not to lead to a simple and untroubled metaphysic of the sign, so it ought not to lead to a sense of literature as the untroubled reflection, or representation, or imitation, of a reality happily guaranteed by God. (Not that this worldly optimism is in any way confined to the literary theory of Christians: it is quite blatant, for instance, in I. A. Richards's *Principles of Literary Criticism*, written explicitly in opposition to theology.) What is needed, I have been suggesting through this work, is a Christian dialectical theory of literature; and I should like to close by considering that theory once more, in the perspectives opened by this chapter, and, somewhat unconventionally, in terms of St Paul's experience of law, cultural misreading, transgression, writing, speaking.

Sollers claims that the most apparent form of neurotic illusion is religion, and I take it that this is the case. Paul, or Saul, discovered as much, some time ago. He describes himself in the letter to the Philippians as having been produced by a history, society and culture that were actually more highly structured than most: 'I might also have confidence in the flesh. If any other man thinketh that he hath whereof he might trust in the flesh, I more: Circumcised the eighth day, of the stock of Israel, of the tribe of Benjamin, an Hebrew of the Hebrews; as touching the law, a Pharisee; . . . touching the righteousness which is in the law, blameless' (3:4–6). The history, moreover, was inscribed in texts, and its law was read, by many of the Jews of Paul's time and in particular by the Pharisees, as assuring its reader of a place in a totality, and as providing a means of self-justification, through belonging to the race to whom the law was addressed and obeying its injunctions. Paul came to believe, however, that 'he is not a Jew, which is one outwardly; neither is that circumcision, which is outward in the flesh' (Romans 2:28); and that the purpose of the law was not to justify but to give the consciousness of sin (Romans 3:20) – to teach, indeed, the impossibility of justifying oneself (which would involve keeping the law to perfection) and the need of being justified from elsewhere, not even 'by (one's own) faith' but 'by grace . . . through faith' (Ephesians 2:8). He rejected, not the teaching of the Old Testament ('the law is holy', Romans 7:12), but the reading of it in his culture, a misreading that produced a sort of hallucinated Hebraism, a collective neurosis all the more potent in that it had the true God for its object.

Christianity, from a misreading of the New Testament, can

become the same kind of massive delusion. It may be a law, the belonging to a 'Christian country' or to 'the true Church' and performing one's 'religious duties', which reassures with a sense of well-being in the world; rather than a gospel whose first effect is arguably to disturb the relation of belonging and to nullify effort. It may lay claim to a civilisation, as if from, say, the emperor Constantine the West were really the kingdom of Christ; whereas the gospel surely judges all worldly politics and is never more than fitfully enacted in them. It may be a religion, instead of the practical knowing of God in Christ.

The literature that corresponds to this phase of experience is pretty much at home in the world, or goes about to establish itself in the world.

Realising the groundlessness of his confidence, Paul underwent what seems to have been a complete dispossession, as described in Luke's chronicle of his conversion in *The Acts of the Apostles* and in his own snatches of autobiography in Romans and Galatians: an encounter with the risen Christ, a physical blinding, and perhaps a period of several years in solitude. Endeavouring to obey the law, he discovered his inability to do so, learned transgression, and enacted to perfection the first reversal of the dialectic: 'the commandment, which was ordained to life, I found to be unto death' (Romans 7:10). No longer borne by his culture, he lost, as Sollers would say, his sense of the reality of the subject, and seems to have entered that condition described most famously in the course of Psalm 51 – the knowledge that behind and within any particular action there is an original *misère* of the self, itself originated from beyond the self: 'Behold, I was shapen in iniquity; and in sin did my mother conceive me.'

During this period, as far as we know, Paul wrote nothing. The literature of this phase is exclusively *misérable*, homeless, maybe mistrustful of language, and without issue.

Paul suffered the loss of a world and the loss of self, being considered by his society a perversion and an outlaw ('This is the man, that teacheth all men every where against the people, and the law', Acts 21:28), and agreeing to become that fundamental figure to whom I have often had occasion to refer, that is, the 'fool' (1 Corinthians 3:18). But he also, of course, went beyond the *misère* of the decomposition of culture, and also of nature, by travelling the second reversal of the dialectic. He discovered a new birth for creation and the possibility of a 'new man'; he enjoyed, after life had yielded to death, 'newness of life' (Romans 6:4). He described his new self, originated not from within a fallen world but from elsewhere, with terse intensity: 'by the grace of God I am what I am' (1 Corinthians 15:10).

The literature of this phase is fully dialectical, absorbing the earlier phases and holding up, as it were, a 'dark' mirror to a renewing nature.

The question of reading is illuminated in Paul's providentially thorough experience, in terms of misreading and of the need to un-read and to re-read. So is the question of writing. His own writing practice was in the same way partly a re-writing; and one could argue in fact that the New Testament as a totality is the re-writing of the Old. It sounds the Hebrew scriptures for their Christian import, according to Augustine's notion that the New Testament is concealed in the Old and the Old Testament revealed in the New; it educes their textual possibilities, according to a notion appropriate to our own time, as when John takes the opening of Genesis: 'In the beginning God created the heaven and the earth . . . And God said . . .' and 'translates' it for the opening of his Gospel: 'In the beginning was the Word . . . and the Word was God . . . All things were made through him . . .' (*RV* margin). The New Testament operates (if you will) an intertextuality; it writes out the potential of the Old by what one might call a truly practical criticism; the Old becomes a kind of palimpsest, over which the New is carefully and scrupulously inscribed.

One even begins to see an answer to the puzzling question as to why there are two Testaments. The purpose of the Old Testament is, of course, in Christian terms, to prepare the coming of the Messiah. Since it occurs in a fallen world, however, it too is involved in the dialectic. Although not in itself *misérable*, it under-goes the *misère* of being misread; it is then re-read, and re-written more gloriously. There has to be a New Testament, in other words, just as there have to be 'new heavens and a new earth'. And one notices, to return to the beginning of the chapter, that this process of reading and writing concerns precisely the divine language. The Hebrew scriptures prepare specifically the advent of the Word – they are a word announcing the Word – and 'the word of God' is rewritten in terms of 'the Word of God'.

A final comment on writing and on written language might be that even the word of God, the apogee of writing, passes through a dialectical process. A final comment on spoken language might be that the same dialectical process is undergone by the spoken word of God. Paul's experience led to the realisation that while all our own moves towards the resolution of the dialectic are in them-selves inadequate, they are understressed by a marvellous, baffling language beyond us yet at the same time within us. In a passage of the eighth chapter of Romans which I have several times quoted, he considers the dialectic of the universe, made, unmade and some time to be made anew: 'the creation was subjected to vanity, not of its own will, but by reason of him who subjected it, in hope that the creation itself also shall be delivered from the bondage of corruption into the liberty of the glory of the children of God' (verses 20–1 RV). He continues: 'For we know that the whole creation groaneth and travaileth in pain together until now. And not only they, but ourselves also, which have the first-fruits of the Spirit, even we ourselves groan within ourselves, waiting for the adoption, to wit, the redemption of our body.' The language of desire within us and all around us relates us to the world, deeply and inwardly, in its and our own wretchedness and possibility, being less a language under our control than a kind of proto-language, a universal and inarticulate *stenagmos*.

It is then sustained in its turn by an even more distant language, for Paul continues: 'Likewise the Spirit also helpeth our infirmities: for we know not what we should pray for as we ought: but the Spirit itself maketh intercession for us with groanings which cannot be uttered.' Our words, being fallen, are no longer capable of addressing God correctly, and our breath is that of a body 'subjected to vanity'. So a greater language inhabits us, that of the Spirit, or of the Breath itself. The limits of our world, defined, according to Wittgenstein, by the limits of our language, are transcended by a language that has no limit – by the divine language, itself dialectical, which, having given us life and preserv-ing us in death, groans towards resurrection.

Notes

NOTE: References to the Bible are to the Authorised Version *(AV)* unless otherwise stated. *RV* – Revised Version. *NEB* – New English Bible.

CHAPTER 1   LITERATURE, LANGUAGE, LIFE
1.   I shall be referring mainly to fragments 116, 119, 130, 192, 241, 397, 471 and, in particular, 131 and 149, according to the numbering adopted in Pascal, *Pensées,* trans. A. J. Krailsheimer (Penguin). I frequently retranslate.
2.   Romans 8:20–1 *(RV).*
3.   2 Peter 3:7–13.
4.   1 Corinthians 15:44.
5.   Genesis 3:17.
6.   Genesis 3:22–4.
7.   Revelation 2:7.
8.   Revelation 22:2.
9.   1 Corinthians 15:45–7.
10. Ephesians 4:24, Colossians 3:10.
11. The most Pascalian writing occurs at the opening of Epistle II:

> ...A being darkly wise, and rudely great:
> With too much knowledge for the Sceptic side,
> With too much weakness for the Stoic's pride,
> He hangs between; in doubt to act, or rest,
> In doubt to deem himself a god, or beast, *etc.*

12. Romans 1:18.
13. 2 Peter 1:4.
14. For instance in fragment 733. He is not really concerned, however, to make distinctions among the kinds of contrariety that he uncovers. All – whether they occur at the collision of life and death, or death and rebirth, or rebirth and the continuance of death – are amalgamated into a vision of universal 'contradiction'.
15. References to Genesis in this section will be to the first four chapters.
16. *Paradise Lost,* Book VIII, lines 352–3 and 439.
17. Any theology of language must of course start from, or work round to, the doctrine of the 'Word of God'. I work round to it in the final chapter.

CHAPTER 2   THE DIALECTIC OF TRAGEDY
1.   T. R. Henn, *The Harvest of Tragedy,* p.266.
2.   Luke 22:22.
3.   Acts 2:23.

4. He suggests, in the *Traité de la Connaissance de soi-même,* that there exists a multitude of ideas, feelings, passions, which never rise to 'the surface of the mind', and which nevertheless constitute what is 'most essential and most important' in us.

5. Of course, Pascal's choice of words is deliberately commonplace, since he is writing of the common places of the human condition. In the sixteenth century Garnier had already caused Polyxène, in his tragedy *La Troade,* to describe herself as 'De telle grandeur chute en misère profonde', 'from such greatness fallen into deep misery'. Another, related, tragic common-place – that the greater the hero's elevation the greater will be his fall – also chimes with Pascal's Christian account of man in general. As, in another sixteenth-century tragedy, Jean de la Taille's *Saül le furieux,* Saül understands his rise to the throne: 'Le sort m'a élevé pour tomber de plus haut', 'Destiny raised me to fall from a greater height', so Pascal claims that our wretchedness is increased by our former eminence: 'c'est être d'autant plus misérable qu'on est tombé de plus haut' (fragment 122).

6. Here again, the nature of tragedy corresponds to the nature of the human condition as analysed by Pascal. The mutual growth of the tragic contraries recalls fragment 613: 'The more light one has, the more greatness and baseness one discovers in man'. Their interaction recalls those fragments which claim that greatness and wretchedness can be deduced from each other. Fragment 116, quoted in the previous chapter, is of particular interest: 'All those very miseries prove his greatness. They are the miseries of a great lord, the miseries of a dispossessed king *(d'un roi dépossédé)'*. The agents of tragedy are also great lords and kings; and the dispossessed king – Pascal is thinking, via Perseus king of Macedon, of Adam uncrowned and of every man – inevitably reminds one of Oedipus, of Lear. Some four years after the publication of this fragment, a servant in *Iphigénie* says of Racine's version of Agamemnon king of kings: 'Le roi de son pouvoir se voit déposséder'.

7. The paradox of tragedy recalls, once again, Pascal's investigation of the human condition, and in particular one of the formulas by which he analyses greatness and wretchedness: 'The greatness of man is great', he claims in fragment 114, 'in that he knows himself wretched'.

8. See Helen Gardner, *Religion and Literature,* p. 98.

CHAPTER 3   COMEDY AND POSSIBILITY

1. Philinte's role, surely, is that not of straight man but of accompanying funny man. He is a 'humour', his comic *phlegm* being the opposite and the foil to Alceste's comic *bile* (see line 166). If Alceste, despite his Greek-derived title of misanthropist, falls short of being a true 'hater', Philinte, despite his similarly Greek-derived name, falls even further short of being a true 'lover'.

2. Molière wrote these roles for himself: he played Jourdain, Argan, Pourceaugnac, and also Alceste, and many others. He was not only an actor – he was, deeply, a Clown.

3. On the Fool, see Enid Welsford, *The Fool,* and William Willeford, *The Fool and His Sceptre.*

4. It is remarkable that the origin of the whole genre of medieval French

farce, on which these plays partly draw, seems to have been precisely a comic mingling of languages and dialects.

5.   The later *School for Scandal* includes a perfect instance of the power of the imagination to bound further and further into triumphant fantasy, in Crabtree's retelling of the rumours surrounding the supposed duel: 'Charles's shot took effect, as I tell you, and Sir Peter's missed; but, what is very extraordinary, the ball struck against a little bronze Shakespeare that stood over the fireplace, grazed out of the window at a right angle, and wounded the postman, who was just coming to the door with a double letter from Northamptonshire.' The bullet of the imagination loses no opportunity to hit off the smallest conceivable, unnecessary detail.

6.   A. E. Dyson, *The Inimitable Dickens*, p.84.

7.   Hugo often comes to mind in reading Dickens. The statement is in the preface to his drama *Cromwell.*

8.   Comedy can be taken, of course, fully into the depths of evil, death, despair, as when Lear makes jokes about Gloucester's blindness.

9.   As well as the laughter by which we outface our fallen condition, and the laughter which sees possibility beyond it, there is, of course, satanic laughter – a delight in evil, a revelling in the Fall.

10. See especially Paul's letter to the Galatians.

CHAPTER 4   STORY

1.   Compare Raymond Queneau, in *Une histoire modèle:* 'Literature . . . points metaphorically to Paradise Lost' (p.103), and especially, 'All narrative is born of human misfortune', *Tout le narratif naît du malheur des hommes* (p.21).

2.   Frank Kermode has written powerfully on the subject, as on other aspects of fiction close to my concerns here, in *The Sense of an Ending.*

3.   Curiously, Marguerite de Navarre's *Heptaméron,* written in emulation of Boccaccio in Renaissance France, also defines the conditions for the existence of its stories, manoeuvres them likewise between death and salvation, and creates a special story-place for them. The ten story-tellers have been to the baths at Cauterets in the Pyrenees – they too have been concerned for their health – but are prevented from returning home after their cure by rains 'so marvellous and so great that it seemed God had forgotten his promise to Noah nevermore to destroy the world by water'. Through this deluge they make their several ways to an abbey, all of them escaping death in a number of separate adventures. Having been 'miraculously assembled', they set workmen to build a bridge across the nearby river, and decide to imitate Boccaccio in the meantime by telling stories. In this holy place, this refuge which is both in the world and out of it, and which protects them like the Ark in a time of apocalyptic upheaval, they enter a story-world beyond danger and death, 'while waiting for [their] bridge to be completed'.

4.   This tends to confirm Gabriel Josipovici's view that Chaucer is centrally concerned with questions of writing and reading. See the chapter, 'Chaucer: The Teller and the Tale', in *The World and the Book,* a rich and stimulating study of relations between fiction and reality.

5.   The same occurs in Malory's source, the *Queste del Saint Graal* from thirteenth-century France. See 'The Quest of Narrative' in Tzvetan

Todorov's *The Poetics of Prose.*

6. *A la recherche* also moves towards a particularly suggestive end-as-beginning. Marcel's decision to write is both a return to the opening of the story which has already been written, and a project for the future – as much for the reader as for Marcel himself. The reader, for whom the process of reading the book has been in part a process of learning how to read it, can only begin to do so correctly when he has finished, and must therefore begin again. The end of the novel is big with the promise of the novel. One might suppose that Marcel's future is merely to decline, since he has completed the one book of which he claims to be capable. Yet the last words of the novel: 'le Temps', connect with the very first word: 'Longtemps', and expansively transform it into a foretelling of the 'long time' of the book; in achieving the book, Marcel constructs time and inhabits it triumphantly. And the time that follows the novel is a strange, hardly imaginable, time of the imagination. Since Marcel is present both as having written the novel and, more forcibly, as being about to write it, what ensues is both the time after its writing and the time during which it is to be written. The past is projected teleologically into the future, time is redeemed, and for Marcel too tomorrow is great with story.

7. In *The Thousand and One Nights* need is decidedly the mother of story, in the special sense that only by telling tales can Scheherezade avoid dying. Her stories arise, in a painfully precise way, from a world of mortality.

8. See *The Comedy of Errors, The Two Gentlemen of Verona, The Tempest.*

9. See *The Merchant of Venice, Much Ado About Nothing, All's Well that Ends Well, Pericles.*

10. Of course, Dante himself called it explicitly a comedy rather than a tragedy (in a letter to Can Grande della Scala), on the grounds that its beginning is 'horrible' and 'foetid' and its end 'prosperous', 'desirable' and 'agreeable', while tragedy, on the contrary, begins 'calm' and 'wonderful' *(admirabilis)* but ends 'foetid' and 'horrible'. Dante's idea of tragedy, however, is based on the tragedies of Seneca, and on the restrictive definitions to which they gave rise in the Middle Ages.

11. See the second chapter of Josipovici's *The World and the Book.*

12. Narrative self-consciousness is not only enacted in major, 'cultural' works: it is just as present in popular ones. Consider the detective story, and in particular the kind where an enigma is posed at the beginning so as to be resolved at the end. As Todorov suggests, in 'The Typology of Detective Fiction' *(The Poetics of Prose)*, it actually contains two stories, the crime and the investigation; the second story constitutes the novel, while the first precedes the novel and engenders it. Remarkably, the second is a quest for the first. Like *The Tale of the Sankgreal* or *A la recherche,* the detective story is a search for story, and the detective even functions as a novelist in search of the story to tell. He is likely to tell it, moreover, with all the trappings: with careful timing, to a circle of listeners and in a well-chosen venue. Again as in *A la recherche,* or as in *Finnegans Wake,* the story also homes to its origin: our concern as readers is to find out less what will happen than what has already happened, and when the story achieves its end it discloses its beginning. Furthermore, the second story is even a number of stories, a series of different attempts by the detective, and perhaps other characters,

to tell the first story accurately. Several more stories are probably composed by the reader, in the course of his own investigation. A detective novel is therefore another compilation of stories, all of which appeal to our desire for story, and each of which is a version of the one true tale. It is that last fact, of course, which is specific to the genre: the function of the final story is to reassure, by removing uncertainty – an uncertainty that it has itself pleasantly aroused – and by locating truth, in the single story which relates 'what really happened'. Strangely, what happened is usually that somebody killed somebody: the decisive characteristic of the detective story is the most obvious, that it deals in murder – in a paroxysm of violence, fear, death. Like *The Decameron, The Heptameron* or the *Commedia,* it is mothered by *misère.* As a popular genre, involved in a particularly revealing way with the deepest of issues (like farce), it uses story comprehensively as a means to manage evil. It draws the reader into an elaborate though undemanding story-world, by gathering several paradigms of story; it sends its hero off to contend with evil and to overcome it; and by its final story, ministered by an all-powerful, all-comprehending voice, it relieves the reader by saying who really did it, and thereby pinning the guilt on someone.

13. One notes also, here as throughout Sartre, that the atheism is actually Protestant rather than Catholic.

14. Actually from a Renaissance writer, Luis de Granada, quoted in chapter 16, 'The Book as Symbol', Ernst Robert Curtius's *European Literature and the Latin Middle Ages.*

CHAPTER 5   ELIOT/LANGUAGE

1. 'T.S. Eliot at the Cross-Roads', *Critical Quarterly* (Winter 1970).
2. Robert Creeley, *Contexts of Poetry: Interviews 1961–1971,* p. 28.
3. Donald Davie's expression, in 'T. S. Eliot: The end of an era', from *The Poet in the Imaginary Museum.*
4. *The Sacred Wood,* 'Imperfect Critics'.

CHAPTER 6   WRITING AND RE-CREATION

1. My attention was drawn to this by Douglas Oliver.
2. George Steiner's expression, in the remarkable fourth section of the chapter 'Word Against Object', in *After Babel.*
3. Compare Borachio in *Much Ado About Nothing,* speaking to Don Pedro about Dogberry and his men: 'what your wisdoms could not discover, these shallow fools have brought to light'.

CHAPTER 7   TRANSLATING

1. For *Directions in Italian Poetry*, a special number of the review *Prospice.*
2. The translations appeared in an issue of *Prospice* devoted to Queneau.
3. I have attempted a small something along these lines: seven variations on Yves Bonnefoy's poem 'Lieu de la salamandre' published in the review *Samphire* for spring 1980.

CHAPTER 8   RENGA

1. The comments on Baudelaire and Laforgue are in *To Criticize the Critic,* in

the essay 'What Dante Means to Me'.
2. See 'From Poe to Valéry' in *To Criticize the Critic*.
3. 'What Dante Means to Me' in *To Criticize the Critic*.
4. See Leonard Forster, *The Poet's Tongues*.
5. Actually that fourth line is 'mine', since I wanted to point to the fact that the same word, Paz's 'lenguajes', opens and closes the poem. Tomlinson, by a large act of transformation, translates the first instance as 'the gift of tongues'.

CHAPTER 11   WORD, BREATH
1. Page 73 of the English translation by Gayatri Chakravorty Spivak, which I sometimes retranslate.

Index